PENGUIN BOOKS

THE TENTATIVE PREGNANCY

Barbara Katz Rothman is Associate Professor of Sociology at Baruch College and the Graduate Center of the City University of New York. She is the author of *In Labor: Women and Power in the Birthplace* (published by Penguin under the title *Giving Birth: Alternatives in Childbirth*) and has contributed articles to *Woman's Day*, *Ms.*, *Mothering*, *Self*, and elsewhere. She lives in New York City with her husband, son, and daughter.

THE TENTATIVE PREGNANCY

Prenatal Diagnosis and the Future of Motherhood

Barbara Katz Rothman

PENGUIN BOOKS

PENGUIN BOOKS
Viking Penguin Inc., 40 West 23rd Street,
New York, New York 10010, U.S.A.
Penguin Books Ltd, Harmondsworth,
Middlesex, England
Penguin Books Australia Ltd, Ringwood,
Victoria, Australia
Penguin Books Canada Limited, 2801 John Street,
Markham, Ontario, Canada L3R 1B4
Penguin Books (N.Z.) Ltd, 182–190 Wairau Road,
Auckland 10, New Zealand

First published in the United States of America by Viking Penguin Inc. 1986

Published in Penguin Books 1987

LIBRARY OF CONGRESS CATALOGING IN PUBLICATION DATA
Rothman, Barbara Katz.
The tentative pregnancy.
Bibliography: p.
Includes index.
1. Amniocentisis—Social aspects. 2. Prenatal
diagnosis—Social aspects. 3. Choice (psychology)
4. Loss (Psychology) I. Title.
RG628.3.A48R68   1987   618.3'2075   86-18709
ISBN 0 14 00.9486 5

Printed in the United States of America by
R. R. Donnelley & Sons Company, Harrisonburg, Virginia
Set in Palatino

To the memory of my grandmother,
Rose Colb Charnow

ACKNOWLEDGMENTS

Well, here it is. The moment that makes book-writing worthwhile—sitting down at the typewriter, manuscript completed, and writing the acknowledgments. Acknowledgments are like a will you don't have to die to have read: a public thank-you, a wrapping-up, a final gesture of appreciation.

Especially important to any book are the people who had faith in it early on, when it was loosely formed, not written, and very fragile. The encouragement of Mary Cunnane was essential to the existence of this book. Mary Brown Parlee made a research assistant available to me at an early and crucial moment. Audrey Heimler and Peggy O'Mara MacMahon helped establish connections to concerned women. And it was Charlotte Muller who first pointed me in this direction.

The BHE-PSC grant program of the City University of New York provided funding for research and clerical assistance. Joan Liebmann-Smith was research assistant in the initial stages of the project, and helped to formulate the work on genetic counselors.

Melinda Detleffs was research assistant for the rest of the project, and was an invaluable help. I am particularly grateful for her sensitive interviewing.

I thank my colleagues at Baruch College, including Norman Storer for his helpful clippings and references, and most especially those who listened while I ranted, raved, cried, and generally ruined their peaceful lunches: Susan Maisel Chambre, Glen Peterson, and Michael Plekon.

A number of people have read and commented helpfully on various chapters. I wish to thank Sue Fisher, Janet Glass, Marsha Hurst, Judith Lasker, Julius Roth, and Brenda Seals for their insights. Janet Gallagher has introduced me to people and to ideas that have profoundly influenced my thinking, as she has herself.

Irving Kenneth Zola and Ruth Hubbard each read through the bulk of the manuscript shortly before its completion. Their detailed comments and helpful criticisms went far beyond academic obligations. I have found in Ruth Hubbard a continuing source of wisdom and strength.

There are certain friendships that shape one's life and work. Such are my feelings about Kit Gates, Judith Lorber, Maren Lockwood Carden, Betty Leyerle, Eileen Moran, and Rosalyn Weinman Schram. Each brought unique insights and skills to this book, and each gave me the kind of personal support for which no expression of thanks could be adequate.

I am grateful to Mary White, who kept the home fires burning.

My family and friends helped me live through this book, which often felt more like an illness and convalescence than like scholarly work: they called to find out not how the work was going, but how I was doing. My appreciation for their concern goes to all of them, but especially to my husband, Herschel Rothman. This has not been easy for him, either, and I am deeply grateful for his support, nurturance and steadfast presence in my life.

My children, Daniel and Leah, taught me, as children will, the meaning of motherhood, a lesson that lies beneath all that I have written here.

To the many women who shared with me their thoughts, feelings, beliefs, fears, anger, and grief, I offer my gratitude, and I offer this book.

CONTENTS

* The author urges those readers who are currently pregnant to read the appendix first.

THE
TENTATIVE
PREGNANCY

1

THE PRODUCTS
OF CONCEPTION

It troubles me when a pregnant woman, suspecting a bout of beer drinking may have harmed her baby, aborts, saying, "It'll only set us back three months."

It troubles me when a friend talks about hiding her pregnancy from her daughters until after she has gotten her amniocentesis results because, "How could I explain an abortion to them?"

It troubles me when I am introduced to a pregnant woman and after giving her name she pats her belly and says, "And this is Heather."

It troubles me when a disabled woman says prenatal diagnosis is wrong because had her mother used it, she might have been aborted.

These issues that trouble me provide the impetus for this book. Taken together, they speak to an evolving American value system regarding our children, our parenthood, and ourselves. I see them as representing further movement toward the commodification of life, toward treating people and parts of people—our organs, blood, energy—as commodities. When we talk about the buying and selling of blood, the banking of sperm, the costs of hiring a surrogate mother, we are talking about bodies as commodities. And when we talk about being able to "afford" a second child, like a second car, then we are talking about children as luxury items, fine if you can afford them. And if all children are luxuries, then special children are special luxuries, as when we talk about how many extra dollars a year it costs to raise a child with sickle-cell disease.

In this value system, in this developing ideology, we are learning to see our children as products, the products of conception. Even while they still move within us, they are not part of us—we have learned to see them as other, as separate, as products. We work hard, some of us, at making the perfect product, what one doctor calls a "blue ribbon baby." Modern adoption practices have long encouraged us to think of babies as commodities: they are, after all, available for purchase.

The new technology of reproduction is building on this commodification. Rather than buying whole babies, we can now buy the parts. Sperm is relatively cheap. It is sold by students for approximately the cost of a textbook, or of an evening out. But it is the woman who supplies all the work, the labor as it were. Purchasing the woman's services, if you can supply your own sperm ("surrogate mothers") is considerably more expensive. Egg donations are being done only on an experimental basis now: will they eventually become purchasable too? And what of embryo transplants: doctors have tried to patent the embryo transfer process. How long will it be before human embryos, like some animal embryos, are up for sale?

Even in a more usual, "naturally" occurring pregnancy, the new technology of reproduction encourages and reinforces the commodification process: genetic counseling serves the function of quality control, and the wrongful life suits are a form of product liability litigation.[1]

What is the underlying ideology that permits the development of such a technology? And what does it do to us to think this way? These are the questions that I grapple with in this book.

I am not claiming that the technology itself is harmful. I think that the new technology of reproduction offers us an opportunity to work on our definitions of parenthood, of motherhood, father-hood, and childhood, to rethink and improve our relations with each other in families. Freed from some of the biological con-straints, we could evolve better, more egalitarian ways of relating to ourselves and each other in reproduction. The technology is a promise, beckoning us with new possibilities, limiting the role of chance and accident in reproduction, giving us new control. And the technology is a threat: control toward what end? For what purpose? For whose purpose? Or will the technology simply be incorporated into the social order and bring no social change? Technological change in reproduction, whether the current abil-ity to diagnose genetic disease in utero, the future ability to grow babies in test tubes, or the well-established ability to substitute artificial milk for mother's milk, does not necessarily mean social change. Think of how the invention of infant formula might have changed men's and women's roles in childbearing.

But technological change can represent social change. Techno-logical change can force us to confront questions we never before faced, to see ourselves and each other in new ways. The techno-logical revolution in reproduction is forcing us to confront the very meaning of motherhood, to examine the nature and origins of the mother-child bond, and to replace—or to let us think we can replace—chance with choice. Amniocentesis for prenatal diagnosis is the fulcrum on which the reproductive revolution turns: with this technology we move from motherhood as we have always known it to a new vision of the mother-child bond.

Amniocentesis for prenatal diagnosis is an increasingly im-portant part of the new technology of reproduction, affecting more and more pregnancies each year. By the 1990s it may very well become a standard, routine part of all prenatal care.[2] In this procedure, a small amount of the amniotic fluid that surrounds the fetus in the womb is withdrawn during the sixteenth to twentieth week of pregnancy, and fetal cells are cultured. Stud-ies of the fluid and fetal cells can detect chromosomal abnormalities, notably Downs Syndrome, but many others as well; hundreds of other genetic diseases, including sickle-cell anemia and Tay Sachs disease; and also the neural tube defects such as hydrocephalus and spina bifida. If the fetus is found to be diseased or damaged, in almost all cases abortion is the only treatment available.

For parents who have watched one child suffer and slowly, inevitably die with a condition like Tay Sachs disease, the availability of prenatal diagnosis can fundamentally change their reproductive options. When both parents are carriers of such a disease, in each pregnancy they have a one-in-four chance of producing a fetus with the condition. Very few parents are faced with such high risks of reproductive tragedy. The much more common uses of prenatal diagnosis are for the neural tube defects, such as spina bifida, and for chromosomal disorders, especially Downs Syndrome.

The chances of bearing a fetus with Downs Syndrome, which causes mental retardation and is associated with some physical problems as well, rises with the age of both the mother and the father. There is no particular age at which the risk jumps dramatically, but rather a steady increase. For a woman at age 30, the chances are roughly one in 1000, at age 35 one in 350, and at age 40, one in 100. It may well be that other age-related factors—perhaps diet, general health, exposure to environmental toxins and radiation—are the real causes of Downs Syndrome, and not age per se. But so far age alone has been the only factor demonstrably linked to Downs Syndrome in the general population.

When amniocentesis for the diagnosis of Downs Syndrome was first introduced, it was for women over the age of 40. Within ten years the medical standard dropped to age 35, and is currently inching its way down to 33 or even lower in some centers.

Although some people have discussed the value of being forewarned of genetic or other diseases even in a pregnancy the woman intends to carry to term, abortion is an integral part of this new technology. Fetal treatments do not exist for these diseases. The overwhelming majority of people who are told of serious disease or damage in the fetus do abort. These abortions, abortions to prevent the birth of a handicapped or disabled child, are among the most socially acceptable of abortions. In the

United States, more than 80 percent of people approve of the use of abortion in this situation.[3] Because these abortions are socially acceptable, many people have assumed that they are psychologically more acceptable than are abortions for what is called "less reason," abortions because a woman does not want to be pregnant. That is not true. The reasons lie in the meaning of abortion for the woman who uses it.

Women's willingness to use abortion for unwanted pregnancies has been perceived as a devaluing of motherhood. That it is not. On the contrary, it is because women continue to take motherhood so very seriously that abortion is necessary. Women understand motherhood to change their lives, to involve a deep and permanent commitment. If women did not take motherhood seriously, other options for managing an unwanted pregnancy would be available, from simple abandonment to the sale of babies. The current market rate for a newborn baby is upward of ten thousand dollars—but very few women are willing to bear babies to give them away.

In a sense, the motherhood-abortion paradox parallels the marriage-divorce paradox. The divorce rate is highest when expectations for marriage are highest. If marriage were considered less important, less central to one's life, divorce would be less common. Thus the paradox is that the high divorce rate demonstrates not a devaluing of marriage, but a commitment to the importance of the marriage relationship; and abortion as a solution to an unwanted pregnancy, demonstrates the importance to women of the mother-child relationship.

Abortions to prevent the birth of a disabled child may be more socially acceptable, but they are not in any sense easier. They present a deeper, more fundamental challenge for both the individual woman and the society at large. The challenge is to the meaning of motherhood.

The meaning of the abortion lies in the meanings the pregnancy holds for the woman. If a woman sees a pregnancy as an accident—if, for example, her pregnancy is a by-product of contraception that did not work—then in her definition the fetus is not a person and not meant to be one. The abortion is the solution to the problem of failed contraception.

But if the fetus is to be her child, if she has chosen to have this

baby—chosen by consciously and purposively becoming pregnant, or by willingly and openly accepting an unintended pregnancy—then she considers that fetus to be a person. It is her
baby. She means it to be her baby. To abort an accident is one
thing. To abort your baby, even your very imperfect baby, is
something else again. And that is equally true of two fetuses who
are identical in size, in ounces, in "viability." There is an understanding in sociology, and a deeply held belief for me, that situations defined as real are real in their consequences.[4] If a woman
defines the products of conception within her as accidental, then
that is what they are to her. If she defines it as her baby, then she
treats it as her baby.

The problem, or one of the problems, with the technology of
amniocentesis and selective abortion is what it does to us, to
mothers and to fathers and to families. It sets up a contradiction
in definitions. It asks women to accept their pregnancies and
their babies, to take care of the babies within them, and yet be
willing to abort them. We ask them to think about the needs of
the coming baby, to fantasize about the baby, to begin to become
the mother of the baby, and yet to be willing to abort the genetically damaged fetus. At the same time. For twenty to twenty-four
weeks.

Women suffer in this contradiction of demands. They want to
have amniocentesis to identify and to be able to abort a damaged
fetus, but are afraid of the procedure's possible harm to their *baby*.
As one couple said during a counseling session, as they struggled
with the (remote) possibility of miscarriage caused by amniocentesis and the (equally remote) possibility of having a child with
Downs Syndrome:

HUSBAND: We really want this baby. . . .
WIFE: . . . and if it's a healthy baby I really hate the thought
of losing this person.

If it is healthy, if it is genetically acceptable, then it is a person,
her baby. If it is not, then it is just a fetus, a genetically damaged
fetus.

Parenthood demands such total acceptance from us. We expect mothers to love, to accept their babies unreservedly, with

the fullness of their hearts, no matter what. We joke about it: "a face only a mother could love." It is not that women have always been able to achieve that unconditional love. Indeed, the fear of having a child one cannot love is one of the more common fears that haunt pregnancy. But never before have we asked women to make rational, intellectual determinations based on that fear. What does it do to motherhood, to women, and to men as fathers, too, when we make parental acceptance conditional, pending further testing? We ask the mother and her family to say, in essence, "These are my standards. If you meet these standards of acceptability, then you are mine and I will love and accept you totally. After you pass this test."

The amniocentesis comes so late in the pregnancy. The problems will be very different when fetal testing is done earlier in pregnancy. But now there are months that women wait in this limbo of "tentative pregnancy," unsure whether they are "mothers" or "carriers of a defective fetus." For some women the amniocentesis comes too late:

> . . . by the time the results came in the baby had been leaping in my womb for a month. . . . During one of the sleepless nights before the results were in I decided I would raise the child if it looked like E.T.[5]

A face only a mother could love.

An irony in all this is that the technology still cannot guarantee a "blue ribbon baby." A fetus can pass all of the tests and still be far from perfect at birth. A child can be born or become retarded, disabled, disfigured from thousands of causes. One can rationally decide to abort a fetus with spina bifida because life in a wheelchair is not acceptable—and then have a baby's back broken in a car accident. One can choose not to carry to term a fetus with Downs Syndrome because the quality of life of the retarded is not acceptable—and then have the baby suffer permanent brain damage from some illness. There are limits to control, and our children are always "hostages to fortune." Does the conscious, deliberate emphasis on control and "standards of acceptability" prepare us for the *reality* of parenthood?

Another of the problems with the commodification process

and its ensuing technology is that it allows some people, the richest and the most powerful, to buy their way out. Individual solutions are found while leaving social problems intact. Let us take as an example the situation of having a retarded child. Why do I recoil at the thought of having as my son a grown man who drools and behaves like a child? If the person is, as most people with Downs Syndrome are, able to learn to walk, to talk, to do simple tasks, then why do we so fear retardation?

One reason is what it does to our lives. You cannot even afford to die if you have a retarded child: what will become of her or him? This is just the extreme case of what is true of all children in our society—they are private property, and their economic and social burden is not shared. Support services for children in the United States are abysmal: it is United States policy to allow children to live in great poverty unless their individual parents and families can provide for them. With retarded or other damaged children, the stakes rise. One may be able to afford twenty years of expenses for a normal child, but a lifetime of expenses for a damaged child is just too much. The economic burden of a retarded or disabled child is beyond most of us. And the emotional burdens are inextricably tied up with the financial burdens.

The economic ties are basic. Most of the causes of disability and retardation among children are related to class position: one's chances of having a healthy child kept safe in a safe environment increase as we go up the socioeconomic scale. The children of the poor suffer disproportionately from premature birth, from illness, from lead paint poisoning, from pollutants that parents in factories bring home on their clothes, from starvation and deficiency diseases, from cold apartments, from overcrowding, from poor medical care. One of the few causes of disability and retardation that seems truly *not* to be class-linked is genetic disease: Downs Syndrome, for example, appears to be associated exclusively with maternal and paternal age, and not class position; hemophilia brought in by Queen Victoria destroyed the royal house of Russia.[6] As we increasingly solve genetic causes of disability, the population of the disabled will become even more disproportionately drawn from the population of the poor. As the wealthiest, most powerful in society increasingly buy their way out of retardation and disability, what will happen to the support services that do exist? Who will monitor the state schools for the retarded then?

Retardation and disability are social issues[7] threatening the stated values of the society: the value of equal opportunity and a fair share for everyone. We treat these social issues as individual troubles, to be individually solved. We treat them *clinically*, not *politically*. It fits in with the private property idea of children: the needs of *your* children are *your* problem.

From the point of view of the individual pregnant woman and her family, amniocentesis and selective abortion make great sense. I am not suggesting that we force wealthier and more educated people to have retarded children so that they will make that their political issue, their fight. I cannot accuse the people who offer the services or those who use them of doing the wrong thing. Mostly they are doing the only thing they can do. They are absolutely right when they say that they cannot afford, emotionally or financially, the burden of a disabled child. It is equally true that the infertile couple who can afford to buy a baby or to buy surrogate services may be making absolutely the right choice in purchasing such a baby or such services. But individual solutions are not the answers to the social problems.

We cannot solve the social issues of dealing with the less-than-perfect people by making disability an individual trouble. We live in a society designed for the physically and mentally competent. Part of the issue then is redesigning the physical and social environment to meet the needs of all people. This is what the people in the disability rights movement are calling for. The decision to abort a fetus with spina bifida when you live in a fourth-floor walkup in a city designed without access for wheelchairs is not really an exercise in free choice.

But there are other issues as well. We must consider what it means to us to commodify life, to affix price tags to body parts. I include semen, ova, embryos, and fetuses as body parts. An important lesson can be learned from what happens when other body parts are available for purchase. Richard Titmuss's study of blood donation in England and in the United States, *The Gift Re-*

lationship, provides a model.[8] In England, where there is still resistance to total commodification of life, there is a right to health services, and blood is free. It is freely given. In the United States, blood is purchased either for money from paid donors, or for insurance, blood donors earning access to free blood for themselves and their families as needed. Blood is purchased twice then, once from the donor and once again from the blood bank. Titmuss's most dramatic finding is that the commodification of blood does not work: where blood is purchased, it is scarce where needed, wasted where hoarded, in uneven, unreliable supply. Where blood is given freely, it is made freely available, and the supply is more even, with considerably less waste.

Titmuss's conclusions are not merely pragmatic, regarding the most efficient way to distribute blood. He reaches beyond to analyze the social bond, to claim a *right to give*, a right to be "my stranger's keeper," a right that is violated when social policy supports commodification. He says of the altruistic English blood donors:

> In not asking for or expecting any payment of money these donors signified their belief in the willingness of other men to act altruistically in the future, and to combine together to make a gift freely should they have need for it. By expressing confidence in the behavior of future unknown strangers they are thus denying the Hobbesian thesis that men are devoid of any distinctively moral sense.[9]

I want to argue from blood to gametes, to embyros, to fetuses, to children. The commodification of life and bodies feeds upon itself and destroys, as Titmuss claims, the right to be altruistic. In a society that claims little joint responsibility for children, children are inevitably private property, and just as inevitably it follows that they will be sold and it further follows that they will carry different price tags based on social desirability. And some will be rejects, not salable at any price: too damaged, or the wrong color, or too old, too long on the shelf.

In a world that does not value children, I do not know what it means to be altruistic with my seed. Could I give away an embryo, as many men have given or sold semen, when I know that child may grow to have needs that will be unmet? Is that kind of giving away altruism, or is it abnegation of responsibility? One of the things mothers who have given up babies for adoption often say is that they just wish there was some way that the child could reach them if (s)he needed them. In this world, in this society, we do not, cannot trust that the needs of all children, of our children, will be met. Thus the right to give is lost.

As we lose the right to give, so too do we lose the right to accept, to accept our less-than-perfect, our needful children. In gaining the choice to control the quality of our children, we may rapidly lose the choice not to control the quality, the choice of simply accepting them as they are. The new reproductive technology is offered to us in terms of expanding choices. But it is always true that while new technology opens up some choices, it closes down others. The new choice is often greeted with such fanfare that the silent closing of the door on the old choice goes unheeded. To take a simple example, is there any meaningful way one could now choose horses over cars as a means of transportation? The new choice of a "horseless carriage" eventually left us "no choice" but to live with the pollution and dangers (as well as the convenience and speed, of course) of a car-based transportation system.

It happened first with *quantity* of children. The oldest and most basic reproductive technology is the technology of fertility limitation. Self-imposed limits on fertility, through contraception or abortion, are the *sine qua non* of the reproductive rights movement. Without such control:

> . . . women cannot gain access to or participate effectively in the political and social processes which shape every aspect of their lives. The degree of control women are able to exercise over their reproductive lives directly affects their educational and job opportunities, income level, physical and emotional well being, as well as the economic and social conditions the children they bear will experience.[10]

Nadine Taub, professor of law at Rutgers University, quoted this as an "understood premise" of a Reproductive Rights Symposium at Rutgers in 1982. I think it is a statement with which most feminists and most liberals would agree. It is a statement of choice and control: to be free, women must be able to choose to control their fertility.

Wait a minute. Did I say to be free women we must be able to choose to control our fertility? Then what of the choice *not* to control fertility? At that same symposium, in a related but different context, Ruth Hubbard said, "As 'choices' become available, they all too rapidly become compulsions to 'choose' the socially endorsed alternative."[11]

I have been troubled in recent years by reactions, including my own, to unlimited fertility. A woman I see each summer was pregnant this year. Again. It was her fourth baby in five years. I know that she is having problems with money (and who wouldn't, with four kids?). I know she is overworked and tired, trying to find affordable child care so she can work part-time. Four babies, I thought. My god. And then we talked. She's the classic case: the woman who has gotten pregnant with every birth control method, in place, used correctly. This last pregnancy, the doctor said, "C'mon, I'll abort it right now, you can go home not pregnant and forget it." She was tempted, sorely tempted. But no, she chose not to abort. She really didn't want to have an abortion. She had had several, years ago, before her children, and she didn't want any more. It was a choice she made, an unpopular reproductive choice, one that is not, in her community of friends, socially endorsed. And if her educational and job opportunities are severely reduced, if she's physically and emotionally exhausted, if the economic and social condition of her children suffers, well, that's her choice, isn't it? And if another woman in these circumstances chooses to abort, she too is exercising her choice.

While on the one hand we worry, with very good reason, about losing the option of legal abortions, on the other hand we are losing the option not to abort. When women are not allowed, or cannot afford, safe and legal abortions, that does not mean that they can afford children: what they resort to is their "only choice," abortions that may be neither legal nor safe. This woman who kept her fourth pregnancy made a choice, but it is a choice that may be rapidly slipping away from us. She is suffering not just the inevitable consequences of four children, but the consequences of her poverty. If she were rich, if her husband made a fortune, she would still be tired, I'm sure, but she would have many more choices in how she lives her life as the mother of four young children.

The choice of contraception simultaneously closed down some of the choices for large families. North American society is geared to small families, if indeed to any children at all. Everything from car to apartment sizes to the picture-book ideal of families encourages limiting fertility. Without the provision of good medical care, day care, decent housing, children *are* a luxury item, fine if you can afford them. So it is a choice all right that contraception gave us, and a choice we may very well experience as being under our control, but it may well be a somewhat forced choice. In its extreme, legislation has repeatedly been introduced to punish "welfare mothers" by cutting off payments if they have more children. Sterilization abuse is the flip side of the abortion battle: the same sorry record. And, at a different place in the economy, just sometimes, when I think wistfully about another baby, a bigger family, and realize I could never "afford" it, afford the schools, the private medical care, the trappings of middle-class life expected of, and for, and by me for my children, I almost envy my great-grandmother her eight children. Does the choice not to be burdened with continual childbearing have to be paid for with the choice to have larger families?

So there may be choice brought to us by information and technology, the choices we get when we learn how to use contraception and backup abortion for fertility control, but the choices may very well be heavily weighted for, or against, us.

And so it may also be with the technology of *quality control*: the ability to control the quality of our children may ultimately cost us the right not to control that quality. It probably won't be done, as some fear, by state mandate, as Nazi Germany did, through forcible sterilization or compulsory abortion. It happens instead through a narrowing and structuring of choices. Issues of basic values, beliefs, the larger moral questions are lost. Decisions become pragmatic, often clinical, always individual. Irving Kenneth Zola puts it this way:

Bombarded on all sides by realistic concerns (the escalations of costs) and objective evidence (genetics) and techniques (genetic counselors), the basic value issue at stake will be obfuscated. The freedom to choose will be illusory. Someone will already have set the limits of choice (cuts in medical care and social benefits but not in defense spending), the dimensions of choice (if you do this then you will have an X probability of a defective child), and the outcomes of choice (you will have to endure the following social, political, legal, and economic costs).[12]

Amniocentesis and selective abortion, like embryo transplants, surrogate motherhood, and other new reproductive technology, are all being used to give the illusion of choice.

On an individual level they certainly solve some very grave troubles. People who have successfully used the new technologies have had their choices expand, have gained control over their lives. In just the same way, contraception and abortion provide us with the very real and very true experience of controlling our fertility. Choices open and choices close. For those whose choices meet the social expectations, for those who want what the society wants them to want, the experience of choice is very real.

Perhaps what we should realize is that human beings living in society have precious little choice ever. There may really be no such thing as individual choice in a social structure, not in any absolute way. The social structure creates needs—the needs for women to be mothers, the needs for small families, the needs for "perfect children"—and creates the technology that enables people to make the needed choices. The question is not whether choices are constructed, but *how* they are constructed. Society, in its ultimate meaning, may be nothing more and nothing less than the structuring of choices.[13]

The new technology of prenatal diagnosis and selective abortion offers new choices, but it also creates new structures and new limitations on choice. Because of the society in which we live, the choices are inevitably couched in terms of production and commodification, and thus do not move us to see new levels of genuine choice.

What do these new choices and limitations mean to women who would be mothers? It is not what selective abortion or the sale of gametes and fetuses do to the fetuses that I will address in this book, just as it was not the rights of blood that Titmuss addressed. It is what this technology does to mothers and motherhood that concerns me. It is women, women as mothers, who are most directly and powerfully affected by this technology. As committed as any couple may be to sharing parenting, to raising children together, at twenty weeks of gestation, waiting for prenatal diagnosis results to come back, it is *women* who are pregnant, not couples.

This book is about women's experiences with prenatal diagnosis, but it is about more than that. It is about motherhood and the meaning of human commitment. It is about choices. It is about loss and grief. It is about the world we are creating, and what it is doing to us.

About the Research

The research reported in this book is based on interviews with four groups of women: three are the recipients, or intended recipients, of genetic counseling and prenatal diagnostic services. The fourth group consists of genetic counselors, providers of these services. Today's genetic counselors, sometimes also called genetic associates, generally have a master's degree in human genetics and counseling. They are usually employed by hospitals and work under physician supervision. Almost all are women, as were all twenty-five I interviewed formally, and all I have met and interviewed in less structured situations. They are the women who are the most familiar with the uses and choices in prenatal diagnosis.

I spent over a month observing three different genetic counselors at work, providing prenatal diagnosis counseling. That is not very long, just long enough so that sessions began to blur, and I could anticipate what each counselor would say next. Routine pre-amnio counseling for "advanced maternal age" (pregnancies over 35) is boring. Counselors say so, and I can see why. The same information is given over and over, the same questions asked again and again, and the chances of finding a problem are wonderfully, blessedly remote. At age 35 the risk of Downs Syndrome is just one in 350 pregnancies. That means that counseling seven such women a day, five days a week (which, considering the amount of paperwork involved, is a very heavy schedule), would yield only five cases of Downs Syndrome in a year. Among the counselors I interviewed, the average was approximately two cases of Downs per year. Some counselors, of course, work for two years without ever seeing a case of Downs, and another might have two in one month.

The month I spent observing counseling sessions was my introduction to the area. I said nothing, asked nothing, just sat in a corner and took notes. The counselors were kindly and often warmly accepting of my presence. Clients of course were asked their permission for me to sit in, and all agreed—people are accommodating, and observers in such settings are not uncommon. As I sat and listened, I came to see more clearly what the questions were that I needed to ask of both clients and counselors.

My second step was to interview genetic counselors. With the aid of two research assistants, Melinda Detleffs and Joan Leibmann-Smith, I conducted interviews with twenty-five genetic counselors. The interviews the research assistants did were tape-recorded for my benefit.

The observations and interviews of genetic counselors were the background, and while I will refer to that work throughout the book, the bulk of my research is based on interviews with women who had had or who had refused amniocentesis with pregnancies medically defined as "at risk." For most, this meant a pregnancy after the age of 35. For some, it was a pregnancy in which both parents were carriers of a genetic disease, or where a previous pregnancy had resulted in the birth of a child with a genetic disease.

Finding women who had had or were going to have amniocentesis would not be hard for me. As a professional woman in my mid-thirties, I am surrounded by colleagues and acquaintances who are pregnant and having amniocentesis. Like maternity blazers, prenatal diagnosis is a hallmark of the professional woman's pregnancy. But I wanted to get past this particular population, the entirely urban, well-educated, career-committed group of women I knew. I wanted to reach women from around the country, women who were experiencing pregnancies in different places and circumstances. And hardest of all, I wanted to find women who had thought about prenatal diagnosis, who knew it was an option, but who had chosen not to have it. Some women were reached by word of mouth: friends of friends, a colleague's sister-in-law, someone's ex-husband's second wife, and the like. But particularly helpful in reaching women with a variety of backgrounds and experiences were pieces placed in two magazines. *Ms.* magazine ran a classified ad, asking for women who were interested in sharing their experiences with amniocentesis to write to me. And *Mothering* magazine ran a two-page article about some of the questions raised by amniocentesis, questions about who should have it and under what circumstances. The article concluded by asking people who were willing to discuss their experiences with prenatal diagnosis to write to me. *Ms.* magazine is addressed to a feminist audience. *Mothering* might best be described as an "alternative lifestyle" magazine. There are regular sections on home birth and midwifery, on schooling children at home, and ways of working from home. *Mothering* readers were the largest part of my sample.

Interestingly, roughly half of the women in each group—the *Ms.* readers, the *Mothering* readers, and the word-of-mouth contacts—chose to have amniocentesis, and about half refused. The use of prenatal diagnosis does not break down neatly into a feminist-traditionalist division. Some of those who had amniocentesis fully and totally identify themselves as full-time wives and mothers, devoted to home and family in the most traditional way. And some of those who are committed, active feminists, some whose names are well-known in feminist circles, chose not to have amniocentesis.

In all, I interviewed over sixty women who had amniocentesis, and sixty women who were equally "at risk" but refused the amniocentesis. Most of these interviews were conducted by mail—I sent out a ten-page questionnaire, with lots of space for long answers. Most women used up all the space, and many sent long letters besides. Questionnaires and letters came back filled out in crude pencil with poor grammar and many spelling errors, in flowing handwriting, in cramped writing wrapping around the margins and over the backs of pages, in long typed essays, and even done on a word processor. Some came with photos. And besides the letters there were phone calls. I gave the women my telephone number, and some called to talk more. I asked for their phone numbers, and most gave them. Some I called to explore an unclear point, to discuss an issue further. Some women were more comfortable corresponding in writing, and some few did not have telephones, and so we wrote letters back and forth. I feel as if I have come to know these women from all over the United States, from virtually every state in the country and some from other countries as well.

One final source of respondents was reached through a particularly helpful, thoughtful genetic counselor. I was interested in hearing from more women who had received bad news from prenatal diagnosis. One of the counselors I interviewed was especially concerned with these women. I made copies of a letter explaining the research that I was doing, enclosed self-addressed stamped envelopes and my phone number, and the counselor mailed these to those of her clients who had received bad diagnoses. Those who were interested or willing to talk to me mailed me their names and addresses, or called me. In all, I interviewed fourteen women who terminated pregnancies following prenatal diagnosis. Some few of those interviews were conducted entirely by mail, some by combination of mail and phone, some I did in person, and some were done by Melinda Detleffs. And, as with the interviews with genetic counselors, those done by Melinda Detleffs were tape-recorded.

Let me point out some of the advantages and limitations of this kind of research. There is one kind of research that is often described in terms of marbles in a jar. If we want to know what the proportion of black and white marbles are in a jar, we can draw out a random handful, and the proportion in that sample represents the proportions in the jar. That technique is called "representative sampling." That is *not* what the research described in this book accomplishes. Picture instead a box with marbles of many different colors. You reach in your hand and pull out a scoop of marbles: red, yellow, blue, another red, a purple, two more blues, another yellow. With all those different colors, and just one scoop, we cannot be at all confident that we know the proportions of the various colors. What we do learn is something about the variety and kind of marbles in there. That is the research described here: it is exploratory research. I will not be able to tell you what percentage of women thought this way or that, had this feeling or that about their experiences with prenatal diagnosis. But we can, from listening to these women, learn something about the variety of ways the women have of thinking about the issue.

I know that my sampling of women is not representative of all women who have had or who choose not to have a prenatal diagnosis, and not representative of all the women who receive bad diagnoses. Because the women had to respond to me, answer my call, at least two groups of women are almost certainly missing: those who were the least troubled, and those who were the most. If having amniocentesis was genuinely not an issue for the woman, if it was no big deal at all, then there would be no reason for her to respond to me—no more than there would be responses if I called for women to talk about their experiences with, say, having a tooth filled. If it was a routine, nontraumatic event, then the woman might feel there was nothing to discuss. On the other hand, if the experience was genuinely traumatic, if it was deeply disturbing, it might be too painful to discuss. I know that that was the case with several women who received bad diagnoses and were asked by others whether they would talk to me, but said that they could not.

These then are the women who were bothered enough so that they were motivated to talk about it—or were pleased enough that they wanted to share the experience. And these were the women who were not pained so much that they were unable or unwilling to talk about it.

One response I got over and over again was an expression of appreciation for doing the research—so very many of the women told me how grateful they were to have the opportunity to talk about this experience, how much they appreciated my listening, taking it seriously, giving them a chance to let others know what it was like. Again, we must remember that these were women who *chose* to respond to me—the ones who didn't think it needed discussion didn't respond. But even with that understanding, it seems that many women feel that the seriousness of this situation and event is unrecognized. In a strange way, this got in the way of my writing—after having woman after woman say to me how grateful she was for the opportunity to be heard on this subject, I found myself wanting to quote all of them, each and every one. Early drafts of some chapters were filled with repetitious quotes, a dozen different women making each point. Having been told by a woman that "nobody else wants to hear about this," I couldn't bring myself to say, "me, neither," and silence her voice, however much she repeated what others said. It was only months later, going back to do rewrites and editing, distanced from the immediacy of each woman, that I could prune off the repetitions.

What you now have before you in this book are the voices of women who have been offered the choices brought by the new reproductive technology, women who accepted and women who refused to use the technology. They are thoughtful, reflective, caring women. They want to be heard, and I want very much for you to hear them.

Some of what they say is troubling, some deeply distressing, and some even horrifying. The technology of prenatal diagnosis is usually presented to us as a solution, but it brings with it problems of its own. Does that mean that we should discard the technology? Could we do so if we wanted to? These are questions I cannot, will not answer. This book is a description and an exploration. Mostly it is an opportunity for the women who have experienced the solution to be heard.

The Organization of This Book

In the next chapter I will review some of the social and technological changes that have brought us to this new technology and the way that we use it. The second half of the chapter will focus on the contemporary context in which prenatal diagnosis is offered. The chapter will draw upon interviews with genetic counselors, and my observations of genetic counseling sessions.

Chapter 3, "Making Choices," is on how women decide whether or not to have amniocentesis. The reasons and values the women have for their choices are presented, and the implications of new and developing technology for prenatal diagnosis are considered.

The following two chapters focus predominantly on the experiences of women who chose to have amniocentesis, drawing upon the experiences of the women who refused the tests primarily for contrast. I explore the effects of waiting for a diagnosis through the first half of the pregnancy in the chapter called "The Tentative Pregnancy." The effects of the prenatal diagnosis on the second half of the pregnancy are considered in the chapter on fetal sex: what happens to women's experience of pregnancy with the knowledge of fetal sex?

For most women, the prenatal diagnosis brings good news. It is only a very tiny minority who receive bad diagnoses. Chapters 6 and 7 deal with the experiences of those women. Theirs is the minority experience, but they are what this entire process is all about. It is the women who receive bad diagnoses who can be said to have benefited at all from the procedure: they are the ones who are offered new choices. The meaning of such a choice, the way such a choice is made, and the pressures brought to bear in making it teach us a great deal about our society. The responses, and especially the grief that accompanies the choice, teaches us a great deal about motherhood.

Chapter 8 concludes the book by reconsidering the issues raised by prenatal diagnosis. An appendix offers some personal strategies in using the technology. I urge those who are currently pregnant to read the appendix first.

2

PRENATAL DIAGNOSIS
IN CONTEXT

There are many different histories one can write for the new reproductive technology, and specifically for prenatal diagnosis. As I pick and choose my way back, following different strands of the story, I realize that each history casts its own light on the present. Whichever history I present here will provide a context for understanding prenatal diagnosis—and different histories give very different contexts. These histories are not only different; at times they are quite contradictory. Prenatal diagnosis is part of the history of the loss of medical mystique and control, as physicians lost the exclusive power over the abortion decision. But prenatal diagnosis is also part of the history of medicalization, as physicians sought to gain control over pregnancy and the fetus. This is not simply a shifting of ground, but, as I will show, the outcome of two very separate movements. There is another, more fundamental contradiction. Prenatal diagnosis is part of feminist history, woman's increasing right to control her own reproductive capacity. But prenatal diagnosis is also very much part of the history of patriarchy, men's struggle to gain control over their "seed," and thus men's control over women's reproductive capacities. So this chapter will not, cannot, present *the* history of prenatal diagnosis—it will present some of the many histories.

The History of Abortion

Legalized abortion is a necessary part of prenatal diagnosis as we now know it. For the overwhelming majority of conditions that are prenatally diagnosable, there are no prenatal treatments. While an individual woman might consider prenatal diagnosis worthwhile just for the benefit of preparation, the social support, including the funding of programs, has come for prenatal diagnosis as a preventive measure. Since the prevention can occur only after conception, and most of the conditions themselves can be neither treated nor modified in pregnancy, abortion is the preventive measure taken. In the unlikely event that abortion were to become illegal, it is hard to envision the continued existence of legal prenatal diagnosis programs. It is possible, maybe even likely, that these services, like abortion itself, would continue to be available outside of the law.

Because of their dependence on legalized abortion, and because of the strong links between legalized abortion and the contemporary women's movement, those engaged in prenatal diagnosis can and often do lay claim to a feminist basis for their services. Using these services, in turn, is sometimes seen as a "feminist" or "liberated" thing to do. As the women themselves will make clear in later chapters, nothing is all that simple. But because the connections are drawn, and because the dependency on legalized abortion certainly does exist, it is important to look at the history of abortion for the light it casts on prenatal diagnosis. Much of the discussion that follows draws upon Kristen Luker's fine book, *Abortion and the Politics of Motherhood.*[1]

Physicians in the nineteenth century used abortion as a wedge toward gaining their own professional status. Abortions were apparently widely available in America at that time, advertised in newspapers, and performed by people with a variety of backgrounds. In driving out the "quacks," physicians were in one sense doing what they were doing in other areas of practice. They replaced midwives at childbirth and a host of other practitioners who were supplying services that only later became defined as "medical" in nature. But with abortion, another dimension was added. Physicians argued that their knowledge of embryonic and fetal development (really quite minimal at that time) enabled them to know what the women having abortions presumably did not know: that the embryo was a baby. Having made this claim, doctors were able to say that the abortionists were not only incompetent, dirty, backward—all the charges they leveled at midwives and other competitors—but also that what they were doing was fundamentally wrong, immoral.

The physicians, however, did not want an absolute ban on abortion. What the doctors claimed, a contradiction highlighted by Luker, was that abortion was wrong, but physicians, and only physicians, could determine when it was *necessary*. Abortion was *necessary* when pregnancy threatened the life of the mother—a determination over which the physicians claimed technical expertise. Thus there were two kinds of abortions: the ones the doctors did not do, which were "immoral" and "criminal," and the ones that the doctors did do, which were both moral and, almost by definition, "therapeutic."

As the overall health of the population improved, and as medical technology improved, abortions literally to save the life of the mother became increasingly rare—but abortion itself did not become correspondingly rare. Rather, it seems, the categories of therapeutic abortion broadened to take into consideration the woman's general health: physical and, eventually, emotional health. While some physicians and hospitals were doing abortions only to preserve the life of the mother in the strictest interpretation of that phrase, others did them based on broader definitions of life and health. A gap opened between what Luker calls the "strict constructionists" and the "broad constructionists," in the way they defined the preservation of the mother's life. In one of life's stranger ironies, it was these "broad constructionist" physicians who opened the can of worms that abortion reform meant, which eventually lost the medical profession its control over abortion. They did so by seeking legislation to legitimize their broad interpretation of the law. They did so, Luker argues, without realizing that their view of abortion was not universally held, without even realizing that strict constructionists still existed, let alone existed as a potentially powerful political force.

It is not all that uncommon for a reform to open the door to an out-and-out rebellion, and that is what seems to have happened with abortion. Once a "broad" interpretation, or "liberal" abortion law was allowed, the inherent and often arbitrary power of physicians to do the interpreting was laid bare. And thus what Luker claims to be a new force entered the abortion discussion: women, as women, claiming abortion as a *right*, not dependent upon the approval of their physicians, but as a basic human right to control their own bodies.

The rest, as they say, is history.

Part of the legacy of the history of abortion is the rather strange language with which we are left. Abortions that are most clearly "medical"—that is, abortions based on medical considerations of *any* sort—are called "therapeutic." Still. That includes those abortions that are based not at all on the condition of the woman's health, but on the health of the fetus. This language itself makes abortion following prenatal diagnosis an easy target for attack by those opposed to abortions: it is hard to claim that abortion for genetic defect is "therapeutic" for the fetus aborted, and the mother is not sick. The more the "right-to-life" movement attacks abortions for fetal indication, the more the "pro-choice" movement feels called upon to defend such abortions.

For those who are neither in the right-to-life movement, nor particularly concerned with abortion as a specifically *feminist* concern, other considerations come into play. Fears of disability, extreme repugnance toward the mentally retarded, and deeply embedded cultural ideas about health combine to make abortions when the fetus would be "defective" among the most acceptable of abortions to most Americans.

Politics, as they say, does make strange bedfellows. Those in the disability rights movement are courted by those in the right-to-life movement. The feminist movement, loudly proclaiming that biology need not be destiny, calls upon notions of biology as destiny, disability as doom, to support the continued availability of abortions. It is perfectly understandable that people would call upon "worst-case" scenarios to defend abortion, the "what if your 14-year-old daughter was raped and got pregnant" variety of argument. Given social attitudes toward disability, the temptation to call upon abortions following prenatal diagnosis as support for all abortions is also clear: what if you or your wife were pregnant and going to have a "cripple," a "retard," a "defective" child? What if she had taken thalidomide, a "teratogenic" drug? Teratogenic means "causing fetal abnormality," but it comes from the root meaning "monster." Very deep feelings are being called upon.

The Fetus as Patient

The early part of the history of abortion which I just presented, abortion in the 1800s, is part of the history of the *medicalization* of reproduction. In spite of having lost its control over abortion, the power of medicine as a profession is still considerable. In her book on the new reproductive technology, *The Mother Machine*, Gena Corea writes of the "pharmocrats," the physicians and bio-technicians who control reproductive technologies.[2] Just as "theocracy" refers to political rule by a priesthood, "pharmocracy" refers to political rule by medicine. As more and more aspects of our lives have come under medical supervision—i.e., are "medicalized"—medicine has become even more clearly an institution of social control.[3] Reproduction has come under medical control, as first abortion was seen as a medical decision and childbirth as a surgical event, and then pregnancy as a disease, and now the fetus has attained the status of patient.

Control over reproduction is not quite like other forms of medicalization. Compare the medicalization of pregnancy with the medicalization of alcoholism. Declaring that people who drink too much alcohol are ill and therefore "patients" has not the same far-reaching effects as declaring fetuses to be patients. One can negotiate the "alcoholic" label, argue about who is and who is not "really" an alcoholic. But declaring fetuses to be patients, as medicine now does, is the most inclusive categorization possible: we have all been fetuses, and there is no other entry into life but passage through the status of fetus; in the beginning, we are all fetuses. As medicine gains control over fetalhood, it controls the gates of life; in the beginning, we are all patients.

How has this view of the fetus as a patient come about, and what does it mean for women—women as the people in whom fetuses grow?

Perhaps it really began in earnest with the by-now familiar techniques for fetal monitoring in labor. Not all that long ago, just back in the 1970s, the way that medicine "monitored" or to put it simply, *watched* a labor, was to watch the laboring woman. Her heart rate, blood pressure, the frequency and intensity of her contractions, and the rate at which her cervix, the neck of the uterus, was opening up, provided the information on how the labor was going. In addition, there was one other measure that was taken, one that was more directly a measure of the fetus: by putting a stethoscope to the mother's abdomen, one could hear the heartbeat of the fetus.

Electronic fetal monitoring was introduced for use with "high-risk" pregnancies, but as is so often the case, it rapidly came into widespread use. Electronic monitoring was used to provide more direct information about the status of the fetus in three ways: (1) externally, by ultrasound monitoring of the fetal heart rate and uterine contractions; (2) internally, by fetal electrocardiogram obtained with electrodes attached to the fetal head and uterine monitoring by means of a catheter passed into the uterus through the cervix; and (3) by direct sampling of fetal scalp blood, obtained from an electrode screwed into the fetal head.[4] As it turns out, electronic fetal monitoring may not really provide all that much more information on the condition of the fetus than does good nursing care. It certainly does look like more information, though, with endless strips of printout for the duration of the labor.

But I think more important than the sheer quantity of the data, impressive though that was, was that the information came in a new context. Instead of having to approach the woman, to rest your head near her belly, to smell her skin, to feel her breathing, you could now read the information on the fetus from across the room, from down the hall. While there was still one being on the bed, medical personnel came to see the woman and the fetus as separate, as two different patients. The continued development of a technology that renders the fetus visible, that gives obstetricians more and more direct access to the fetus itself—the fetal tissue, blood, and the direct observation of the fetal movements that sonography allows—exacerbated the problem. More and more doctors developed a relationship with the fetus, the separate patient within.

This technology came at just that point that women were rejecting the patient role for themselves in pregnancy, often to the irritation and even distress of their doctors. As pregnant women increasingly declared themselves healthy and rejected the label of pregnancy as an illness, the doctors were looking more and more closely at the fetus within, the tiny, helpless, dependent fetus.

In part as a response to this new technology that enables the obstetrician to see, and perhaps diagnose, and perhaps even treat the fetus; and in part as a response to the changes in the status of women as patients; and in part as a continued growth of men's domination of reproduction—because of all of these, pregnancy is increasingly becoming seen, as Ruth Hubbard has pointed out, as a conflict of rights between a woman and her fetus. With the fetus seen as a separate patient, the obstetrician has come to see the mother as a potential adversary, a potential barrier to the optimum medical care of the fetus. The special irony introduced in the case of prenatal diagnosis, as it is used in early to mid-pregnancy, is that there is as yet no medical care available for the fetus. Still physicians may claim the right of the fetus to diagnosis, or conversely, may feel their right as physicians to diagnose their patient, the fetus. Some physicians see the development of diagnostic techniques as just the first step toward ultimately developing treatment techniques. What happens when treatments are developed that are experimental, that may be harmful to the woman?

The potential conflict in this situation has recently been dramatized in court-ordered caesarean sections. When women in labor or late pregnancy have disagreed with their physicians (or who they thought were *their* physicians) over how to manage labor, the physicians have turned to the court.[5] In several bedside juvenile court hearings, with a lawyer appointed to represent the unborn fetus, another representing the pregnant woman, and yet others representing the hospital, women have been ordered to submit to caesarean sections, the fetus within them claimed by the state as a "dependent and neglected child."[6] In 1981, *Obstetrics and Gynecology*,[7] writing to an audience of obstetricians, carried an article reporting one such case in which the woman, although found to be psychiatrically competent, was forced to undergo a caesarean section very much against her will. The article quoted the current edition of one of the classic obstetrics textbooks, *Williams*, which states that the fetus has "rightfully achieved the status of the second patient, a patient who usually faces much greater risk of serious morbidity and mortality than does the mother."

Caesarean section is one of the most common operations done on women. Caesareans are very, very occasionally done to save the life or the health of the woman herself. Much more commonly, caesareans are done in response to fetal indications, because obstetricians, rightly or wrongly, believe that the laboring uterus is potentially quite dangerous to the fetus. Major abdominal surgery is conducted on the body of the woman to help her fetus. In the crisislike situation of a labor going poorly, or which doctors believe is going poorly, the conflict of rights and interests between the mother and fetus may well be blurred.

The situation becomes more dramatically fraught with possibilities when surgery is suggested on the fetus itself, with the mother opened up only to gain access to the fetus. Several procedures of this sort have been done, including placing a shunt in a hydrocephalic fetus to prevent fluid from building up in the brain of the fetus. The procedures are experimental and have had little real success. Doctors, lawyers, and philosophers have somehow anticipated women's possible objections to such procedures, and begun to talk about "fetal advocates," people who can make decisions on behalf of the fetus, represent the fetus's interests, presumably particularly in those cases where the mothers resist experimental surgery.

But is that the way it really works? I was amused—no, I laughed out loud—at a presentation by a noted ethicist at a meeting of the Society of Law and Medicine.[8] The topic was experimental fetal surgery, and the ethicist was holding forth on the intense feelings of all those involved in such procedures: the prayerful, beseeching mothers, trying to save the babies dying within them; the pioneering, new-frontier excitement of the doctors repairing a fetus and replacing it in the womb. Someone asked the ethicist: but what about those fetal advocates you have called for in the past? Ah, he said, there seemed no need. The doctors and ethicists were surprised to see that the mothers were acting as advocates for the fetus. The mothers themselves were pleading for the surgery—the ethicists found themselves, he said, reminding the mothers of how dangerous the surgery was for them, for the mothers, trying to prevent mothers from risking their lives and health without good cause.

He discovered motherhood! Mothers are fetal advocates! Mothers will risk sacrificing themselves for their babies! Whatever will science discover next?

To be surprised by the willingness of mothers to risk themselves for their children—this takes a special kind of training. It takes the kind of context that medicine has been developing, a context in which mothers and their fetuses are separate patients, with separate needs and separate rights.

While the most recent roots of this perspective may lie in the development of a new technology that enables, and indeed encourages, us to see the fetus and the mother as two separate patients, the roots truly go much deeper. The roots go to the very history of patriarchy. In an earlier work[9] I discussed the way that patriarchal ideology has influenced the provision of modern maternity care. But it is not only in our management of pregnancy as a "stress" or "risk" condition, in our management of childbirth as a surgical event, that the influence of patriarchal ideology can be seen. That perspective or ideology, which takes men as the dominant group, and men's views as the dominant view of the world, influences all of our reproductive technology, and all of our ideas about reproduction.

Patriarchy

Someone recently said to me, as if it were a generally recognized principle, that abortion was "inherently" feminist. So closely have these two movements been linked that she could only see abortion—the actual procedure itself—in the context of a woman's right to control her own body.

But what have been the conditions under which women have had abortions? It has certainly not been, invariably, out of their own needs and wishes. At the extreme, we have the situation of women forced to abort female fetuses because their husbands want sons. While rare among Western populations, with the introduction of amniocentesis Eastern women do face just this situation.[10] *No* technology can be "inherently" feminist; all technologies exist in a social context. In our own society, one of the most widely recognized reasons for abortion, a reason we see as basis for abortion "on demand," or the more "liberated" woman's abortion, is pregnancy in an unmarried woman. A woman without a man *needs* an abortion. Abortion prevents "illegitimate" births. This, like abortions of unwanted females, is hardly an inherently feminist justification for abortion, even if it does indeed meet the needs of women in the system.

Obviously, reproduction can be controlled not only to meet the needs of women but also to meet the needs of men, both men as individuals and men as a class. Thus prenatal diagnosis and the new reproductive technology can also be seen in the light of the history of patriarchy. Patriarchy has meant many things, but at its core is the recognition of paternity, the concept that children grow out of men's seeds. Recognition of paternity changes the way men and women see themselves and see each other, changes the way we see the world. Without paternity, the distinction between seed and soil hardly matters: plants spring forth from the earth, children from the mother. With paternity, with the primitive "seed" concept of paternity, seed and soil separate: the farmer sows the field; Daddy plants a seed in Mommy. The seed is the source of life, and the soil, now "dirt," is only the receptacle; the woman, the vessel for men's seed.

Patriarchy begins with paternity, but it moves beyond, to an encompassing world view. With recognition of the seed, people are seen as *on* but not *of* the earth. The seed penetrates the soil, breaks into the crust of the earth, but is not drawn from the earth. With patriarchy, man rules over the earth. Unlike the earth goddesses, the God of patriarchy is the God of all the world, the one God, above whom there is none other, and below whom lies the earth and all its inhabitants. The God of patriarchy gives hierarchical order to the world. That which was interconnected and interdependent becomes hierarchical and ranked.

From a cycle of being comes a great chain of being, a line of domination and hierarchy—from God to man, from King to subject, from Man to beast. The cycle of the world straightens out into a line, and time itself, no longer cyclical, straightens up and marches on. Tomorrow is not yesterday again, the earth continually reborn, but each day a step forward, a progression.

In such an ordered world, different ways of thinking develop. Erich Fromm, in his analysis of myths and fairy tales, contrasts the matriarchal with the patriarchal principles:

> The matriarchal principle is that of blood relationship as the fundamental and indestructible tie, of the equality of all men [sic], of the respect for human life and of love. The patriarchal principle is that the ties between man and wife, between ruler and ruled, take precedence over ties of blood. It is the principle of order and authority, of obedience and hierarchy.[11]

It is this principle that determined that to be worthy of God, Abraham had to be willing to sacrifice his son Isaac, to place obedience before blood. Abraham may have experienced anguish, but he was willing to do it, willing to sacrifice Isaac, and patriarchal religion praises him for that willingness and obedience. Echoes of Abraham's dilemma can be heard in the voices of the women in this book.

The History of Eugenics

What is a seed? A seed is potential, pure potential. Given the right environment, the seed can *become*: the acorn, the oak tree;

the bulb, the tulip; and the sperm, the man. One of the earliest uses of the microscope was to look at sperm, to see the little "homunculus," the tiny little man the scientists believed they saw curled up inside each sperm. Spilled on inhospitable ground, the seed becomes nothing. Planted in a welcoming, nurturing soil, the seed can become all it was meant to be.

The more we focus on genetics, on the seedlike qualities, the more we think of potential: what the person can become. One effect of the focus on potential has been to see the mother not as a source of nourishment, a source of energy and strength, a protector, but the mother as a barrier to full potential. The seed has in it all it can become—but the very idea of a seed as potential tells us that it cannot become more, only less than its full potential. Is the infant less than its seed might have been? Then how has the mother harmed it, how has she failed it?

But there is another thing that happens when we focus on the seed: we think of different seeds as having different potentials. The history of prenatal diagnosis has roots in the eugenics movement, in various attempts to "improve the race." It is certainly one of the less flattering lights in which to view prenatal diagnosis, but part of its history has been an attempt to control the gates of life: to decide who is, and who is not, fit to make a contribution to the "gene pool," whose seed is worth passing on. Thus began eugenics.

The study of eugenics in the United States attracted a large number of prominent scientists and physicians, including Alexander Graham Bell, and crystallized in the activities of a eugenics movement, whose headquarters was The Eugenics Records Office at Cold Spring Harbor, Long Island, established in 1904 by Charles B. Davenport. From this early eugenics movement came the impetus and the scientific rationale for legislation permitting forced sterilization of certain kinds of "undesirables" and, later, limiting immigration. Indiana passed the first state sterilization laws in 1907, requiring compulsory sterilization of inmates of state institutions who were insane, idiotic, imbecilic, or feeble-minded, or were convicted criminals, upon recommendation of a board of experts. By 1931 thirty states had similar legislation, to include such "hereditary defectives" as sexual perverts, drug fiends, drunkards, diseased, and degenerate persons.[12] Harry Laughlin, Davenport's assistant, was the most active eugenicist in the sterilization campaign.

The Immigration Restriction Act of 1924 extended the eugenics concept to racial differences. The act contained a eugenics provision, again argued for by Laughlin, the appointed "expert eugenics agent" of the House Committee on Immigration and Naturalization. This provision for selective restriction dramatically limited the entry of individuals from Southern and Eastern Europe, the "biologically inferior," in favor of the "Nordics." And in Germany in 1933 Hitler decreed the Hereditary Health Law, or Eugenic Sterilization Law.

One of the people influenced by the eugenics movement was a physician, Charles F. Dight, who in a 1927 will left his estate to the University of Minnesota, "To Promote Biological Race Betterment—Betterment in Human Brain Structure and Mental Endowment and therefore in Behavior." The university was to "maintain a place for consultation and advice on heredity and eugenics for the rating of people, first, as to the efficiency of their bodily structure; second as to their mentality; third, as to their fitness to marry and reproduce."[13]

The Dight Institute for Human Genetics began to function in 1941, with family consultations used more as the basis for future studies than as a eugenics program. In 1947 a man named Sheldon Reed began working at Dight, and genetic counseling was born. Reed rejected the older names for his work, such as "genetic hygiene," and substituted *genetic counseling* "as an appropriate description of the process which I thought of as a kind of genetic social work without eugenic connotations."[14]

Reed's claim was that he could divorce genetic counseling from eugenics, and could put the clients' needs at the center:

> Genetic counseling, in my conception at least, is a type of social work contributing to the benefit of the whole family without direct concern for its effect upon the state or politics.

By 1951 there were ten genetic counseling centers in the United States. Through the 1950s genetic counseling developed as a form of preventive medicine. As such it moved from the academic centers to the major medical centers. Genetic counseling became medicalized, and physicians began claiming turf. The bulletins of the Dight Institute shifted title from "Counseling in Human Genetics" to "Counseling in Medical Genetics."

Genetic Counseling: The Contemporary Context

All of these historical strands come together in modern genetic counseling: the medicalization of reproduction and reproductive decision-making, the availability of abortion, the world view of patriarchy, and perhaps, some fear, the remnants of eugenic thinking.

Genetic counseling and genetic testing are, as I pointed out in the first chapter, rapidly becoming a routine part of prenatal care. It began with women who were at high genetic risk, including women over 40. The age has moved down to 35, and is now inching its way down to the early thirties. I think genetic counseling of some sort will ultimately reach everyone who seeks prenatal care.

The remainder of this chapter will examine contemporary genetic counseling. Most of this book is based on interviews with the women who chose to have, or chose not to have, prenatal diagnosis with pregnancies medically defined as being at risk. This chapter is different: here you will hear the voices of genetic counselors.

As genetic counseling has become more widespread, more routine, physicians are beginning to turn the work over to lower-status, and very much lower paid, workers. As genetic counseling becomes a more standard part of prenatal care, these counselors take over more and more of the counseling from physicians, "freeing" the physicians for other work. Counseling is not high-status, technical work: it is "just talking." We now consider what it is that is discussed, and how counselors talk to clients.

The Genetic Counseling Session

Genetic counseling sessions are most often initiated by the obstetrical services. The private obstetrician or the clinic refers the woman, uniformly called "the patient," for genetic counseling based on information gathered in the obstetrical history. Most commonly the only indication is "advanced maternal age," standardly taken to mean 35 years or older at "e.d.c.," estimated date of confinement. Occasionally someone is referred because of a history of birth defects in previous pregnancies or because of some specific familial indication, but far and away the most common referral nowadays is for advanced maternal age.

Genetic counselors are one of those specialty service providers that most people see only once, and so no ongoing relationship is established. But because the topic under consideration has the potential for becoming intensely personal and emotional, it is important to establish some rapport right away. Like people in any other occupation that has to "meet the public," counselors develop their own style for breaking the ice. Some begin with chit-chat about the weather, the location of the office (usually in some hard-to-find place, it seems), or some other neutral topic. Others plunge right in with a question like "Do you know why you have been sent here?" That question is mostly reserved for clinic patients, who might very well *not* know why they are there, having gotten used to going where they are sent in the hospital system. While some counselors prefer to counsel a couple together, the fact is that more often than not the woman is there alone, or accompanied by her children. In more than one session where I came to observe, I found myself babysitting for a preschooler, so the mother could devote her attention to the counselor. Non-English-speaking patients have to bring their own interpreter in many medical settings. That can get awkward, particularly when the interpreter is a near-adolescent child, as I observed on occasion. Once everybody has been settled in, with appropriate introductions and translations arranged as needed, the session begins.

There are three basic parts to a genetic counseling session for advanced maternal age: genetic/medical history; information about the test; and making the decision whether or not to have prenatal diagnosis. Some counselors begin with the first, some with the second, but each session ultimately has to cover all three parts.

The paperwork involved—particularly the medical history forms and the informed consent forms—in some ways structures the interaction, becoming as one observer of medical record-keeping has called it, "a third participant in the interaction."[15] Sometimes the forms do seem intrusive. One group of counselors, for example, was working with a family history form which had them asking, "How many children do your brothers have?" and "How many children do your sisters have?" because it listed these separately. That required people to sort out their nieces and nephews in an unfamiliar way. ("Let's see, my older brother has two and my younger brother has three and my baby brother has none. That's five. Now my sisters . . .") Some counselors stick more closely to the forms, trying to get things filled in "right," and others deviate and skip over things that do not seem pertinent.

The "information giving" part of the session, as opposed to the history, or "information taking," has the most room for variation between counselors and between patients with the same counselor. When I asked counselors what they typically covered, some specifically said that they had "short versions" and "long versions" of explanations for things like "what sonograms are," and then, depending on the patient and the amount of time available, they presented one or another version. Language barriers naturally tend to shorten explanations. The essential information to be conveyed was summed up by one counselor as:

> What the amnio can tell you. The risks of the procedure. The fact that we can come up with an ambiguous result— we may not be able to tell them in black and white. For me, these are the high points.

Most counselors would probably agree with her first sentence, but most do not seem to want to raise the issue of ambiguous results. Most do not want to raise *any* ambiguous issues. When I asked counselors what they covered in a typical pre-amnio session, asking specifically about the major topics, almost all agreed that they described what the amnio feels like (not painful); what Downs Syndrome is (sometimes with pictures of people with Downs Syndrome if the client seems unsure); what neural tube defects are (with frequent reference to the March of Dimes poster children or occasional pictures again if it seems necessary); what the test can and cannot tell; what the miscarriage rate or complication rate is after amnio (some give the figure of 3 in 1000 additional miscarriages due to the amnio; others give the "less than one-half of one percent complications" rate); and what chromosomes are, also sometimes with pictures. Almost always the risk rate for Downs Syndrome, as it increases with age, is presented.

Of equal or greater significance are the issues that are not or may not be raised. Some counselors say they "always these days" discuss what sex chromosome abnormalities are, including XXX, XXY, XYY, and XO. Most said they "rarely," "never," or "maybe never" raise these, or raise them "only if asked." One said, "Never—it scares people."

I asked if they discussed "what the choices are if Downs is found." Some always raise that, saying things like:

> They can continue the pregnancy knowing it has Downs or they can terminate, but there's nothing we can do to change the status of the fetus.

> That it cannot be cured. That the parents have the choice to decide if they want to keep the pregnancy and raise a Downs child or terminate, and either way the staff will support their decision.

I also asked "Do you raise the issue of termination or do you wait for them to?" Some do:

> Always—it comes at the end of the session, with reference to when the results are ready. I ask if they've discussed what they would do if the results were abnormal.

I do, at the beginning, because I want it clear to them that we cannot cure these diseases.

And some don't:

Sometimes it's assumed, and I don't push it.
I initiate it enough so they would ask.
I just say that if we find anything that needs explanation they will see a medical geneticist.

While observing sessions, a number of times I got the distinct impression that the client had no idea what this was about. This was particularly a problem when there was a language barrier, but not limited to that. For example, right near the end of a session with a middle-class, intelligent, competent-looking couple, the father finally asked, "So, tell me, what if you do find something? What can you do about it?" And another woman, there by herself, also quite bright and articulate with no language barrier, asked toward the end of a session, "I'm just so curious—if something is wrong, what could I do at this point?" In both cases the counselors (two different counselors, with quite different styles) gave the answer that the choices were between continuing or terminating the pregnancy. But the information was not given until it was requested.

Similarly, almost no counselors discuss how the abortion would be done in a pre-amnio session, "unless they ask," and a number added that "most people don't want to know." The one counselor I interviewed who does raise it routinely says she asks the client if they would like to know, and "75 percent ask to know." It is not easy to raise a discussion of how a late abortion would be done with a pregnant woman who wants her baby. And it is not easy for the pregnant woman to raise the discussion with the counselor.

Sessions end by coming back to the forms. The informed consent, with its descriptions of all that can go wrong, needs to be read and signed, which is a "downer," "a bad way to have to end the session." The "informed consent" forms repeat some of the information of the session. They vary somewhat from institution to institution, but typically cover the possibility that a second tap might be needed, that there are conditions that the tests cannot predict, that if there is more than one fetus present the results might pertain to only one of them, and that in any case the results might be wrong or "not accurately reflect the status of my fetus." Consent to the amniocentesis tap includes the awareness that the tap itself might cause damage, including a miscarriage. Most clients seem to decide whether or not to have the amnio before they ever come in, and some decide during the session. By the time the forms come out, the decision is usually made. But some do go home to think about it, or go home to discuss it with their husbands, partners, or families.

In almost all cases the results are normal, go to the patient through her obstetrician three to four weeks later, and the client and the counselor never see each other again.

On Nondirective Counseling

What is the point of prenatal genetic counseling? Is it to prevent birth defects? If your initial response is yes, then you are thinking of what is called "directive counseling." That is not the dominant mode of genetic counseling in America today. The value is on "nondirective" counseling, counseling that presents information, but allows the patients/clients to reach their own decisions. Only one of the counselors I interviewed said she was a directive genetic counselor: "Without any question. A firm believer in directive counseling." The others might have said that they have become a little more or a little less directive over time, but nondirectiveness was a strongly shared value: "I'm not going to be taking that baby home—they will," said one. And another: "I can't make their decision. I would never presume."

Many expressed an awareness of the impossibility of being totally nondirective; as one of the counselors I interviewed said, "I am aware that I can do a very subtle thing, and make a decision for somebody, and I really work at not doing that—it's really terrible. It's not appropriate."

In the early days of genetic counseling, when genetic counselors were physicians, the situation was different:

> Neutrality is unusual in medical practice and is a difficult attitude for many physicians to adopt, and may even be confusing to some patients who expect to be guided by their physicians.[16]

Eighty-five percent of the genetic counselors interviewed in 1973,[17] most of whom were physicians, considered it important that counseling achieve prevention of disease or abnormality, and "64 percent felt it was 'always appropriate' to inform counselees in a way that would 'guide them toward an appropriate decision.'" But what *is* an "appropriate" decision? The counselors I interviewed kept stressing that the decision must be one that is "right for that woman." So many of them told me, "I'm not an amnio saleslady." Asked about what reasons people have for refusing amniocentesis, and how they (the counselors) feel about it, most echoed the counselor who told me, "Whatever their reason, I respect it."

But of course many of them were uncomfortable with some reasons: being afraid of the needle was not a good enough reason to refuse. Nor was simple faith that "God would not give me an abnormal baby." Nor was "My mother/sister/friend had a baby at 43 and it was okay." And certainly some things just seem wrong to the most nondirective of counselors: one told a couple whose fetus was diagnosed as having Downs Syndrome that no, they couldn't go on vacation and then have the abortion when they got back.

Because nondirectiveness is a value among the counselors that is supported at so many levels—the medical consumerism movement, the feminist movement, the American value of individualism—giving examples of their directiveness looks like muckraking. But counselors are bound to be directive sometimes—avowedly so in some circumstances, perhaps unwittingly so in others. If I write now about the times and ways in which they are directive, please do not lose sight of the fact that most of them do truly value nondirectiveness, do truly seek it as a goal.

But they are faced by women who are making decisions that may change the course of their lives:

> When I see a woman who is genetically considered to be at high risk in her pregnancy, who has two children she loves and adores, there's no father, there's no means of support, no money, and she's looking at me and saying, "Should I keep this pregnancy?"—what do you do?

What this counselor does is say things like, "Well, let's look at this," and "Let's think about that," pointing out the problems to the woman until she comes to her decision. Others talk about building scenarios, "How are you going to feel if?" or "trying to act as the devil's advocate—'what if? what if?'"

It would be naive to think that the women are free agents with only the counselors' directiveness to worry about. Some women want the amnio but their husbands "won't let them" have it. Others are pressured by family into having the test. As a result, one counselor said, "When I feel that a patient really wants to do something but they're getting pressure from their families to do otherwise, then I feel that if I'm more directive they'll do what they really want to do."

This is the thing about the counselors' directiveness—they are trying, if directing at all, to steer the woman in the direction they think she wants to go. Mostly that is toward amnio and ultimately toward aborting affected fetuses. But sometimes it is the other way: "What bothers me is when young women come in here having the test because their doctors said they have to have it whether they want it or not. . . . Most make up their mind to do what the doctors say anyway."

A number of counselors said that they tried to steer women with a history of infertility or repeated miscarriages away from the amnio, or from doing anything that might disrupt the pregnancy; and some said that they were most clearly directive when it came to Tay Sachs disease. Tay Sachs is a kind of touchstone for genetic counseling. A normal-looking baby deteriorating over a period of years to an inescapable but lingering death is so horrifying that nondirectiveness tends to fly out the window. They feel: *of course* the couple should be tested for carrier status.

What follows is that if a carrier married to a carrier is now pregnant, *of course* she should have amnio, and *why ever not* abort an
affected fetus?

These are the extremes, the conditions under which many
counselors feel most justified in saying what a client should do.
Most everything else falls somewhere between, where the stakes
are lower and the pressures more subtle. When counseling for
advanced maternal age, just how old the woman actually is is
probably going to have an effect on how the counselor conducts
the session: 46 is not 35. As one counselor said, "When they're
forty, then I'm putting much more pressure on them."

Probably when forty was the starting age for amnio, it was
women in the mid-to-late forties who got the pressure.

The larger concept of riskiness, not just age, comes into question here—just how much of a risk is "high risk?" Partly it is the
disease: "For Tay Sachs, one in a million is high." But there is
some general understanding of what "high risk" and "low risk"
means, and here, too, there has been change over time. The current counselors see riskiness somewhat differently than did those
physicians doing genetic counseling in 1973. Risk rates of one-
in-two, or one-in-four—the risk rates found for genetic diseases
for which parents can be carriers, like Tay Sachs or hemophelia—are seen definitely as "very high," just as they were by the
earlier counselors. But even by one-in-ten a shift in perception
begins, with more of the current counselors seeing higher riskiness at every risk rate. A risk rate of one-in-fifty is called high or
very high by almost half of the counselors I interviewed—and by
only 20 percent of the earlier group of counselors. Twice as
many now call one-in-100 high or very high (21 percent vs. 9
percent) and twice as many now call one-in-200 high or very
high (13 percent vs. 6 percent). And look at the flip side: what is a
low risk? Among the earlier counselors, three-fourths called
one-in-100 low or very low. Among the counselors I interviewed,
less than half thought that low or very low. In fact, only three-
fourths of the counselors I interviewed thought one-in-*400* was
low or very low. In 1973 the researcher never even asked about
risk levels lower than one-in-200. Perhaps in the 1990s one-in-
400 will seem like a very high risk.

The implications are striking. One counselor, for example,

said that she was most directive when "I feel that a couple is at very high risk and they don't realize it or if they're at very low risk and don't realize it." This counselor considered a one-in-200 risk to be moderate, one-in-300 or -400 to be low, and *nothing* to be "very low" risk.

When counselors feel their clients are at high risk, I believe it inevitable that there will be some direction given, some subtle pressures exerted. What then are the techniques available to counselors who will not say "you should"? One of the ways they can direct their clients is by separating the decision to have the amnio from the decision to have an abortion if an affected fetus is found. While the two tend to go together, the decision to have an amnio can be separated out. Some counselors say that people who say they will not abort for any fetal abnormality should not have amnio. For one thing, why take the risk of interfering with the pregnancy? The miscarriage rate, while small, is there. For another, the knowledge that something is wrong could make the pregnancy very difficult for the woman and her family.

But others saw that as precisely the reason why even women who do not plan on aborting for abnormalities should have the amnio: once the woman actually knows she is carrying a fetus with Downs or some other disabling condition, she may think differently about abortion.

Some counselors also feel that the test is likely to be reassuring, and so should be done on that basis. They think of pregnancy as a time of great anxiety, and themselves as relieving anxiety. This viewpoint can coexist with the idea of being "nondirective," because the counselor is not trying to influence the more crucial decision to abort, just the decision to have the amnio. In part, how a counselor sees this issue depends on how safe she feels the amnio itself is. Some counselors are concerned about the risks of causing a miscarriage, and that does discourage them from leading a woman toward having an amnio if she will not make use of the results. Others are much less concerned with the risks of the test itself: they feel that "miscarriages after the test probably would have happened anyway."

By avoiding the whole issue of abortion, and instead focusing the session on the test, how it works and what it does, counselors can separate the decision to have an amnio from deciding about abortion, and preserve their feeling of nondirectiveness. Unfortunately, when a bad result comes through the counselor often loses control of the situation as the physician steps in.

In addition, this pressure toward skirting the issues is offset somewhat by the very real desire counselors have to help their clients make decisions. They *like* "helping people through problems, helping them make decisions," and "making a difference in people's lives." This creates a very different kind of directedness: trying to make the client feel the need of the counseling. A number of counselors complained about clients "who think they know it all," clients who do not want the counseling but just the laboratory services, or who have very limited needs for counseling. These clients were primarily drawn from the well-educated, professional women, the women who are making up the widely publicized "baby boomlet" among older women. They certainly do not know as much genetics as the counselors, but the information that needs to be communicated from counselor to client has been made widely available in the popular press. The "what chromosomes are" and "how neural tube defects occur" and other standard "raps" are old-hat for women who, as a group, have been said to take pregnancy as a reading assignment. Similarly, spending time on family history may be just as unnecessary among this population: more often than not the Jews know about Tay Sachs, the blacks about sickle-cell, and they've all thought about family history and asked more questions of their parents than the counselors ask of them. They don't even need to hear the details of the procedure, having heard that from friends. And the decision-making is over before it began: for many of these women, amnio is already an expected, accepted part of the pregnancy experience. All that is left then is signing the forms.

At the other end of the spectrum, sometimes the counseling sessions are irrelevant not because of overpreparation, but because the ship has sailed. Clients sometimes come in *after* they have had the amnio—either because their pregnancies have not been recognized until very late, or because they have not felt the need of, or do not have access to, medical services in early pregnancy. Because of the inherent deadline imposed by the progressing pregnancy, a woman who presents herself for prenatal care for the first time at eighteen or nineteen weeks may be scheduled for an amnio virtually at once: test first and talk later. The doctors thus display their priorities: the test is important, the counseling superfluous, a nicety if time permits.

Observing a session like that, it was a little unclear just what was supposed to be accomplished. Which brings us back to the point of prenatal counseling in general: it has to have effects on decision-making or indeed there is no point. The counselors, if not trying to influence the decision, are at least trying to influence the decision-making process.

But how *can* one influence the process without directly influencing the decision? Can it be done by how one defines the decision to be made? Is this a case of a woman deciding whether or not there is a reason to risk a miscarriage, or is she deciding whether or not she "should learn everything you can about your baby"? Is she deciding whether or not she could face a twenty-one-week abortion, or is she deciding how frightened she is of having a needle poked into her pregnant belly?

The counselors shape the session, and thus the decision-making process, by directing the woman's attention toward some questions, and away from others. The counselors themselves, as one might imagine, mostly think that amnio and selective abortion is a good thing, something that expands women's control of their lives:

I honestly do believe and I share with the patient (after a bad result) that they are lucky to get this information at this time, at a time when they can make a choice. I see a child with Downs Syndrome, or another recognizable syndrome—I don't think I ever see such a child without thinking of a couple with that diagnosis who made the decision not to be so burdened.

Most of the counselors I interviewed would have the test themselves. More than half would have, or want their daughter to have, an amnio even at 25, a "low-risk age." They would want the information. Most would have abortions for most abnormalities; half said they would abort for *any* abnormality.

If there was any abnormality diagnosed I would terminate the pregnancy.

All circumstances—any chromosome abnormality.

I wouldn't have anything that was not perfect, not normal, anything with ifs, ands, or buts.

And while that does *not* mean that the counselors think their clients should do the same—they value nondirectiveness too much for that—how clearly can they make the distinction? If your experience with genetic abnormalities is such that you can say, as one counselor did about why she went into prenatal counseling, "I've had enough freaky kids throw up on me. I want to get it before it happens"; if you can say about Downs Syndrome, as another counselor said to me, "Sure they can be sweet children. And they grow up to be ugly adults"; if this is how you see it, how can you *not* influence? If the counselor thinks this woman sitting across from her is going to do something she will deeply regret for the rest of her life, how can she *not* influence her? Just what kind of person would she be if she saw someone heading off a cliff and sat back "nondirectively"?

With all of these provisos, with all these warnings and disclaimers, let me end this chapter with my notes of a session I observed. It was not "typical," and I do not present it as such. It was indeed one of the more disturbing sessions I went through. But this is what can happen, this is what *does* happen, when people try to help people for their own good:

Notes of Observations, 1/83

A 39-year-old Hispanic woman arrives for counseling accompanied by her sister, who also serves as translator. She had been married for 13 years, separated for the last four. This is her first pregnancy. The sister says this several times, adding, "Nothing, not even any abortions." They told her she was sterile. The woman sits quietly. Answers questions about herself in monosyllables. Quietly but firmly refuses to answer any questions about the father. The counselor does not press the point. The counselor does a lot of talking—the chromosome stuff, neural tube defects, etcetera. She explains how the test cannot guarantee everything, just the things that they are testing for. At 39 years the risk of Downs is one-in-140. The counselor puts it that "One-in-140 will have mongolism and we want to make sure you're not that one." The woman does not want the test. She sits, mostly silent, looking down. The counselor spends a great deal of time reassuring her that the test is not painful, that the needle will not hurt. The woman never mentions pain. She says nothing. She never brings up the fear of the needle, it's just the counselor saying she understands she is afraid, but there is nothing to fear, it's just a little pressure, no pain. The sister repeats, she doesn't want the test. The sister is shaking her head, aligning herself with the counselor. The counselor says, "Tell your sister to think of the benefits, the advantages of the test. She would know that the baby doesn't have mongolism, doesn't have an opening in the spine." The woman says, for the first time in English, that she's afraid. She doesn't say of what. The counselor doesn't ask. The counselor says: "You have to think of the advantages." The sister jumps in in Spanish, obviously trying to talk her into it, obviously irritated with her unreasoning silence. The sister is young, has a child. The counselor interrupts the sister's argument: "A woman has to decide for herself. No one can decide for her. It has to be a very personal decision."

At the end of the session, after fifty minutes of listening to this, I do not know if this was a deeply wanted pregnancy—a miracle thirteen years in the making—a pleasant surprise, or an unwanted accident. The sisters get up and leave. We don't know if she will have the amnio.

3

MAKING CHOICES

In this chapter you will hear the voices of women making choices. Most of the voices are troubled, full of doubts, the voices of women wrestling with ambiguities. But here and there a very clear voice comes through, a woman who is terribly sure of herself. I found myself distressed by these few women. While the rest struggle, the sure ones seemed almost arrogant in their clarity.

The arguments of the ones who are sure start off in a way that usually made sense to me. Later in this chapter Valerie explains her decision to have amniocentesis. She describes with great passion and eloquence the tragedy of severe disability, the grinding, unending sucking away at the life of the family, particularly the life of the mother. The tortured, unhappy child, supported and maintained through to an unhappy adulthood, with no end in sight, at the cost of all else that might have been the mother's life—the image compels. But then Valerie goes on, and it is no longer the tragedy of these lives that she describes, but the costs to society, the drain on our resources, and the next thing she has gone on to is identifying the criminally insane before they reach their teens, and how we must get on with that . . . and I begin to recognize Valerie's argument, and I say, "Ah, the voice of eugenics, a dangerous, dangerous voice." Having put a label on what she is saying, I want to dismiss it.

There are women on the other side who are just as certain of the rightness of their decision. Cynthia, very sure of what she is doing in refusing amniocentesis, begins by talking about how tests like this change the way we feel about our children, make us think of them as possessions, to be created to our liking. And then she goes on. If we can abort them for not being perfect, Cynthia asks, can we not also beat them as children if they are not perfect? Soon she is drawing conclusions about abortion as the murder of millions of babies and how that is the real cause of child abuse. And this too is familiar, easily labeled—the "right-to-life" argument.

But labeling these arguments, knowing how dangerous they can be, is not sufficient basis for me to dismiss them. I cannot stop hearing the reasons, the sanity, in *both* of these arguments— as they start. These two deeply contradictory views *both* make sense, up to a point. They stop making sense to me when each woman loses sight of the possible validity of the other's argument. It is not that the answer lies somewhere in the middle. There is no middle. We cannot construct a "compromise" position between these two arguments. All we can do is stand here in the middle of the ambiguity, the uncertainty, the inevitable conflicts of interests, of needs, that is life itself, and make choices.

DECIDING TO HAVE AMNIOCENTESIS

have the amniocentesis
not have the amnio
have the amnio
have an abortion
have the amnio
    (from letter from Irene, requesting interview)

Why do people choose to have amniocentesis? In framing the issue that way, in the very act of asking that question, I begin to distort women's experiences.

What I am calling a "decision" to have or not to have amniocentesis may be more or less consciously experienced as a decision, an opportunity for choice. One can simply show up for all scheduled doctor's appointments and have the amnio without any more of an experience of decision-making than attends, say, the routine blood tests and urinalyses of pregnancy management. Or, conversely, one can just "do nothing," including seeking no medical care at all during pregnancy, and not have amniocentesis without ever having made a deliberate decision. For none of the women I interviewed was the decision that fully routinized, but it was clearly more of a conscious decision for some women than it was for others.

When you ask women who are over 35 why they chose to have amniocentesis, most just say that the reason is their age. People do not often need well-thought-out answers for why they do the accepted, expected thing. It is rather like asking someone why they wash their hands. The only necessary answer is: "Because they get dirty." It is self-evident, and does not warrant a discussion of the meaning of dirt or the value of cleanliness. Hands get washed when they are dirty; amnio gets done when you are over 35. It is routine.

Social Support and the Decision to Have Amnio

When pressed to think more about *why* they chose amniocentesis, medical encouragement is often mentioned: trusted doctors recommended it, saying "If I were you I would." Doctors themselves may also simply present it as a "routine procedure," not calling for thought or discussion, hardly needing a decision at all. Probably the most common form of medical encouragement is just a strong presumption on the doctor's part that amniocentesis is automatic. For example, I spoke to one woman obstetrician with a large proportion of her practice over 35, who said that she cannot remember anyone ever refusing amniocentesis. But medical encouragement can also take the form of more direct pressure, as happened to Helen:

This may sound odd, but I already felt quite sure he was fine. I had a psychic reading after I became pregnant and asked about amniocentesis. But because I live in the real world and it's hard to convince a doctor of this (and myself sometimes) I decided to go ahead. . . . I think a lot of it had to do with wanting reassurance but sometimes I'm not really sure why I went through with it. . . . The home birth doctor I was seeing at the time was fairly aggressive and I felt particularly vulnerable at the time I saw him. I felt judged somewhat (36, unmarried, and on top of it trying to tell him some nonsense about a psychic reading). I think he thought I was a little nuts. At the time, I guess I was. Anyway, he very pointedly said, "Are you willing to raise a retarded child?" and then gave me the line about the costs to the state. So much for my intuition or guidance. I went along with it because I wanted to be labeled okay (and sensible) for a home birth.

Among the women I interviewed who chose to have amniocentesis, almost all had medical encouragement, and in those few cases where they did not, the medical providers were neutral. No woman felt she received *any* discouragement at all from *any* medical representative, though in many cases one medical provider remained neutral while another encouraged her. Sometimes it was an obstetrician who encouraged the amnio while a genetic counselor (M.D. or master's level) remained neutral, and sometimes the other way around. Some women saw a midwife in addition to or instead of an obstetrician; a couple of the midwives encouraged amniocentesis and the rest remained neutral, but meanwhile an obstetrician or a genetic counselor or even both were encouraging the woman to have the amniocentesis. Although I do not assume any kind of prearranged or conscious conspiracy on the part of the providers, the resulting pattern often sounded like the old "good-cop, bad-cop" routine. One puts the pressure on, and the other "cools the woman out," telling her to make up her own mind.

Medical encouragement is not the only encouragement for women who choose to have amniocentesis. Almost all were also encouraged by their husbands. A few husbands were, in the woman's opinion, neutral, or "wanted it only if I wanted it," and an occasional woman felt her husband "insisted on it." I have found no woman who felt she was discouraged by her husband from having an amniocentesis she wanted.

I asked women whether people encouraged, discouraged, or remained neutral in the decision to have amniocentesis, or on the other hand did they not discuss it with them at all. The groups I asked about specifically, in addition to medical providers (obstetricians, midwives, and genetic counselors) and husbands were the woman's mother and/or father, her siblings, her intimate friends, casual friends, and co-workers. The circle of people included in the decision-making by women who decided to have amniocentesis was relatively small. While invariably it included the husband and at least one member of the medical community, for some women these were the *only* people with whom she discussed the test. Intimate friends were often involved in some discussion, less often the woman's parents, and others relatively infrequently.

Most women did discuss the decision with at least some of their intimate friends, most of whom encouraged them to have the amniocentesis. Some felt that their intimate friends tried to remain neutral, but only two felt discouragement from any of them.

The women's parents followed a somewhat similar pattern. About half of the women who had amniocentesis discussed the decision with their mother and/or their father. About one-third of those encouraged the amnio (though one woman added, "but I didn't ask their opinion"). The others felt their parents remained neutral. The sole exception was Sally, who said that she discussed it with both her parents and her priest, and felt "they tried to appear neutral, but I felt they discouraged it."

Siblings were less commonly consulted, but among the few who were, most encouraged the woman to have amnio. No sibling discouraged the amniocentesis, though a couple remained neutral.

Most women do not discuss amniocentesis with casual friends

or co-workers. Only one woman, Lois, reported any discouragement:

> I guess I would say that we live in a very conservative climate here in Mid-America. When I first began to consider the test, a few of the people I mentioned it to were mildly negative. I heard things like "they are special people" about retarded individuals and even the question "would you do anything about it if something were wrong?" implied criticism. It was very important for me to feel I was doing a responsible and moral thing. For that reason, the support of my husband and good friends—one of whom even congratulated me on my decision—was *very* important and I think I shall always appreciate it. Since abortion, which should be a personal, often painful, decision has become a sensationalized political topic, that sort of personal support is extremely important to the woman involved.

In addition to her husband and good friends, Lois's obstetrician and her genetic counselor also encouraged amniocentesis. The rest of her family remained neutral.

Stepping back and looking at social pressures or social support as a whole, I found only four women among those who chose to have amniocentesis who experienced any discouragement from any source at all. One was Lois. Another was a woman discouraged by her intimate friends while encouraged by her husband and, she says, "too aggressively encouraged" by her obstetrician. The third was Sally, discouraged, she felt, by her parents, priest, and some of her intimate friends:

> Some of my friends were very judgmental, implying that if I was spiritually in a good place, I wouldn't be worried and anxious, and certainly wouldn't have an amnio. The ones that weren't (including a neighbor who had had two amnios) were, it seemed, at the opposite extreme of having no compunctions about having an abortion if the baby had problems. So I felt very isolated—like no one felt like me.

Sally's encouragement to have amniocentesis came from her husband, other good friends, her obstetrician, and her genetic counselor. Sally's experience reminded me of a couple I observed during pre-amniocentesis counseling, who truly agonized over their decision. They saw both sides of it, the advantages and disadvantages inherent in any decision they made. And they saw that split in their social world as well:

> WIFE: The world is really split on this. Half of my friends are one way, half the other, half the doctors one way, half the other.
> HUSBAND: I'd still rather make the decisions ourselves than have them made automatically.
> WIFE: I'm not so sure.

Most women choosing amniocentesis do not experience such social conflict. The only other source of discouragement among all the women I interviewed who had amniocentesis was added into the "other" category: "a much older pregnant woman I met on the bus." That was the only source of discouragement for Rita, who was encouraged to have amnio by her husband, mother, siblings, co-workers, intimate friends, genetic counselor, and obstetrician. It stuck in her mind.

All of this encouragement, this pervasive atmosphere of assumption that amniocentesis will be done as a matter of routine, may carry the woman straight through without second thoughts. Or the woman may, as Deirdre did, come to question it as she learns more about amnio:

> I honestly didn't think about it too much; it was understood, assumed by my OB that I would do it; I didn't feel I had an option. . . . When I got to the medical center for the test and had all the risks spelled out is when I almost backed out.

What was first experienced as support, even welcome support, may begin to feel like pressure as the pregnancy progresses. This is what happened to Sally:

Before pregnancy, and before I understood fully all that was involved in an amnio, I thought it was a good idea and my husband agreed and we didn't discuss it further. I ignorantly assumed you could find out results before three months, before it really felt like carrying a baby. But the more steps I took in the direction of the amnio, the more of a "bad dream" it became. This is primarily because I felt trapped by an earlier agreement with my husband to have an abortion if the baby was defective. As the pregnancy progressed, I was less and less sure I could "terminate"—which seemed like a euphemistic term for killing the baby and then delivering it. I was afraid that it would be devastating to learn the baby had an abnormality and even more afraid my husband and the doctor would put pressure on me to abort. Instead of being able to lean on my husband for support, I felt myself drawing away from him in anger and feeling alone and isolated.

Thus the decision to have amniocentesis occurs in a social context in which the support is more or less overt, more or less welcome, but consistently there.

The Reasons: What Amnio Can Offer

While some people never do think about it all that much—just having the amniocentesis because it is expected, and never really expecting any problems—others think long and hard about what they are doing, and choose to have amniocentesis fully aware of what it can offer them.

Since my husband and I both have full-time careers, we felt we couldn't do justice to a baby with "special needs." (Vicki)

I live in a rural area with no medical, social, or developmental help for birth defects. All children with problems that I know of live elsewhere if the parents live here. The nearest medical help—major—is 75 minutes away, over hard-to-drive roads. [Also] this is my husband's second

family and he did not want any problems with the child.
(Ida)

Bonnie wrestled with the decision, and with all the strong feelings it entailed:

The central feeling about my amniocentesis was the difficulty around aborting any fetus and so interfering with the
natural order of things, and the wish to have a normal
healthy child. I didn't have to make a decision about abortion, but felt terribly worried about whether it was right,
whether I would have the strength to do it, etcetera. I still
wonder. On the other hand, I was most happy that I had the
opportunity to have a safe amniocentesis and be given an
opportunity to choose. For me it was a grave and profound
choice. I had had an abortion at the age of 22 as I was not
interested in the father and too young, and although it was
the right thing, it was and still is a source of sorrow. To have
an abortion at 41 under completely different circumstances
(very wanted baby and deeply loved husband) would have
been infinitely more sorrowful. And after all, why shouldn't
all babies be given a chance? I felt that Downs Syndrome
children could have a happy life and enrich their parents
but I didn't want one. So all these intense feelings came to
the fore.

However much one's eyes are open going into the amniocentesis, it can be very hard to know, or even to think you know, what
you would do if the results showed Downs or other birth defects.
Ida, the woman living in a rural area whose husband "did not
want any problems," said:

At my age I just didn't want any problems if I could avoid
them. I work full-time and my husband is eight years older
and already a grandfather. We looked upon the procedure
as a tool. A positive one. It's easy to look back and say I
would have aborted if such and such was the test result. But
deep down the total decision would—for us—only be made

at the time, using the test result as a tool to help make the decision.

Realizing that she could not really know whether or not she would terminate the pregnancy until she faced the decision, Paula felt her own uncertainty was not a reason for her to forgo the amniocentesis:

> I also reasoned that at my age and my husband's [56] neither of us felt we wanted to spend the rest of our lives caring for a child that might be severely retarded and ill. We also felt it wouldn't be fair to our very active and demanding first child. Also, both of us continue to be involved in careers and have many other interests. However, we did not know what we would actually do if the results showed we would have a Downs child. But I felt I should be prepared. . . . Some people tried to tell me that it would do no good to have the amnio if I would not be willing to have the abortion, but I felt the advice that the two decisions should remain separate was valid and logical.

Even if women start out expecting to abort for Downs Syndrome, the very act of going through the amniocentesis procedure itself may make considering the need to abort more difficult. As Joanne said:

> I was not sure that I would be able to go through with an abortion and I am still not sure what I would have done if the results had been negative. During the procedure I saw my baby very clearly on the sonogram and I saw her move her arms and fingers. Then before the results came in, I felt the movements. Those two factors made me very attached to her, much more than before the amniocentesis. Also knowing her sex made her so much more like a real person.

Bea puts it more bluntly:

> It was easy to say at the beginning of the pregnancy that I would have an abortion. However, as part of the procedure

an ultrasound is done. We could see the baby and she became real to us. After that it was extremely difficult to think of abortion. . . . The procedure is performed so late and the pregnancy is advanced enough that abortion is not a simple matter. It seems more like murder.

Does the language of "murder" from a woman who *chose* amniocentesis surprise you?

Other women who chose amniocentesis are fully convinced that they are doing the right thing. They do not speak of murder, but of being free from guilt, of doing the responsible, appropriate thing. A woman interviewed in another study said:

It's a feeling that . . . I have done all I can do that is medically feasible and advisable, at my age, to ensure that any baby I have will be fine. There still may be defects beyond amniocentesis—indeterminable ones. But as I said, I have done what I can . . . and I can't blame myself for what I couldn't have done.[1]

Celia is a trained technician, and identifies herself as such. She values the contribution technology can make, not only to her pregnancy, but to the world:

I am a technician. I wanted the information technology could give me because I did not wish to add another burden to society in this world. . . . Having long contemplated adoption of some of the lovely, healthy children already born but not wanted, I cannot justify denying them a home in favor of an individual (my own) whose life could not help but drain community and personal resources. The earth cannot hold endless numbers of humans and so I believe in loving and nurturing those who are here rather than propogating at any cost, just for the deep, but short-lived experience of nine months of pregnancy. . . . I felt at least we'd *tried* to assure that our issue to the world would be a benefit, not a burden. If the test were wrong, we'd feel no guilt.

Celia is basing her moral argument on her commitment to the community and on the scarce resources available to the children of the world. Audrey addresses the issue of "quality of life," what she owes the unborn child:

> I think that questions about the civil rights of the most severely handicapped and of the unborn are important to ask. Even so I *personally* do not believe in life at any cost. I would prefer not to abort an unborn fetus, but I would do it and would not feel guilty if we had concluded that it was best for us and for the unborn child. The *quality* of life counts for a lot—and decisions about it differ for different individuals.

It is Valerie who makes the strongest case of all the women for having amniocentesis, with no hesitation. She addresses all of these issues: the quality of the child's life, the effects on family, the drain on the society. She would encourage a national program requiring amniocentesis. She goes on at length. Listen carefully to what she is saying:

> My husband [33 years old] has a sister [who is now 23] who has Downs Syndrome. My husband's mother has spent 23 years taking care of a 4-year-old, and she will continue taking care of Ellen until either she or Ellen dies. She buys her clothing, makes her meals, takes her everywhere transportation is required, accompanies her to swimming, bowling, Little League, and the Special Olympics. Her days are filled with caring for an idiot, who will never be able to take care of herself—who will never improve!
>
> My husband's family came to stay with us recently (to see their new grandchild) and they brought Ellen with them. My husband hadn't seen her since she was about 8 years old (when her problems were not so graphic). For anyone who feels it is a possibly edifying or enriching experience to have a Downs Syndrome person in the family, I suggest they visit a home where a Downs Syndrome *adult* lives. From friends who have worked with the children, I understand DS infants and little ones are easily amused and pleasant company. Adults are another matter.

Here is a small, and not very bright child—trapped in the body of an adult. The resentment felt by this mutant being is enormous—knowing that she is an adult in terms of years, but having to be overseen all the time because she is incapable of caring for herself, making rational decisions about safety, spending money, behavior, etcetera. Far from being grateful to her parents (who have not only kept her at home, found suitable training for her, arranged numerous activities and a social life, but also take her on all their vacations!), she is short-tempered and abrupt with them. She acts up, very like a 3-year-old, when things don't go just her way, and is capable of, needless to say, highly inappropriate behavior at any time, in any place.

She expects to have "womanly" clothing, and wears makeup (smeared awkwardly) when she goes out. She expects to be offered an alcoholic drink when the other adults are having one. At a restaurant, she orders steak, takes a bite, pushes the plate away sulkily—people aren't talking to her enough. Then, out of spite, she orders an expensive dessert, tastes it, and refuses it also. She leaves the bathroom a disaster area of puddles and soaked towels each time she showers—and sometimes she decides to shower three times in one day.

In short, she wants all the privileges of an adult (and who can blame her? As she shouts angrily when defied in this, *"Ah twenny free yiss oh!!!"*) and yet is unable to handle the responsibilities of a first-grader. A grotesque situation, edifying and enriching to no one. There is *no* solution to this sort of retardation other than *prevention*. Every time I see romanticized articles in magazines, fund-raising drives for "help for the retarded," I want to rage. The answer to this problem is here, in amniocentesis. A rational society would use this technological advance to *prevent* retardation whenever possible. It's a national disgrace that there isn't a more aggressive program to have amniocentesis become a normal, standard procedure when pregnancy is confirmed. I'm willing to wager that never before in the history of Persons has there been a society as rich as we are and, therefore, desirous of maintaining every bit of damaged, pathetic, psychotic, criminal, retarded, incapable flesh as we are—our attitude toward severely premature babies with dreadful anomalies is another demonstration, as is our attitude toward the criminally insane (yes, there is such a group, and they are capable of being identified before their teens, if we would only get on with it)—the saddest part of all this is that we allow those with real potential to be left behind in our rush to defend and protect the hopeless.

Decisions would be easier if everyone who had amniocentesis felt like Valerie. But other women do it without such conviction. They cannot be so terribly sure, so righteous. Some have grave doubts. Anna said, just after the amniocentesis was done, and before she had the results:

So what made us do it? 1, friend Marion who it did happen to. 2, the remote chance that it could, statistically—no, that's not valid, cause there's so many remote possibilities—no, it was those nice competent people sitting there saying, "we can see if there's a Downs baby in there, and if there is, we'll help get rid of it." That was a tempting plum—ugly, distorted, perverse, but still, to be assured that our lives won't be disrupted by that, was too tempting not to pluck. It feels like an ignoble choice, a choice offered by the devil himself. Pardon my lapse into the biblical, but the whole thing made me sick, the deliberate vote of no, baby, if you are a Mongol, death to you, no right to exist. I see these children occasionally—what's so terrible? That's while they're children, and no, I've not forgotten about growing old with a handicapped adult child to care for. It's truly your right but it's got a moral stink to it that sickens me.

She had the amniocentesis. Three weeks later she learned that her baby did have Downs Syndrome. She had the abortion.

DECIDING AGAINST AMNIOCENTESIS

While women who have amniocentesis are doing the expected thing, the women over 35 or otherwise defined as "at risk" who choose not to have amniocentesis more often have to justify their decision—amniocentesis has that rapidly become part of "standard medical practice." Refusing to take advantage of the latest in medical technology in Western industrialized societies may take some explaining.

Social Support—Or Its Lack—and the Decision Against Amniocentesis

Women who choose not to have amniocentesis are often at odds with the expectations of their own medical providers. This is no surprise to anyone, including the women themselves. Some deal with the potential for conflict by never discussing the issue. Few women who want not to have amnio seek genetic counseling: many of them believe the counselors will pressure them into having the amnio. Some women actively "close off" the opportunity for discussion: they note that there is "nothing to discuss." Their doctors or midwives know how they feel on the subject:

> There was no room for discussion, as I am knowledgeable about amniocentesis, its applications, implications, possible complications and irrelevance to those who believe life is always worthwhile.

The medical personnel consulted by the women who decided not to have amniocentesis did indeed encourage them to have the test (when they were consulted) but there were exceptions. Obstetricians and genetic counselors tend to see a history of infertility or of miscarriage as a "good reason" not to have amniocentesis. Working with a straightforward mathematical approach, that makes some kind of sense. Amniocentesis is often said to be indicated at the point where the risks of the procedure equal that of the risks of Downs. With a history of infertility or of miscarriage, the risks of amniocentesis are perceived as higher: women with a history of miscarriage may be genuinely more at risk from the amniocentesis (though there is no data supporting this commonsensical hypothesis and, depending on the cause of miscarriage, does not even seem likely) but in any case they, like the women with a history of infertility, have more to lose if they lose a pregnancy. Their pregnancy loss may mean that their last chance at having a baby is gone.

While some of the women who refused amniocentesis did indeed refer to a history of miscarriage or infertility as a reason, other women—and their medical providers—may use that same kind of history as a reason *to have* amniocentesis. With such a history, the women's faith in their reproductive capacity and competence may be badly shaken. If this much has gone wrong, some women think, then who knows what else might also go wrong. Similarly, women with a long history of infertility are sometimes told by their obstetricians that they are more prone to genetic abnormalities and to birth defects. Since very, very few cases of infertility have anything to do with genetic problems, that is misleading.

In any event, cases of infertility and of miscarriage were the exception. We must look beyond the medical community for the sources of social support in decision-making. For those who refused amniocentesis and went against medical advice, these outside sources may seem even more important.

While all of the married women who had had amniocentesis discussed the decision with their husbands, about one-fifth of those who did *not* have it never discussed their decision with their husbands. Of those who did, almost half of the husbands were neutral. The rest, agreeing with the wife, wanted her not to have the amnio. Only one husband wanted his wife to have amniocentesis, among those women who did not. This was the *only* case reported by any woman where the husband and wife disagreed on any aspect of the process, and the wife won. They flipped a coin, since no compromise seemed possible, and each agreed to be fully behind whichever way the toss went. (The baby was fine.)

With the husband often neutral or not consulted, and medical people only rarely discouraging women from having the amnio, where did the social support come from for those women who refused amniocentesis? Slightly more than half of the women discussed their decision with their intimate friends. In some few cases these friends encouraged them to have the test; in more they were neutral, and in the remainder they actively discouraged it—this last, accounting for about one-fourth of all the women who refused, provided active support for the decision not to have the procedure.

Few women mention any other sources of social support for the decision not to have amniocentesis—few friends, co-workers, siblings, or other family members actively supported the woman. On the contrary, more women received some encouragement to have amniocentesis—from co-workers, casual friends, parents, in one case a mother-in-law, and in another a "high school friend seen at a reunion who'd had it done." Victoria points out the difficulty and loneliness of making an unpopular decision:

> I want to mention that within my "reference group"—friends who are professional women in their 30s and pregnant or with young children, mine was the unusual decision. I kept trying to see things the way the others did, but for me their reasoning just didn't work. Once I had made my decision (not to have amnio) I tried to avoid the subject and I felt lonely with my decision.

Doing the unexpected requires people to be ready to account for themselves, to defend and explain the reasons for their actions. When women "at risk" who have refused amniocentesis are asked *why*, they more often have thought-out answers.

The Abortion Question

It is generally understood that women can refuse amniocentesis if they see it entirely as a prelude to a potential abortion, and see abortion as wrong, a totally unacceptable choice—not a choice at all. That is commonly seen as the "right-to-life" position, and it is by now a familiar argument. As Ruth put it:

> Because in utero treatment is in its infancy, prenatal diagnosis today is used mostly to seek out and destroy "defective" infants. I believe this is morally wrong.

Cynthia sent me a letter, signed by her children as well, with pen scratchings from the youngest:

> I feel that amnio with the thought of aborting must affect your relationship with the baby—make you see it as a possession—not as a human being with her own rights, including of course the right to live even if she is not the perfect human being you envisioned. If you have the right to kill a baby before birth because it is not all you hoped for, then don't we have the right to beat or otherwise abuse this same child after birth if it doesn't live up to all of our expectations? Can you see a link between ten years of a minimum of ten million babies murdered by an approving society and the great amount of child abuse? I am a Christian. Every person has the right to live—no one has the right to decide for someone else that their life is not worth living. But maybe what we are really deciding is that a handicapped child will require too much of us—more than we are willing to give. How sad.

Cynthia places her anti-abortion feelings in her Christianity. The roots of Yvonne's anti-abortion sentiments lie elsewhere. Yvonne had spent years and years and years trying to conceive:

> People frequently assume that I am opposed to abortion because of our infertility. My outlook on abortion was formed long before we were married and attempting a pregnancy, from my upbringing as well as my training in biology. I was convinced that the baby was a separate human being, and not part of my body. I have the obligation to provide as good an environment as possible for the baby—but I do not see this as giving me any right to decide whether the child can continue to live. . . . I knew I would not have an abortion regardless of the findings of the amnio.

Yvonne wants it clear that her position on abortion came neither from her own infertility, nor from an acceptance of traditional sex-role values. She presents her credentials, almost as a challenge:

To tell you more about myself—I am 35, white, Catholic, and consider myself a feminist. I belong to NOW, Catholics Act for ERA, the National Ordination Conference for Women, the National Coalition Against Sexual Assault, League of Women Voters and Girl Scouts, USA. I did hot-line and advocacy work for abused women. Some people see my attitude on abortion as inconsistent with the claim to be a feminist—I see it as a logical extension of my beliefs in an *individual's* rights, which I grant to the unborn as well as the born.

Discomfort with and an unwillingness to have an abortion are by no means limited to women who lay claim to a "right-to-life" argument. Although some women who refuse amniocentesis clearly espouse a "right-to-life" position, probably even more disassociate themselves from it, stating that they are "not a right-to-lifer, but." The "but" usually consists of the distinction between other people's *right* to abort and one's own *personal willingness* to do so, at least under these conditions. Melanie says:

I'm not a "pro-lifer" and believe abortion must be made available to those who choose it, but I discovered some pro-found feelings about it for myself during my first preg-nancy. That is my basic reason for not considering amnio. I can't see taking the risk involved, including physical harm to the baby as well as incorrect results, unless I were pre-pared to abort. There was a program on [a television show] on amnio, for spina bifida, a while ago. The potential error rate was appalling to me; the possibility of aborting a "nor-mal" baby was horrifying, and knowing something about the condition and personally knowing more than one victim of spina bifida, the idea of killing a baby so afflicted broke my heart. As with other defects, there are so many degrees of impairment. Many Downs Syndrome children can live productive lives. Like so many of the new technologies, this has a terrifying potential for misuse. I guess there are no easy answers. I only know what I myself think and feel and have done about amniocentesis.

Melanie is herself a paraplegic, and so has special awareness of disability.

When a woman is not opposed to abortion in principle, when she is not even opposed to the possibility of abortion under some circumstances for herself, she may still reject the possibility of this particular abortion. Often the lateness of these abortions— when, as Gloria put it, "the 'fetus' had become 'a baby' "—distresses some women who might be more tolerant and accepting of earlier abortions. As Sarah says, "Amnio results come back so late, around twenty weeks, the fetus is no longer a 'clump' of cells but a baby. Even if I would consider abortion in the first few weeks, I never could at twenty to twenty-one weeks."

Emily's first child, born when she was in her 20s, has Downs Syndrome. Pregnant for the second time, she portrays with horror her vision of the abortion scenario:

> My main reason for not having the test done was because the results were obtained in your fifth month of pregnancy, which meant not a D&C, but an induced labor with a child being born who dies because it is not capable of existing. This "fetus" is then thrown into a trash can and hauled away. I could never do this to my child no matter what. Also I felt like I would love my child no matter what.

It is not simply the issue of "lateness," as measured in weeks of gestation, ounces of fetus, or "viability." These women are speaking to the problem expressed in the tangled language of "fetus" and "baby," the point at which a "fetus" becomes a "baby," "my child no matter what." Victoria expresses it clearly:

> At some point, I began to feel, more and more strongly, that this fetus *was my baby*, and as this emerged as a strong reality, it no longer depended on the baby's health, normality, or perfection. Just as my older child is my child "in sickness or in health," so was this one. I was then committed to caring for the baby no matter what. Two of the many friends I have who have had amnio had babies who were in need of special care for reasons not detected by amnio, so I knew in

a very real way that amnio was not the guarantee of a healthy child some people assume. It seemed a little strange to me to take a chance on aborting a fetus in order to scrutinize it in this way, once I was committed to the fetus. Lastly, just before the amnio would have been done (I'd scheduled it in case I decided in favor) I began to feel movement. That settled it.

The genetic counselors I observed and interviewed found it hard to understand how a woman who had had abortions "for less reason" could hesitate or refuse amniocentesis. Adrienne explains that reasoning. Like the women who refused amnio because of its lateness, Adrienne too is concerned with commitment:

> This was a child that when we started the child, we wanted the child. The year before I had an abortion. The second child had colic, was difficult. They would have been too close together. We decided to have an abortion. It wasn't terrible, but it wasn't a pleasant experience. We hadn't planned that to be a child, but this one was planned to be a child. It seemed wrong to reject it because it was damaged.

These women are refusing amniocentesis and the potential of *selective* abortion because of their personal commitment to the fetus. For some it is a commitment to fetuses in general, fetuses as people; for others it is a commitment to "my child no matter what"—what Marilyn refers to as the "responsibility a mother has, even before birth, to a newly incarnating being." This belief, she states, "is not, however, one I would try to impose on someone else."

This commitment, responsibility, love if you will, can be entirely secular, a this-world connection. But some women place this connectedness in a religious or spiritual context.

Religion and spirituality can offer an alternative to the value of control over nature espoused by modern society. This alternative belief system says that things happen "for a reason," and the value lies in rising to meet the challenge, accepting what the world offers. It can be expressed as simply as Connie's proclamation that "I was ready to accept whatever God had planned for me," or in Marilyn's view that "I know that babies often bring their 'means' with them—we think we aren't prepared, but we find ways to manage." I think Jane eloquently expresses this view when she explains why she did not have amnio:

> I just didn't feel right about it—even though there seemed rational (statistical) reasons for doing it, intuitively it just felt all wrong. I had read that it was not always accurate and that it could be dangerous. I feel that the main reason to find out if your ~~baby~~ [sic] fetus is defective would be so you could decide if the defect warranted termination of the pregnancy. . . . A soul in a defective body is still a soul and a potential seeker of truth. . . . Conception is a conscious decision (on *some* level) to accept life, to go for life, to trust in the perfection of a universe that takes sexual energy and transforms it via the egg and sperm into a conscious human being with the potential for manifesting truth and love.

Jane's spiritual acceptance does not come without an awareness of the difficulties life has to offer:

> While on the one hand I feel opposed to abortion and would tend to be open and accepting to any baby I carry, I am also aware of the incredible "burden" a severely defective child would be, and how reluctant I would be to take that on. . . . But . . . where do you draw the line? If there is *any* chance for creative potential do I have the right to take the life of a fetus?

Like Jane and Marilyn, Lois says she has "trust in the universal flow of life and death. I do not feel there are any mistakes." This kind of thinking, this acceptance of a universal plan, of lessons to be learned, runs deeply contrary to the prevalent world view, the value of taking charge, making decisions, and controlling one's destiny. Ginger talks about safety concerns regarding amnio, her hopes that things would be fine, and then she says:

I also believe, and this is my main reason, that this babe, already conceived, with his own soul and being, was and is right for us, in our spiritual path, and feel he's God-given and needs to be accepted as is. I find it hard to talk about this main reason. It's easier for me to rattle off as I did because I know it is socially more acceptable. Y'know?

Feeling Safe

Not all people who decide not to have amniocentesis do so out of a solid philosophical grounding. Some just feel *safe*, are confident that there is no problem with the baby. Just as some women draw an unreasonable, irrational feeling of safety from having "done everything" medicine has to offer, including amnio, and now feel like nothing will go wrong, other women make their bargains with different gods. Eating right and living right, having a "healthy life style" makes some women, like Kate, feel secure:

> I eat a very natural diet and get plenty of fresh air. I do not feel that my body is "slowing down" (cell death, et cetera) as rapidly as city-dwelling women. I feel very young. Also I trust my intuition. I felt everything was okay.

Lillian echoes her sentiments:

> Fetal defects have never been a concern of mine because I stay away from unnatural procedures, all medicine and chemicals in food, don't drink or smoke, et cetera, and always felt I would have normal babies.

One of the most common and readily acceptable ways to "feel safe" is to play the numbers game. Thirty-five is the arbitrary cut-off point, but anywhere between 30 and 40 it seems a woman can consider herself "borderline." Some of the women who have amnio say they would not have had it if they were "a year younger," "under 35" (she's 36), "under 37" (she's 38), and so on. On the flip side, women who choose not to have amniocentesis can claim that they are on the "good side" of the borderline.

One can feel safe because the numbers are "on your side," or because you've eaten right, or whatever, but a woman can also feel safe because she just *knows* it is okay. Like Helena, whose spiritual reading made her feel safe, and just went along with the amniocentesis "for verification" and to satisfy her doctor, other women also feel they have alternative sources of knowledge. Not all feel the need for the scientific verification amnio provides. Karen felt that "because I'm a dancer, I feel in touch with my body," and Carol had an "inner belief in the health of my fetus." Rachel seemed the most sure: "We were divinely directed not to have it. We *knew* our baby was healthy." Rachel says she would have amnio if she "did not have access to divine direction."

The Experience of Motherhood

Most women go into pregnancy well aware that lightning does strike even those who think right and feel right. Women may refuse amniocentesis not because they think it won't happen to them, nor because they reject abortion as a possibility, but because they feel confident in their abilities to cope. Just as Ida felt that a lack of support services in her rural area was a motive for amniocentesis and selective abortion, other women's experiences of social support may make them feel more ready to deal with what comes:

> We felt we could handle a problem if it happened—we have a close family and good friends for support. Who can expect perfection? Our two adopted sons both ended up needing extensive orthopedic work after normal adoption physicals.

One would expect that the most significant experience in women's lives teaching them whether or not they could "cope" with the problems of a disabled child would be their experiences of motherhood. Some women are having their first pregnancy after they are 35, but even more already are mothers. Does having a child make a woman more or less likely to have amniocentesis when she has a pregnancy over 35? No one has yet done the kind of representative sampling that could answer that question. But it does seem that the whole question becomes more complicated when one is already a mother. It is as if the stakes rise on both sides of the decision. On the one hand, the experience of completing a pregnancy changes the meaning of later pregnancies for women. Many women say that they would have more trouble with an abortion, now that they have experienced a completed pregnancy and birth, and know their child, than they would have had the first time. On the other hand, there is now another child and another life to consider: the impact of the potential child's retardation on the existing child's needs has to be considered. A decision that is rarely easy is now that much more complicated.

Virginia had refused amniocentesis with her first pregnancy, when she was 35, but had it with her next one a few years later. She represents the point of view that amniocentesis is more important now that another person's life is involved. But while some women will have amniocentesis with a next pregnancy (whether they were "at risk" or not the first time) because they are now mothers, others will not, and for the same reason. Marsha had terminated a pregnancy because of Downs Syndrome, and then gone on to have another pregnancy, with a healthy child. She says:

> John and I want to have another baby, and I am having a difficult inner struggle right now. I have to be mentally prepared to have an abortion if the test results are negative, and now that I have had a baby that decision is more difficult for me. I thought it would be easier, once I had a baby, but it's just the opposite.

Motherhood changes a lot of things. The woman who would have an abortion for fetal defects with a first pregnancy is just not the same woman, not living the same life, once she has had a child. For some women, these changes produce changes in their need or willingness to have amniocentesis. Rochelle says of her first pregnancy:

If the fetus had been Downs Syndrome I would have aborted for the purely selfish reasons of not wanting my possible only child to be less perfect. At my age I didn't want my life so drastically changed for that. I would have taken the chance of no children. But now that I have a child and a changed life, the decision to abort would be more difficult to make. At this point I speculate that I probably would not, but who knows what my emotional state would be then.

Suzanne directly addresses the way the experience of parenting can give a woman new confidence in her abilities to "cope":

We had serious concerns about being able to care for a "special child"—physically, emotionally, and economically. As it turned out, the results of the procedure indicated no genetic problems, but she has had other health problems and we've learned that we can indeed handle these problems and continue to thrive as a "healthy" family.

It is very likely that if someone *does* do the representative sampling necessary to determine the effects of previous children on the decision to have amniocentesis, they will find out that these conflicting feelings cancel each other out: some women will abort more readily for fetal defect once they are mothers; and some women will abort less readily. Each woman may be acting out of her experience with motherhood—but in a large-scale statistical study previous motherhood may appear to make no difference.

The Meaning of Downs Syndrome

What happens to women who have already had a child with Downs Syndrome? These are the most strongly encouraged of all to have amniocentesis, and many of them do, fully prepared to terminate pregnancies with Downs Syndrome diagnosed. But others have been more fortunate in their experience—maybe they have had less severely affected children, maybe more supportive environments. Both Arlene and Emily had children with Downs Syndrome when they were young, when they had no reason to believe they were "at risk." With subsequent pregnancies Arlene chose to have amniocentesis and Emily chose not to, but their basic thinking is very similar. Arlene said:

> Having a Downs Syndrome child greatly influenced my decision for amnio. I was 21 years old when Charles was born and the thought of having an amnio while I was pregnant was the furthest thing from my mind because I was so young. If Charles had been a "normal" child, I would never have had amnios performed on my following two pregnancies. . . . Charles is the love of our lives, a complete joy. I had amnios done so that if I were carrying another DS child I would be warned ahead of time so that the baby's birth could be a happy experience. I could *never* abort a DS child. The amnio does give peace of mind to some extent.

Emily also did not have amnio with her first pregnancy:

> When I heard my child wasn't normal I didn't believe it. I had no experience to compare him so I didn't accept it until eight or nine months. I never thought of giving him up. I knew I would love him the same. So when I was pregnant again I knew I could love my next child regardless of how she was born. I also decided, though not a church-goer at all, that I would pray for my unborn child and I asked others to pray also. The only reason I considered amnio for a little while was because if it came out for the best I wouldn't have had to think about it for the rest of the nine months.

Arlene and Emily are not dismissing the seriousness of their children's problems: they prayed for healthy children, and felt they would want to be warned if they had to face Downs Syndrome again. Emily says that because of her age and being at risk, she and her husband have decided to have no more children, and he has had a vasectomy. Both women acknowledge the seriousness of the problem, but neither was unwilling to accept another Downs Syndrome child.

Ruth, who is opposed to all abortions, would not want to know if the baby was going to have Downs Syndrome:

> Knowing ... adds stress to the remaining gestation and does not give the parents the opportunity to see the *whole* child, the child who is more like other persons than unlike them. The parent can only focus on what's *wrong*, not what's *right* about the child.

Women like Ruth, Arlene, and Emily are trying to see Downs Syndrome in the context of the child as a whole, a child whose birth could be a "happy experience." Many—including many other mothers of Downs Syndrome children and adults—would say that it is an overly optimistic picture of Downs Syndrome, but some women after seriously considering the possibility of bearing such a child are not frightened of it:

> I read a lot on Downs and decided that not only was it not so bad a condition as made out to be but that one could do something about it—raise a Downs kid as normal.

> My main concern was Downs Syndrome. Before test "eligibility" at sixteen weeks I read a lot pertaining to the syndrome, and decided I would not abort for this reason. To me therefore the test would be useless.

Some women feel that a diagnosis of Downs Syndrome is not specific enough to be used for decision-making:

> I didn't feel I would have an abortion, give up the baby, even if I knew it was defective, since even the term Downs Syndrome implies a whole spectrum of possibilities from mildly retarded to severely so, and a similar spectrum of physical ills possible.

Then there is Judith. She chose not to have amniocentesis with her fifth child, born when she was 36:

We chose not to have amniocentesis. We had a Downs
Syndrome baby. I have no regrets. I love him very much.
Every developmental milestone is a source of great joy.

Her baby is two months old.

So these are the reasons people choose not to have amniocentesis with a pregnancy medically defined as "at risk":

abortion is not acceptable to them
amniocentesis results come too late for them to abort
they have made a commitment to the baby/fetus
there are no mistakes, and they accept what is given
they feel safe; it won't happen
they are not that frightened of Downs Syndrome

But running over and through and around almost every answer is one constant refrain, a word that hums and buzzes and
swoops and excuses and justifies and props: *risk.*

. . . risks outweigh the benefits at 35–36.
. . . possibility of injuring, however subtly, the fetus.
. . . so why take the risk involved?
. . . the chances of amniocentesis hurting the baby were al-
    most as great as the baby having Downs Syndrome.
. . . I didn't want to risk losing the baby or even the remote
    possibility of it.
. . . and I thought amniocentesis might hurt it.
. . . fearful some harm might come to the baby when the
    needle was inserted.
. . . nothing to be gained . . . and possible risk to fetus.
. . . so why take the risk for the baby?
. . . it wouldn't at all be worth the risk.

Over and over and over, from almost every woman, there is a
constant refrain: amniocentesis poses a risk—a risk to the continuation of the pregnancy, a risk to the baby, a risk of hurting
the very thing one is trying to achieve: a healthy baby.

CHANGING TECHNOLOGY, CHANGING CHOICES

What happens to all of the decision-making arguments, the bases for choice, if the risk factor changes? The choice of amniocentesis now involves three choices: (1) the choice to get a prenatal diagnosis, to learn whatever is knowable about the condition of the fetus; (2) the choice of selective abortion, because there is no fetal therapy for almost all of the conditions; and (3) the choice or the willingness to use *this particular technology*. To choose amniocentesis a woman must both want the information, and be willing to accept the waiting and the risks involved to get it. Given the risks, for many women all three aspects must be in place before amniocentesis is acceptable. For many women, risking amnio without a willingness to abort "doesn't pay."

The risk of amniocentesis comes from its inherently invasive nature: to get the information a needle has to be put inside the amniotic sac and fluid must be removed. The risks are minimized with highly trained, competent, and very experienced workers, but are still there. Further, to do this with any immediate safety, ultrasound, with its long-term unknown risks is used. The second technical problem, the lateness of the results, is also built right into the technique. A highly efficient lab can speed up the turnaround time, but drawing the fluid must await the middle of the pregnancy.

There is currently an experimental technique that at least partially overcomes these problems: chorionic villi biopsy. Chorionic villi develop out of the union of egg and sperm, and so can be tested for chromosomal status; but, like the placenta they become, they are not part of the fetus. Sampling this tissue, which is inside the uterus but outside of the amniotic sac, can be done in the first trimester of pregnancy. Results are available early, before fetal movement, before the woman looks pregnant, before many women have experienced a commitment to the pregnancy.

Chorionic villi biopsy differs from amniocentesis in more than timing: the amniotic sac is not entered; the fetus is not at risk of needle damage; the amniotic environment is not changed. But entering the uterus during pregnancy is still distressing to some women, may still "feel" unsafe. Tammy, for example, refused amniocentesis because she "value[s] the womb as a sacred place that should be off-limits, especially to technology."

An even more impressive technological change that the next decade may bring will be the recovery of fetal cells from maternal blood: not amniocentesis, not biopsy, but just a simple blood test from the mother, and a wealth of information about the fetus will become available. What happens then to the objections and hesitations some women have about amniocentesis? Will an early blood test resolve those concerns?

I think that an early blood test will strip the problem down to its bare bones. I think it will take us past questions of risk, of date and of technique, to confront the essential moral and ethnical issues. It will take us straight to the meaning of motherhood, the ethics of abortion, and the human ability to control nature.

I think that the "risk" issue in amniocentesis is a widely used, socially acceptable excuse for not having amniocentesis. Risk is almost always cited by women who, for a variety of reasons, do not want to have the test. Their own reasons, their feelings, their intuitions, their sense of discomfort—these are not acceptable, rational reasons for rejecting medical procedures. But playing the numbers game is ever so much more rational.

For example: one often hears a woman comparing the risks of Downs Syndrome, the one-in-350 at age 35, with the risks of losing the pregnancy due to amniocentesis, a risk presented as three-in-1000. The two numbers are the same. That is the break-even point, and that is one reason that 35 has been institutionalized as the magic age. I think we have here something of an apples and oranges problem: they don't add up. Can the risks of miscarriage be weighted against the risks of Downs Syndrome and be declared equal when the numbers are equal?

If a woman gets pregnant fairly easily, then what *does* a miscarriage mean to her? To some women, very little. A woman I observed in a genetic counseling session, who aborted because some beer drinking may have harmed her fetus, said, "It'll only set us back about three months." An early blood test and selective abortion can just turn a June baby into an October baby. No big deal. Other women, however, are horrified. They are devastated at the thought of a miscarriage. In recent years there has been an outpouring of women's feelings about pregnancy loss. A selective abortion, early or late, is more than a few or even many months delay on the way to the goal of a healthy baby. If that is all it was for most women, then there would be little hesitation in risking that against a lifetime of caring for a disabled child. If there is any lesson we can learn from women's greater openness about reproductive tragedies, it is that pregnancies and babies do not cancel each other out. For their mothers, fetuses are not often "fungible," as some of the philosophers claim: interchangeable and replaceable. The woman who is afraid of risking a miscarriage, of "losing this baby," is not talking about a delay in achieving the goal of a healthy child. She is talking about her early and developing commitment to *this* child.

Moving the time of the potential abortion to an earlier point in the pregnancy means moving it to a point where the commitment is less solidly established. It may not make the problem go away, but it certainly makes it easier for most women. Asked whether they would have an earlier blood test for prenatal diagnosis, most women who refused amniocentesis thought they probably would use such a blood test. Some spoke directly to the issue of commitment, and the point in pregnancy results are available:

> Probably. I might have an abortion. It's real hard to say. It's very hard to think of aborting a baby you've consciously and lovingly conceived. (Naomi)

> I feel I could abort if a test revealing a severe defect had been done very early in pregnancy, before I became "attached" to the fetus. (Gloria)

> If it could have been done in the first ten weeks, that would get rid of most of my objections. (Adrienne)

Adrienne has hit the nail right on the head. If it is safe, and if it is early, that does get rid of most of most people's objections. Maybe not all, but most.

The people whose objections are still not being met are those who are totally opposed to abortion, who make no distinction between abortion and murder. But here we have to consider the information-giving quality of prenatal diagnosis, as distinguished from the abortion potential. Some women who are absolutely opposed to abortion insist that they would not have a blood test for early prenatal diagnosis because they "wouldn't have an abortion anyway," or because "there's no point." Some specifically say that knowing will do more harm than good:

> I have enjoyed my pregnancies and births, and learning early on of a defect would only make me anxious and I can't see the point of that. (Melanie)

And Ruth's objection to prenatal testing still stands: that it prevents people from seeing the "whole child," and focuses us on the disability.

But there are very powerful arguments for having a noninvasive, completely safe, and early test, even for women who do not plan or are not sure about abortion. The arguments the genetic counselors use to separate the amnio decision from the abortion decision come in to play. The simplest is the argument for reassurance. Once we are talking about a blood test, then it is likely that age will cease to be an issue, and the test will be offered even to very-low-risk women. Since the chances are overwhelming that the woman will receive good news, why, she will be asked, should she not avail herself of this opportunity to be reassured? It is a very convincing argument:

> I might consider a test with lower risks to the fetus to be reassured that the fetus is healthy so I would not worry, but not to abort should the fetus be defective. (Beverly)

Reassurance, preparation—these are the bases on which amniocentesis is urged on women who are quite sure that they will not abort.

In asking these women whether they would use such a test, in talking about a technology that has not yet been developed, I am encouraging them to think about this as a decision. In practice, I am sure that it will not be handled that way. Blood tests are a common part of early pregnancy. Time is not spent, for example, in discussion of what the options will be if the rubella titre indicates recent exposure. The idea that one would *not* want information is so counter to the medical profession's world view, that I think only rarely would an early blood test be presented as itself an opportunity for decision-making.

Most women are not altogether sure of what they would do faced with the knowledge that their early pregnancy fetus is damaged—just as most women have ambivalencies about what to do if the amniocentesis indicated Downs. "It depends" is the most consistent answer: it depends on the kind of damage, disorder, or disease that is diagnosed; it depends on the life situation of the woman at the time. It depends.

> I would want to know if there were any defects. I don't know whether I would choose to abort—the concrete facts of the situation would come into play and so would my feelings . . . it depends on when I'd have learned of it [the defect] and what kind of information I obtained. The potential suffering of the child would have to be figured into a decision too. (Victoria)

Removing the issue of risk, the value of information, of informed decision-making comes to the fore:

> If there were a test with no possible risk to the fetus or pregnancy, I would have it and then, either relax in the knowledge that my child would not have certain diseases, or if the results showed a problem, wrestle with the moral and emotional question of abortion from an informed position. (Louise)

When risk is removed, the last completely socially acceptable reason for not wanting to know fetal defects will be gone. A genetic counselor said that many Hispanic women find the risks of miscarriage not acceptable, and so refuse amniocentesis on that

basis. Counselors usually do not argue with that basis for decision: it is considered realistic. But this counselor went on to say:

> I'm sure they have reasons, but not very well thought out.
> They'll latch onto anything. They don't want the test and
> they want a reason not to have it. . . . They don't want to be
> confronted with the choice—but it's not a moral reason be-
> cause they don't think that far.

Look, if you can, beyond the counselor's disturbing prejudice
about Hispanic women, to hear what she is saying about which
are "moral" decisions, which issues are framed as moral questions. To reject the test for moral reasons requires what another
counselor called "always thinking three steps ahead," thinking
straight to the abortion question. We do not even have a language of morality that allows us to talk about the moral nature of
information itself. Moral questions, as we generally phrase it,
come with the problems of what to *do* with information. There
may be moral (and immoral) decisions to be made, but whether
or not to enter into the decision-making process itself is not
widely recognized as a moral dilemma.[2] This is what enables
counselors to consider themselves "nondirective" because they
are not pushing abortions ("a very personal decision") while
strongly encouraging the woman to have the amniocentesis and
"get the information."

We are entering into what has been called the "information
era," and it is reflected in the very way we think. Something beyond knowledge for its own sake is involved: it is the idea that
action is based on information, and the fullest possible information is needed to determine action responsibly. Informed consent
is more than a legal requirement: it is a developing social norm.
If there is information to be had, and decisions to be made, the
value lies in actively seeking the information and consciously
making the decision. To do otherwise is to "let things happen to
you," not to "take control of your life." Such is the contemporary, secular definition of mature, responsible behavior. When a
wife in a counseling session expressed her discomfort with having to make such momentous decisions, her husband said he'd

rather they make the decision themselves, "because when we have our baby, having had the amniocentesis or not having had the amniocentesis, we'd have so much more to do with it."

Women who have chosen amniocentesis call upon this same value to justify the choice. We may not like it, it may not be easy, but we are better people for making the choices: that is the value being put forth. Refusing amniocentesis, on the other hand, is turning *away* from the value of choice, and even more profoundly, turning away from the value of information.

More and more we believe one should have all the information, one *should* be prepared, act rationally, not bury your head in the sand. The pressure to get information comes from all sides. Even with the problems inherent in amniocentesis, with the lateness, with the possibility of miscarrying or damaging a healthy fetus, the pressure was and is there. Adrienne was made angry by it:

> There's a strong assumption toward it ... pressure on women to go through something which would be a horrible experience. People seemed to think it was a normal, okay thing to do. What bothered me was the assumption that it was normal, denying that it would be a very difficult thing. They treat it like it was common, like going to the bathroom.

Adrienne lumps together the amniocentesis procedure, the long waiting period, and the possibility of a late abortion. When these are separated out, when all that one needs to do to get information is to have a blood test and "then decide," the pressure will mount.

And so I am making a prediction here, a prediction that before very long the receipt of information on the status of the fetus—as much information as science can provide—will be an expected part of pregnancy. Information on chromosomal disorders, sex, and a variety of diseases and conditions will be made available. As chromosomal analysis becomes more sophisticated, more information will be made available. What will be the effects of having all of this information?

The next chapters address the effects of the information currently gleaned from prenatal diagnosis, the effects on the pregnancy experience of seeking, waiting for, receiving, and processing information. Seeking and waiting for information changes the pre-information stage of pregnancy, creates what I think of as a "tentative pregnancy." It incorporates the issue of abortion right into the route to motherhood and institutionalizes conditionality in mother love. Getting "good news," getting the information that the fetus is, as they say, "a normal male fetus," or a "normal female fetus," changes the second part of pregnancy, making the baby more "real," more finite, more limited in its potential. And getting bad news changes everything.

4

THE TENTATIVE
PREGNANCY

Prenatal diagnosis changes women's experience of pregnancy. That is obviously true for women who receive bad diagnoses, but in this and the next chapter, I will show that it is also true when results are normal, when the baby is fine.

The first part of this chapter will describe women's experiences with the amniocentesis itself. When things go smoothly, as anticipated, there really is not very much to say. The woman lies down on an examining table, the ultrasound scanner is used to observe the location of fetus and placenta, a needle is inserted below the woman's umbilicus, fluid is drawn up into the syringe, and the needle is withdrawn. But when things do not go as planned, the women—a minority—have a great deal to say. They are angered, upset by the problem, and often surprised. For example, while more than 10 percent of the women I interviewed who had amniocentesis had to have at least two taps, and often more, to get the fluid, almost every woman to whom this happened seemed to think it was very unusual, almost unique to her. It is perhaps unfortunate, but I think inevitable, that my description of the amniocentesis procedure will emphasize these problems, from multiple taps to spontaneous miscarriage, which in total were experienced by more than one in five of the women I interviewed.

But even the smoothest and most perfect of amniocentesis tests changes the pregnancy experience: The possibility of a bad diagnosis casts its shadow back over the early months, and the flow of time in pregnancy itself is changed with mid-pregnancy diagnosis. Most important, the mother's developing relationship with her fetus is affected by the new technology of reproduction.

Having Amnio: Experiences with the Procedure

Genetic counselors often reassure their clients that the amniocentesis procedure itself is usually not painful, and not as difficult as they may fear. In one joint session I observed, the counselor described to the two women and the one accompanying husband that people may fear the pain of the needle, may fear miscarriage, the needle hitting the baby and so on, but "ninety-eight women out of a hundred say they worried for nothing." The woman there alone muttered: "That's *after*." We all laughed.

A small percentage of women experience some significant pain; a few have leaking of fluid or other problems. For most women, it is *not* a painful procedure. It is hard not to be uncomfortable with the thought of someone piercing your pregnant womb, but once it is over, it usually doesn't seem like it was "that big a deal." Besides the simple relief of having it over and done, some women get pleasure out of the sonography that accompanies the procedure, and sharing that experience with the father. Lynn said: "My husband went with me to the amnio. It was especially exciting for him to see the baby on ultrasound and helped him feel closer to the baby." Helen felt it brought her and the father, to whom she was not married, closer together. And for Paula:

The best part about the test the first time was actually seeing the baby on ultrasound, watching it move and seeing
that the essential large parts all seemed to be there. I wish I
could have had a copy of one of all the pictures they took of
my baby at three months after conception.

A genetic counselor who works with women who have terminated pregnancies for genetic defect expressed her concern to me
about the way sonograms are treated. She wonders, if they are
going to have to abort this fetus, does it really make sense for
them to watch it moving? To the untrained eye, the sonogram is
confusing. This counselor discourages the technicians from
pointing out details. This is serious, she says. We are not playing
games. It makes things harder if one has to abort, having
watched the fetus sucking its thumb—"You can live without
that," she says. But people do get pleasure out of it. Katherine
had a very hard time with her amniocentesis, having to have repeated tests done. After going through it over and over again, she
has strong ideas about how the test is best done, and wants to
share them with others:

Insist that your husband, partner, friend, etcetera, be allowed to be there with you if that will make you feel better.
Our hospital had a policy that only the patient could be in
the room because of cramped quarters. I insisted that my
husband be there and got our doctor to support us on this,
but every time we went back we had to argue with the technicians even though they knew all the problems we were
having. Also, most women don't know this, but the ultrasound pictures can be obtained after the baby is born. I requested one and we have it in Jennifer's baby book—she's
fifteen weeks in the picture. Also get the ultrasound technician to move the screen so you can see the fetus. Some of
them don't want to be bothered, but it is thrilling to see, so
insist.

The problem that Katherine was having was that her doctor
was not able to remove enough fluid for testing. Some would say
he started too early in the pregnancy:

According to the doctor who performed my amniocentesis, I may have had more done for one pregnancy than almost anyone else [two at fifteen weeks, one at sixteen weeks, and one at eighteen weeks]. He is a pioneer in this area and said he rarely does more than one and it never took four before. Actually we had a fifth try—I was all prepped but he decided not to try that day. Therefore we were in uncharted territory. At that point I wanted a second opinion, but there was no one else in————who had as much experience as our MD in this area. Having had two previous miscarriages, I was very concerned about each test provoking another one. Each week—between tests—I was nervous about having a miscarriage and at the same time had to decide whether to go back for another test. Because the tests were not working right and my uterus would contract, the tests were painful and I was bruised and sore for a day or so. For me, I couldn't have handled the anxiety I would have felt going through the rest of the pregnancy and not knowing if the baby had a problem. . . .

At the eighteenth week:

Another thrill was that the nurse didn't adjust the table correctly and during the last test the table slipped while the doctor was performing the test and almost blew the whole thing again.

By that point, Katherine and her husband were taking no chances; they took the amniotic fluid sample to the lab themselves in order to guard against mixups.

Having four taps *is* uncommon, but it is not unusual for women not to have a successful test on the first try. Sometimes the problem lies, as it did for Katherine, in withdrawing the fluid. Carla reports that:

During my amniocentesis the doctor had to pierce the uterus three times in order to withdraw enough fluid (which contained a little blood). Also, when the technician did the sonogram, before the amniocentesis test, she asked the doctor to step out of the room with her. I found out at my next medical checkup that the technician had discovered a uterine fibroid tumor.

Another woman says:

My experience with the amniocentesis was rather traumatic. My doctor planned to do it himself, although he didn't do many of them. He spent an hour attempting it—he inserted the needle twice with no success. By the end of this time I was very upset and fearful about harm to the baby. The doctor was very apologetic and concerned. I was referred to a doctor in————who specialized in the procedure. . . . I really agonized about going through it a third time and was quite depressed. . . . The doctor there was quite expert—it took him about fifteen minutes to complete the procedure. He was very informative and reassuring, and the experience was completely painless. If I had been referred to him in the first place it would have been much easier for me.

About 10 percent of the women I interviewed had to have the tap repeated to get fluid for testing.

Problems can also arise at a later stage of the procedure, in the analysis of the fluid, as happened to Paula:

The traumatic part of the whole process for me came upon discovering after nearly three weeks had passed and I was already hoping to get the results soon, that the first test had not "taken" and would have to be repeated. That day I cried out "why me?" I was already beginning to feel very attached to the child and felt that by the time I did get any results I would feel it was too late to do anything. I almost decided I would not repeat the test, but then decided that that did not make sense either. This time they put me on "rush." I was amazed. I thought every amniocentesis ought to be a "rush" case.

One of the fears people have during amniocentesis is that the needle will hit the baby. Irene had her amnio done at a teaching hospital:

> They said a doctor was doing it—she was a doctor, but an intern. She did the test twice, and on the second try she said, "Oops—I hit something," and still didn't get any fluid. At that point I had to wait for another doctor for two to three hours, and have a third test done. One or two wouldn't have been so bad, but three was pretty hard.

One of Jackie's twins was born with a dimple mark on her leg, which she thinks might have been a needle mark.

Georgia has had amniocentesis with two different pregnancies, and reports that, at the two hospitals where she had the tests, they were "largely carried out by students, and if it was in a clinic it was solely carried out by students, although it is not presented that way to the patient." In addition, her first test was temporarily lost.

Needle stabs, dry taps, slipping tables, lost samples, bumbling interns—it is not reassuring, but probably inevitable. If enough procedures are done in enough places by enough people, eventually all of these things will happen. I don't know if my sample of sixty accurately represents the proportion of problems, but I am not really surprised to find that about one in five women had some kind of problem with the test.

Even when things go well, when fluid is properly drawn the first time, some women find the situation distressing. Several women were disturbed by having to take the sample to the lab themselves. Alison and her husband had to drive it to another hospital over thirty miles away. Francine had a particularly bad experience with this. She was only 30, and had had early pregnancy bleeding, thus putting her at greater risk of a miscarriage. Her doctor had said that he would have the amnio if he were she, but:

> Later he said he thought I was asking for his okay because *I* wanted to . . . I really hadn't thought about the possibility of

danger to the baby or read enough about the amnio. . . . So after the amnio I felt invaded and that I was putting the baby at great risk. I was very shaken. I then had to take the fluid to the analysis center, which is on the grounds of a state mental institution, where I saw retarded adults selling vegetables. I then had a talk with the genetic consultants who after they heard my history were amazed that I had the amnio done. This further upset me. I then faced another drive to my husband's work. I was sobbing all the way down the highway. I couldn't believe I had put my baby under *any* risk, we had given up so much those first few months to keep her safe. I was so nervous for three or four days fearing a miscarriage. . . . When we found out the results, my husband came with me to the doctor's. We tried to explain my emotional response. He was extremely defensive and could not understand my feelings. Apparently he had delivered a Downs baby recently and seen the sorrow of those two parents—and wanted to avoid that again. The other woman doctor told me that later.

Deirdre had none of these unusual problems, just a straightforward tap, but she calls it "creepy":

Amniocentesis itself is a very *creepy* procedure. The two specialists I had do it at the University of————were intensely serious, dour and clinical. To break the tension (I was very nervous), as the doc was drawing up what seemed like a *huge* amount of amniotic fluid, I said, "Hey, don't drain my kid's swimming pool!" Nothing, silence, no response. An empathetic woman's presence would have been helpful.

All of these are relatively minor problems, concerns that fade beside the greatest fear, that irrecoverable damage will be done, that an otherwise perfectly healthy fetus will be lost due to the procedure. That can happen when the amniocentesis itself causes a miscarriage, and it can happen if a laboratory error results in the abortion of a healthy fetus. Both are rare events, the latter much more so than the former. In all my research I have only heard of it happening once.

The more common tragedy is to lose a fetus to an amnio-caused miscarriage—or to suspect that you may have. The figures cited by genetic counselors are that *without* amniocentesis thirty-two out of a thousand women will spontaneously miscarry pregnancies after the sixteenth week, the point at which the test is usually done. With amniocentesis, the number rises to thirty-five out of a thousand. The amnio can thus be held accountable for three miscarriages among one thousand women. The trick is in figuring *which three*.

Sometimes it can be obvious. Two counselors shared with me the same story, involving a doctor who had never done an amnio before. The woman became infected, ran a fever the next day, and miscarried shortly thereafter. And sometimes it can be equally obvious that the amnio was not to be blamed. Occasionally when a very severe defect is diagnosed, it turns out that the pregnancy miscarried before the results came back. That is what is often called "nature's way" of handling severe defects.

But there are other times when it is hard to say just what happened. Most of the thirty-five women out of a thousand who miscarry following amniocentesis will probably suspect the amnio as the cause of the miscarriage. Stacey was in that situation.

Stacey describes herself as one of those "Baby Boom babies who waited till late in life to have children." At 35, married, and living in the home she designed and built on a farm, she decided to have a child. She had amniocentesis, and three weeks later, on her seventh wedding anniversary, the results came back that everything was fine.

But things were far from fine. She thought her abdomen looked flatter, and then she began to bleed. The bleeding stopped and started again. She went to the hospital to use an ultrasound machine to detect the heartbeat: "The only one was mine, at 140 lying down. Nerves, the nurse said. I believe it."

Further ultrasound showed what she feared: the baby had died. A painful prostaglandin abortion of her dead fetus followed, with repeated morphine shots for pain. The placenta did not come out, and had to be removed by D&C, completely fragmented. Stacey says:

What I believe happened is that during the amniocentesis
the needle went through the placenta, pulling it away from
the uterine wall. . . . Probably then the placenta started to
disintegrate, and the fetus died.

Patricia Leff also lost her baby in the weeks following amniocentesis, and she too thinks the amnio caused the miscarriage.
She is angry, very angry, not only about the loss, but about the
way that the physicians responded to the loss. Patricia Leff and
her husband are both physicians themselves. She feels that she
and her husband were inappropriately counseled by her obstetrician, and had no idea that the amnio was potentially lethal to the
fetus. They registered their complaint with the county medical
society, with no real response. She says, "I feel that I am crying
out to the wind. So few people, especially among my colleagues,
are willing to take my grief seriously." Patricia Leff wrote up the
story of what happened to her, and called it "Routine Lessons."[1]
Here is an excerpt:

Our baby was dead. Yesterday's empty sonogram screen
and the frightened, blank stares of my obstetrician had sig-
naled her death. Her dancing shadows and flickering heartbeat had abruptly faded out of my life. Was she nothing
more than a brief TV mirage?
I sat frozen in my doctor's office and calmly made plans
for today's second trimester abortion. From the numbness
of my grief, I whispered, "It was the amniocentesis." The
obstetrician, who had so eagerly, so cavalierly, so routinely
(within minutes of confirming the pregnancy) scheduled me
for the amniocentesis, the obstetrician who had so eagerly
pursued the prized amniotic fluid despite two punctures
and a massive uterine contraction, now turned to me and
matter-of-factly pontificated, "After a medically invasive
procedure, it is possible."
Possible. We can't fool you, Patty. You're one of us, Dr.
Leff. We wish that we could deceive you. We wish that we
could concoct some natural, God-given cause for your

baby's death. Anything but our eagerness, our technique, our . . .

A wave of nausea chilled my body. The prostaglandin suppositories were beginning to take effect, to prepare my body to expel the inert, lifeless tissue within me. My normal baby girl.

I pulled the sheet closer to me. My body was shaking. A gentle young nurse introduced herself to me as she took my blood pressure. We talked: Did I have other children? How old was my son? How had this pregnancy progressed? What had happened during the amniocentesis? What had happened after the procedure? Did I want to see the baby?

Tears seared my face: "I know what a normal fetus looks like," I angrily sobbed. Would reality, indeed, force me to see my fetus—the part of me that would never exist? The waters would burst, two or three painful contractions would follow; and suddenly, she would pass away from me to lie motionless on the blood-drenched sheets. I would touch the fragility and utter helplessness. I would touch—where would she go after the delivery? No funeral. No grave. The discarded waste of the pathology lab.

The young obstetrician's mundane workday was coming to an end. I cringed as he patted me on the head. A woman in pain I was; a dog I was not. Perhaps, it was easier for him to think of me as a dog. A dog asks no questions; a dog produces litters en masse, a dog makes no plans for the future. What is one puppy more or less?

Within days of the abortion, she met the obstetrician in the hospital parking lot. While she kept telling him that the parking lot was not an appropriate place for discussion, he insisted on talking to her. He wanted to tell her about a patient, "a woman physician at that," who leaked fluid following an amniocentesis throughout her pregnancy and went on to deliver a normal child.

The story Patricia Leff's obstetrician tried to present as a positive thing, everything "working out okay," is precisely what worries some other people. Betty Levin, an anthropologist studying neonatal intensive care units, observed an infant whose premature birth she thinks may have been caused by amniocentesis. The mother began leaking amniotic fluid after the test, but carried the pregnancy for long enough so that the resulting delivery was the "birth" of a premature baby, and not a "miscarriage." As the age of viability continues to drop, we can expect this scenario to repeat itself more often. Born so very prematurely, the baby faces chances of the kinds of retardation, brain damage, and physical problems that its parents were presumably trying to avoid by having amniocentesis.

But for most women the procedure itself goes smoothly, does not immediately or obviously damage the pregnancy, and provides accurate information. In most cases the information is that the fetus is healthy, and the pregnancy continues.

Marking Time

There are two time-keeping systems operating to keep track of pregnancy. One is the traditional "nine-months" count. Under that system, a woman might speak of herself as "entering her ninth month," or recount some story of something that happened when she was "six months pregnant." The monthly system is the traditional, colloquial way of keeping track of time in pregnancy. The nine-months system also encourages thinking of the pregnancy in terms of three-month "trimesters," which have been the largest generally recognized subdivisions of time in pregnancy. The first trimester is usually thought of as the time before movement and "showing," classically marked by morning sickness; the second trimester as a generally upbeat pleasant time; and the third trimester as the maybe cumbersome, tiring last lap.

The nine-months or trimester system does not mesh with the medical count. The medical system uses a weekly count, with a full-term pregnancy counted as forty weeks. Medical time-keeping begins, oddly enough, not with conception, but two weeks or so previously, with the first day of the last menstrual period. That point is taken as a more "objective" starting date than conception. Doctors have been more willing to trust women's judgment of when they began their last menstrual period than of what day they conceived. So in medical time-keeping, two weeks of pregnancy occur before conception, another two weeks between conception and the day the menstrual period is due, and yet another two weeks before the period is "late" and pregnancy confirmation is possible with standard testing techniques. Pregnancy confirmation thus comes at six weeks, and the pregnancy is always two weeks older than the fetus. A full-term fetus, product of a forty-week pregnancy, is thirty-eight weeks. The first month or six weeks of pregnancy is figured retroactively.

Amniocentesis is placed within the weekly system, with the optimum recommended time being sixteen weeks. Earlier there may not be sufficient amniotic fluid available for testing; later there may not be time for retesting if the analysis fails. Since the cells have to be cultured, test results often take about four weeks, and become available at twenty weeks—or halfway through the forty-week pregnancy. Within this system halves, rather than trimesters, are the larger subdivisions. The pregnancy is marked by its pre-result and post-result status.

Women who have had amniocentesis are more likely than women in traditional pregnancies to think in terms of weeks of pregnancy rather than months. In my interviews I asked both groups of women in which week of pregnancy they first felt fetal movement, and in which week of pregnancy they "began wearing maternity clothes or dressing differently." I asked for month of pregnancy only if the woman could not remember the week. My reason for asking for week was simply for precision—a week is a narrower time span and so more useful for showing if there are differences between the two groups. But the first difference that showed up was how the two groups keep time. Among women who refused amniocentesis, less than 10 percent (and all in their first pregnancies) identified wearing maternity clothes by week of pregnancy. Another 10 percent could not remember or never made a clear switch, just gradually wearing looser clothes. The great majority, though, answered by month. In contrast, among those who had amniocentesis, only about half dated their switch to maternity clothes by month of pregnancy. They were three times more likely to use a weekly measure as were women who had refused amniocentesis. Thus even this entirely non-medical event became located in the time-keeping system of the medical world.

The differences between the two groups in their use of the two time-keeping systems is even more striking with regard to fetal movement. Practically all of the women who had amnio reported fetal movement by week of pregnancy, or in a few cases in reference to the week of the amniocentesis: "Just before the test was done," or "a week or two after results." Only two women used the monthly system to define the first time they felt movement. Most striking of all is that thirteen of the sixty women who had amniocentesis *were not able to remember* when they had first felt the baby move. This had ceased to be a meaningful milestone in the pregnancy. In contrast, among the women who had refused amnio, *all* knew when they first felt movement. And, even though I asked for week of pregnancy, encouraging them to use the medical system, more than half measured in months.

I am interested in these two events—feeling movement and wearing maternity clothes—as representing two different acknowledgments of pregnancy. Wearing maternity clothes marks a public acknowledgment of the pregnant status. Feeling movement is a private acknowledgment of a different and more complex sort. First, let us consider the comparatively simple issue of "going public:" announcing the pregnancy and wearing maternity clothes.

Going Public

There are problems in announcing a pregnancy that may end in an abortion. For some women who have amniocentesis this is a serious concern, although not for all. While one study found no difference in when women who had amniocentesis announced their pregnancies in comparison to women without amnio, another study of seventy-two couples found four who told absolutely no one about the pregnancy, and some delay among some of the others in making the pregnancy fully public.[2] Among the sixty women I interviewed who had had amnio, five told no one but their husbands that they were pregnant until the results came back. Four more confided in just their husbands and intimate friends or parents. There was only one woman with a comparably "private" pregnancy among those who refused amnio. I asked women who they had told about the pregnancies; most didn't want "people's sympathy, pity or gossiping," or declared, "I didn't want to announce in case we decided to have an abortion. I didn't want other people involved in the decision."

The option of a private pregnancy is not available to all who might want it. There are a number of reasons why a woman may not be able to keep her pregnancy private until the results come along, including being obviously pregnant, or being incapacitated by nausea in the first few months, which may require some explanation.

In this context, it is not surprising that I found women who had amniocentesis begin wearing maternity clothes later, as a group, than do women who refuse amnio. This was especially true of women expecting their first babies. As Jackie said, "There was a definite feeling of resisting buying maternity clothes until the results came back."

In the course of the bodily changes of pregnancy, women go through a period where the waist thickens and "shape" is lost, but the distinctive pregnant form is not yet obvious. Because of the very low regard in which being fat is held in modern Western countries, this can be a difficult time for women. They neither look nor feel pregnant—just "dumpy." The switch to maternity clothes, with longer tops, raised waistlines, and generally distinctive styling clarifies the meaning of the body change for people seeing the woman. As a popular maternity T-shirt declares, "I'm not fat, I'm pregnant!" For women in tentative pregnancies, pregnancies that may be terminated, the stigma of fat may be preferable to risking the stigma of late abortion.

The shift to maternity clothing has the potential for being both gradual and selective. Most women have several items of clothing that can be used transitionally—a slightly large pair of slacks, a wrap-around skirt, a loosely shaped dress. A top button can be left open, a belt loosened, all without making a formal or public commitment to the pregnancy status. Women can also be "selectively" pregnant—for example, switch to maternity slacks and tops at home, but continue at work in looser "civilian" clothes. This is one of the reasons why the switch to maternity clothes is expressed in the larger time measure of month of pregnancy, even among women who have had amnio, and the experience of feeling movement in the more precise measure of week of pregnancy. But something else is operating, as evidenced by the fact that women who had amnio were more likely to forget when they felt movement than when they began wearing maternity clothes. Women who refused amnio occasionally forgot when they began wearing maternity clothing, but never when they first felt movement. The switch to maternity clothing exists outside of the medical management of pregnancy, and there is no medical substitute for the social labeling which the "pregnancy uniform" accomplishes. But fetal movement can be both medicalized, and medically superseded in importance.

Suspended Animation

Compared to wearing maternity clothes, feeling fetal movement is a very different kind of milestone in pregnancy. For one thing, while the clothing shift has the potential for being both more gradual and more selective, one goes from not having felt movement to having felt it rather quickly—maybe in the space of the instant the movement is felt, maybe over several days of wondering. There may be, particularly for first-time pregnancies, a few occasions on which one wonders if that fluttering sensation could be "it," but once the woman declares, even to herself, that she has felt the baby move, that is that. She may not be feeling it at any particular moment again, but once felt it cannot be unfelt.

It is not only its abruptness that distinguishes feeling movement from "going public." The significance of maternity clothing and pregnancy announcement lies in the public announcement of the pregnant status. Feeling movement, in contrast, marks the private or psychological acknowledgment not so much of the *pregnancy* as of the *baby*. Before the widespread availability of prenatal diagnosis, there was no distinction to be made between a wanted pregnancy and a wanted fetus. If a woman chose or willingly accepted a pregnancy, the statement "I am pregnant" meant "I am going to have a baby." Of course no one ever knew what the baby would be like (nor do we know even with amniocentesis) but the achievement of the wanted pregnancy was itself cause for celebration and congratulations. And now? Georgia, who has had amnio with both of her pregnancies, says:

> I think that having the amnio test available has turned the idea of pregnancy into a negative situation which formerly was a time of optimism. How many friends faced with the announcement of another's pregnancy have responded with "Are you going to have an amnio?" rather than the usual "congratulations."

How can one offer congratulations if the pregnancy may not continue? "I am pregnant," for women having amniocentesis, means "If everything is okay, I will have a baby." When amnio is planned, with the ever-present possibility of abortion for fetal defect, getting pregnant is just one step in a process leading to "I am going to have a baby."

The new technology of reproduction puts many women into a difficult social state, the condition I think of as a "tentative pregnancy." A woman's commitment to her pregnancy under the conditions imposed by amniocentesis can only be tentative. She cannot ignore it, but neither can she wholeheartedly embrace it. Because she wants the baby, the woman will feel obligated to follow the cultural rituals of early pregnancy. Among women so medically sophisticated as to be seeking prenatal diagnosis, that usually means following medical rituals: the examinations, blood tests, weighing-in and the like. She will also be following the (medically based) food taboos for pregnancy, such as limiting alcohol, caffeine, drug and tobacco use. The tentatively pregnant woman has entered the pregnant status, she is a pregnant woman, but she knows that she may not be carrying a baby but a genetic accident, a mistake. The pregnancy may not be leading to a baby, but to an abortion. The pregnancy is medically acknowledged, made socially real, but the fetus/baby is not.

For some women the situation presents no problems: like some of the women who refused amniocentesis, they feel so strongly that everything will be fine that they are able essentially to ignore the amniocentesis and its implications. They may bow to social pressure, to "rationality," enough to have the procedure, but it does not really touch them. They are pregnant and having a baby. Amnio for them is just one more medical test.

Other women have those feelings of certainty, but they come and go. Gerri says:

> I alternated between being convinced that since statistically the odds were in my favor, everything would be fine, and dreading the possibility that everything wouldn't be fine and I'd have to go through an abortion at my stage of pregnancy. I wanted to know and yet I dreaded the doctor's phone call.

Some women who know "deep down" that everything is fine do learn differently—you will hear from them in a later chapter.

The anxiety *is* there for most women. Very few are able to be fully confident all of the time. Different women have, of course, different ways of dealing with the uncertainty, the stress and anxiety. Some are able to keep busy with other things. Ida said it was a busy time at work, and while the uncertainty was there she didn't dwell on it. Amy tried to put it out of her mind, and since she was working full-time "that was not impossible most of the time." Vicki found waiting "somewhat nerve wracking," but she was "very busy with medical school." The time went fast too for Virginia, busy caring for a toddler. Some women are not able to block it out so well, and report depression, crying, anxiety symptoms. Caroline had "skipped heartbeats" and nightmares. She dreamed of "receiving a computer printout marked *abort*."

Most women manage to keep the anxiety under control, but there is a cost to that. The cost is in the developing relationship with the fetus. Distance must be maintained. Lynn said she tried to keep in mind that she might have to abort the pregnancy; Rochelle tried not to get excited "in case of trouble with the fetus"; and Paula felt she shouldn't plan too much before she got the results. And, in terms of not planning, I recently met a pregnant woman who had amniocentesis and was waiting for the results before she married the father. Nora said she "felt a very tentative relationship to the fetus."

When a woman truly believes that there might be a problem,

and that she might abort the fetus, she may feel she has to keep distance, emotionally and pragmatically, from the baby. How can she begin to relate to the baby within, begin to plan for a child, begin to feel like its mother, if it might *not* be a baby at all but a genetic accident, ultimately an aborted fetus? The situation is what Emma described as "limbo—abortion or baby." Several women used language poignantly expressive of this condition, calling the waiting time a period of "suspended animation." Life, and their commitment to this developing life, must be suspended. For Bonnie, waiting for the results of the amniocentesis was a period of "suspended animation" during which:

> All of my thoughts and energies were concentrated on the results and what I would do if there were an abnormality. There was a sense of unreality as well as a heightened intensity.

And Nancy too called her three weeks of waiting for the results a period of "suspended animation" during which she was:

> . . . trying to deny the reality of the pregnancy to myself because of fear of bad results. It was very difficult especially as the baby had started to move.

Nancy is so right. It is easier to "suspend animation" if the fetus is not making itself felt. The literal "feeling of life" makes the denial of the potential baby very much more difficult. While obstetricians may speak of "fetal movement," women say they "feel life" or "feel the baby." The wanted conceptus is always called a baby—did anyone ever paint the "fetus room," or knit sweaters for a "fetus"? Fetus is the language of abortion. It is difficult, extraordinarily difficult, to acknowledge the movement within and not acknowledge the *baby*.

The old word for the sensation of feeling movement was "quickening," meaning coming to life. With movement, the woman acknowledges both the existence and the separateness of the baby within. Its movements are not within her direct control, but have a life of their own. In an unwanted pregnancy, that can be a very ugly sensation.[3] But in a wanted or accepted pregnancy, it is usually thrilling, a deeply satisfying moment to first feel the baby within reach out to you. The initial movements are gentle, often called "flutters," and women who do not know they are pregnant may not recognize these movements as anything different from the usual intestinal rumbles. Women have, indeed, gone all the way through a pregnancy without ever knowing they are pregnant, and without ever feeling, or more accurately, without ever recognizing fetal movement. But for a woman with a known and wanted pregnancy, the movements are expected, awaited, and welcomed.

Amniocentesis changes the meaning of fetal movement. It is no longer a sign that the baby is there, is real—because if movement is felt before the results are in, the pregnancy may still result in the abortion of a fetus rather than the birth of a baby. One of the ways women have of dealing with the contradiction imposed by amniocentesis is to truly suspend animation: psychologically well-defended women may not feel movement until the existence of a baby—not a chromosomally damaged fetus, but an acceptable *baby*—has been confirmed.

When I first started working on this research I began speculating that women who have amniocentesis might delay becoming aware of fetal movement until after the amniocentesis results. I had a research assistant then who was pregnant, and who had amniocentesis. She had heard me thinking out loud about the significance of women feeling movement at various points in the process, long before her own amniocentesis. She told me later that she had not felt any movement at all until the day the phone call came, telling her that the baby was okay, and was a girl. Within a half-hour, the baby kicked.

Of the 120 women I interviewed for this and the previous chapter, both those who had and those who refused amniocentesis, thirteen women did not feel movement until after the eighteenth week of pregnancy. Eleven of them were women who had amniocentesis, and nine of those were women experiencing their first pregnancies. The option of not feeling movement until results are in is very much less available to women who know what fetal movement feels like. Thus nine of the thirteen women who delayed feeling movement were, as predicted, women experiencing their first pregnancies, and having amniocentesis. But just as interesting, and equal confirmation of the hypothesis that a delay in feeling movement is a response to a "tentative pregnancy," are the four other women who felt movement late.

Judith was one of the two women who did not feel movement until after the eighteenth week who had also *not* had amniocentesis. Judith was expecting her fifth baby, but did not feel movement until the twentieth week—very unusual for such an experienced mother. All of the other women in that category, second or later pregnancies without amniocentesis, had felt movement by seventeen weeks, all but one by sixteen weeks. Within the previous year Judith had had a miscarriage in her fifth month, an experience she called traumatic, and which she gave as her main reason for not having amniocentesis—she could not face losing another pregnancy that far along. Until this pregnancy was past the point at which the last was lost, Judith did not feel movement.

Yvonne was the other woman who had refused amnio who did not feel movement until after eighteen weeks—in her case, at twenty-one weeks with a first baby. All of the other women who had refused amniocentesis and were expecting first babies had felt movement by eighteen weeks. Yvonne had spent eight and a half *years* trying to get pregnant. When I interviewed her, late in her pregnancy, and asked her about her fears during the pregnancy, one of those fears had been miscarriage. When I asked her how much those fears had been resolved by feeling movement, she said, "I don't think I'll really believe this is for real until I'm holding the baby." Both of these women who refused amniocentesis but delayed feeling movement had their own reasons for experiencing tentative pregnancies, pregnancies that they felt may very well not result in a baby.

It is also instructive to look at the conditions under which the two women who did have amniocentesis but who had had previous pregnancies delayed feeling movement. The two women were Marsha and Alison. Marsha was experiencing her second pregnancy, but expecting her first baby. Her first pregnancy had resulted in an abortion for Downs Syndrome, *after* movement had been felt. As she describes it:

> So there I was, all Friday, Saturday, Sunday and Monday with a baby that was very active that I knew I was going to abort. That was the worst few days of my life.

This time Marsha did not feel movement until the nineteenth week, when she knew she could continue the pregnancy.

Alison has a 7-year-old child, and was expecting her second. She says:

> This pregnancy was unwanted because (1) I require cae- sarean delivery and cannot handle the physical and emo- tional pain of that again; (2) I resent a new baby's interference in my lifestyle and ambitions; (3) I resent the drudgery of caring for a baby; and (4) I have difficulty facing child-raising and aging at the same time. I looked at amnio- centesis as an opportunity to escape the pregnancy on terms acceptable to my husband. I guess I can take comfort in what appears to be a normal pregnancy. Results were nor- mal.

After the normal results were in, Alison faced the fact that she would be continuing the pregnancy, and soon after began to feel movement.

Magda Denes, in her portrayal of an abortion hospital in *In Ne- cessity and Sorrow*, noted this same phenomenon. Most patients awaiting saline abortions, she found, claimed that their babies had not moved even as late as twenty-four weeks of gestation. Denes is a psychologist, and felt the women were lying not to her, but to themselves.[4] These too are tentative pregnancies, pregnancies in which the condition of pregnancy must be ac- knowledged, but the fetus/baby denied.

All of the rest of the women who delayed feeling movement were women who had had amniocentesis and were having their first pregnancies. There were fifteen women who were in this category. Only six felt movement before the eighteenth week. The rest waited as long as twenty-two to twenty-three weeks.

This group includes Bonnie, who spoke of "suspended animation" and a "sense of unreality"; it includes Gerri, who alternated
between being convinced that everything was fine and dreading
the phone call; and it includes Katherine, the latest of all to feel
movement. Katherine was the one who had so very much trouble
getting sufficient fluid for analysis. After four attempts at amniocentesis, she finally got her results in her twenty-first week of
pregnancy. She felt movement at twenty-two to twenty-three
weeks, "while watching a movie about ghosts."

To put this in perspective, obstetric textbooks say movement
is felt at 16–18, 18, or 16–20 weeks of pregnancy, depending on
which text you look at. Sheila Kitzinger, a well-known and
widely respected childbirth educator, says fetal movement
begins to be felt around the sixteenth week, and at eighteen
weeks, "If this is your first baby, this is the time when you may
feel the first prod which is definitely nothing to do with indiges-
tion."[5] By twenty weeks movement is externally visible—an observer can see the movement these women do not feel. But most
telling of all is that not one of these women who delayed feeling
movement expressed the slightest concern about it. Here we have
a very well-read group of women, all of whom seem to have a
great deal of information about pregnancy. The knowledge that
movement is usually felt by the eighteenth week is readily available, repeated in almost all of the books for pregnant women.
When I asked specifically about their fears in pregnancy, they
cited data about the connection between coffee drinking and
cleft palate, about cat litter and toxoplasmosis, about all kinds of
obscure conditions and risks. But not one said that not feeling
movement, for as long as twenty-three weeks, was a source of
fear and anxiety. These women were, as Marsha well knew,
doing a good job of protecting themselves from a potentially devastating experience.

The Reassurance of Amniocentesis

Prenatal diagnosis changes more than just the time at which
women feel fetal movement. It changes the fundamental psychological and social meanings of quickening.

Women who have had amniocentesis experience fetal movement in a different way, when they allow themselves to experience it at all. When movement was felt before the results were in, the effect was sometimes to heighten the fears and the conflicts faced by the women. Nancy, for example, experienced "a great sense of wonder and hope, but until the results were back I was perhaps even more fearful that I could not go through with the pregnancy." Similarly, Sally, who was conflicted all along, found that the feeling of movement "intensified my inner conflict. Now that I felt movement the baby seemed more of a person than ever—how could I snuff out the life of this little person inside me, even if 'defective'?"

For women who did not have amniocentesis, the experience of quickening often provided some sense of reassurance, some comfort. About half of the women who refused amniocentesis felt that the movements of the baby resolved, to some extent, their fears. While the women realized that "a retarded baby could still kick," and those whose fears focused on Downs Syndrome knew that movement "didn't prove anything," somehow the moving baby *felt* reassuring: comments to the effect that active and strong movements gave a feeling or a sense of an active and strong, or a *healthy* baby, came up repeatedly among women who refused amnio.

In contrast, almost none of the women who had amniocentesis received *any* reassurance from feeling movement. The reassurance the women did not get from feeling movement came instead from the amniocentesis results—when they were good and indeed reassuring, as they usually are. The significance of reassurance lies not only in the question of how anxious or reassured each group of women ultimately became—both groups seemed to have most of their fears resolved by the end of pregnancy. It is also important to be aware of the *sources* of reassurance. For the women who had amniocentesis, reassurance came from medical science and authoritative reports. For the women who refused amniocentesis, reassurance came from the experience of their own bodies and from their developing relationship with their babies. Both groups of course include women who were "wrong" to feel reassured—that is, their babies were born "with problems."

The question of anxiety and reassurance in amniocentesis is complex—so much so that one genetic counselor said that what she likes best about her job is "relieving some of the anxiety a pregnancy brings," and another said that what she likes least is "causing anxiety." While we must acknowledge the relief and reassurance that amniocentesis provides, it is important to place that in the context of the anxiety it generates. There is of course the specific, heightened anxiety of the waiting period, which is the anxiety the counselor was referring to. There is also, and less generally recognized, the anxiety generated by the destruction of traditional means of reassurance, the anxiety that comes from not being able to take comfort in the baby's movements. But overshadowing these is the anxiety that comes from the selling of amniocentesis—and I use that word "selling" deliberately.

If you look at early advertisements for products such as underarm deodorants, you will note that they were selling not only the product, but also the need for the product: with deodorants, they sold the idea that unpleasant odors came from the underarm. Now that the idea of offensive body odor has been solidly fixed in our minds, the ads sell one deodorant as superior to another in solving the problem. But in the early days, before deodorants were in widespread use, it was the *problem* and not the solution which was being presented. That is a general rule of thumb: before you can sell the solution, you must sell awareness of the problem. This basic rule of advertising is at work in the selling of amniocentesis.

It is not uncommon now to hear women say that they would never have dared a pregnancy at their age without the availability of amniocentesis. I have heard that from women in their early 30s on up. It may very well be true for these women, as things now stand. Pregnancy is just too risky for them to attempt without amniocentesis. But when we talk to women now in their 50s and 60s and older about the children they bore while in their 30s and 40s, they do not talk about the fear of Downs Syndrome haunting those pregnancies. That is not to say that they were not indeed at some risk. I am only saying that the risk was not being brought to their attention, and even if they were aware of the risk, they were not focused on it. In the same way, any mother today might be aware of the risks of, say, Sudden Infant Death Syndrome, or childhood leukemia, or whatever horrid diseases and disabling conditions might occur, but most are not focused on those risks. We would probably consider neurotic any woman who could, off the top of her head, quote you the risk figures for her child for these conditions. Most women do not consider these risks as ever-present possibilities, or our inability to test for the conditions as a reason not to risk pregnancy. For the 99 or so out of 100 40-year-old women of earlier generations who bore children without Downs Syndrome, ignorance may have been, if not blissful, at least relatively peaceful. But those days are gone. One of the costs of having a solution is a focusing on the problem.

Thus amniocentesis is able to allay only those fears it first raises. This point has been made by Burke and Kolker, who also point out that some women take more reassurance from amnio than it objectively has to give.[6] That is, once told that the fetus does not have the abnormalities for which it was tested, some women feel "home free." Such is not the case. Only a small percentage of all birth defects, let alone later causes of illness and disability, have been eliminated. The possibility of spending the rest of one's life caring for a sick or disabled child can never be eliminated by prenatal testing.

While some women take reassurance beyond what amnio objectively provides, others find that the selling of fear of birth defects has surpassed the solutions being sold. They have developed a heightened awareness of all that can go wrong. It is a very precarious balance to have raised only those fears that amnio can allay. About half of the women who had amniocentesis said that the amnio completely or almost completely resolved their fears in pregnancy. Many of them had Downs as their only fear. If all of your fears in pregnancy are focused on Downs Syndrome, then amniocentesis can provide total reassurance. Some other women listed their fear as retardation and felt totally reassured by amnio—an unrealistic situation. Retardation is still possible even without Downs Syndrome. Some women listed spina bifida as a fear, which, appropriately, amnio then resolved. A few women also mentioned fear of other chromosomal abnormalities, also resolved by amnio. Only one woman completely accepted the medical version of what was to be feared and how fears were to be resolved. She listed as her fears *all* of those things and *only* those things for which amniocentesis standardly tests: Downs Syndrome and other chromosomal abnormalities, and neural tube defects. Those were her only fears in pregnancy, and they were completely resolved by amniocentesis. She was Vicki, the medical student.

On Cords and Bonds:
The Meaning of Attachment in Pregnancy

Pregnancy is the quintessential female experience. It is an experience of attachment and separation, both more total than is possible in any other relationship. It is an attachment so complete that it can only be torn apart in blood and pain.

In recent years the importance of the dual themes of separation and attachment in the lives of women and of men have been brought to our attention. Nancy Chodorow's *The Reproduction of Mothering* laid the groundwork for rethinking female and male gender development.[7] What Chodorow did, in a nutshell, was to point out the significance for gender development of women doing the child-rearing for both boys and girls. David Lynn had made much the same point years before,[8] but without embedding it in either a psychoanalytic or a feminist framework. Choderow's work captured the attention of the feminist community, and inspired important further work, notably that of Carol Gilligan on moral development.[9]

The thrust of Choderow's argument is that "from very early on . . . because they are parented by a person of the same gender . . . girls come to experience themselves as less differentiated than boys, and more continuous with and related to the external object-world and as differently oriented to their inner object world as well."[10] Boys "achieve" masculinity by shifting identification from mother to father, or as David Lynn indicated, from mother, the highly specific and individual caretaker, to the more abstract, stereotypical male image.[11] Masculinity develops by the repudiation of feminity. The more general theme of masculinity is thus the establishment of separation and individuation. Feminity, in contrast, requires no such separation—feminity is learned through continued attachment.

Lillian Rubin made use of this analysis to explain some of the difficulties in men and women's relations with each other—why we so often remain, as she titled her book, "intimate strangers."[12] Women, she says, feel threatened by separation; men by attachment or intimacy. The connectedness that women can feel with others, a connectedness from which we can draw comfort and strength, may be experienced by men—who develop their self-image as men by separating themselves from a woman—as smothering, overwhelming, threatening.

Painting the broad pictures this way of course oversimplifies. For one thing, it does not account for the differences in degree of father involvement in infant and early childhood parenting. Nor does it account for the economic demands for a highly mobile, individualistically oriented workforce, which supports the male ethic as the cultural mode. But most people, men and women, were indeed raised predominantly, if not exclusively, by women. And it would seem most women have developed an enormous capacity for attachment, for feeling at one with others. Never is this capacity more needed than in the pregnancy experience. And so we come to Chodorow's full circle: mothers can mother because they were mothered.

In the experience of pregnancy two beings both are, and are not, one. That is an obvious reality, but it is one we continuously deny as we first speak of them as a unit, and then speak of them as separate. The uniqueness of the pregnancy relation eludes our ability to define. We have to learn to see, to express, attachment and separation at once. It is easier to see the shifting balance over time, than to see that all the while, two are one.

In the beginning, the attachment is so total that separation is not possible: for the baby to exist, it must exist as one with the mother. Eventually the balance does shift, and to exist they must disentangle themselves. Both mother and baby can live only if the baby separates. The psychological process of individuation and separation, taken from the point of view of the mother, is also gradual, changing in balance over time. In the earliest part of the pregnancy the changes that occur are experienced as changes in her own body—the sleepiness, the nausea, loss of waistline. With the experience of quickening, the differentiation begins. Early movements are vague, "undifferentiated" rumbles and flutters. As time goes by, the movements become more recognizable—that is, they become the specific movements of another: a foot is felt, the pressure of a head can be differentiated. Moving her hands up and down her belly, the mother may be able to trace the shape of her baby as it lies within.

Traditional social definitions of pregnancy and of the baby relied on those same experiences. Early diagnosis of pregnancy was based on the condition of the woman: recognized signs of pregnancy included darkening of the nipples, cervical changes, and so on, all changes of the mother's body. As pregnancy progressed, a definitive diagnosis was made on the basis of the presence of the baby. All the earlier diagnoses were "presumptive," but feeling the baby move was a "definitive" diagnosis. The midwife or doctor could palpate the abdomen of the mother and feel the recognizable shape of the baby, could feel its movements against their own hands through the mother. Traditional definitions said that before that point, before the point of quickening and felt movement, the pregnancy was a condition of the woman, and on that basis, early abortion was permissible. Thus the social as well as the physical life of the fetus was determined in its relation to the mother: it became a living being, a baby, when it communicated its presence to her, and through her, to us, to society.

In contrast, picture the diagnostic scene now: the woman on the table with the ultrasound scanner to her belly, and on the other side of the technician or doctor, the fetus on the screen. The doctor sits between the mother and the fetus. He turns *away* from the mother to examine her baby. Even the heartbeat is heard over a speaker removed from the mother's body. The technology that makes the baby/fetus more "visible" renders the woman *invisible*. The process works on the woman herself. We now hear women talking about how they felt they "bonded" with their baby when they saw it on the screen. The direct relationship to the baby within them, the fetus as part of their bodies, is superseded by the relationship with the fetus on the screen. The television image becomes more real than the fetus within; it is that image to which they "bond"; it is that image they hold in their minds as they feel their babies move.

These new images of the fetus and even embryo are making us aware of the "unborn" as people—but they do so at the cost of making transparent the mother. Picture to yourself the photos you have seen of fetuses in utero, wriggling, sucking their tiny fingers. Where did they lie in their mothers? Where was that fetus in relation to her body, to her navel, her heart, her pelvis? It existed as if in space. Indeed, the fetus in utero has become a metaphor for "man" in space, floating free, attached only by the umbilical cord to the spaceship. But where is the mother in that metaphor? She has become empty space.

The technology of pregnancy that we as a civilization have developed is a technology of separation and individuation—the technology is geared to recognizing the fetus as separate from the mother. The fetus has, with much public fanfare, become a patient, and fetal medicine the "new frontier." Our medical knowledge so often draws on analogies of war and battle—in fetology, women's bodies become, if not the enemy, then the battleground. The new medical language for mother is "maternal environment," and that particular environment is increasingly seen as only one of the possible locations for the completion of fetal development.

But more important than the way the technology changes the meaning of pregnancy for medical practitioners, I believe, is the way it changes the meaning of pregnancy, and of the mother-fetus relationship, for the mother. A diagnostic technology that pronounces judgments halfway through the pregnancy makes extraordinary demands on women to separate themselves from the fetus within. Rather than moving from complete attachment through the separation that only just begins at birth, this technology demands that we begin with separation and distancing. Only after an acceptable judgment has been declared, only after the fetus is deemed worthy of keeping, is attachment to begin.

Reality has been turned on its head. The pregnancy experience, when viewed with men's eyes, goes from separation to attachment. The moment of initial separation, birth, has been declared the point of "bonding," of attachment. As the cord is cut, the most graphic separation image, we now talk of bonding. The concept of bonding began with the observation that when the attachment between mother and baby was abruptly broken, as routinely occurred when infants were taken off to newborn nurseries, or even more so for prolonged medical care, connection was hard to reestablish, intimacy difficult to maintain. When mother and baby were permitted to continue together through the birth and the first days after, the strong attachment observed was called bonding, as if it just then happened.[14] That attachment might better be seen as the continuation of a long process of disentanglement as mother and baby continue sorting themselves out into two separate beings, thus *continuing* and not *establishing* their relationship. Viewed from men's eyes, the movement of our babies from deep inside our bodies, through our genitals, and into our arms was called the "introduction" or "presentation" of the baby. Only when we touched our babies with the *outside* of our bodies were we believed to have touched them at all—using men's language, we say of women whose babies died or were given away, that they "never touched the baby, never held the baby."

It is the same thing now with the earlier diagnostic processes. As the woman comes to grips with the reality that part of her body, this growing bulge, is a separate and differentiated fetus she sees on a screen, that too is declared not a moment of separation and individuation, but a moment of attachment and bonding.

When the diagnosis is bad, the separation is at once made real and total: the treatment is to abort. When the diagnosis is good, then the women are encouraged to form an attachment, *not* with the fetus as part of themselves, but with the separate baby-person it will become. It begins with the announcement of the baby's presumed health, and its sex.

The technology assumes, and thus demands of women, that our experience parallels men's, that we too start from separation and come to intimacy—and only with caution.

5

ON FETAL SONS AND DAUGHTERS

PROLOGUE: THE SOCIAL CONSTRUCTION OF BABY ZACHARY (A TRUE STORY)

Zachary is a chick counted long before the hatching. Zachary is—or was, or will be, I'm not quite sure any more which is right—John and Linda's second child. Their second child of this their second marriage.

Like Mathew, their firstborn, Zachary is the product of a planned pregnancy. John and Linda planned Mathew for when they felt their relationship was ready, and Zachary for when they felt Mathew was ready. They are a responsible, warm, and loving couple, building their family with care and concern.

Mathew's birth was predictable enough if one follows contemporary trends in obstetrics, but it was not what John and Linda expected. Weeks of Lamaze training notwithstanding, Mathew arrived by caesarean section. Zachary's birth is a planned C-section. His birthday, along with his name, his clothes, and his teddy bear, are all picked out and waiting.

Linda turned 35 during this pregnancy, and so crossed the divider into the age where amnio is routine. She'd had sonograms while pregnant with Mathew, and had had two already in this pregnancy, so that procedure held no surprises for her. She felt no particular fear of the needle, and all in all the amnio was no big deal. There was a little anxiety, waiting for the results, but John and Linda never really believed anything could be seriously the matter with this healthy, planned, wanted pregnancy.

There was perhaps a twinge of disappointment when the letter came, confirming the baby's health, but declaring it a boy, another boy. They only planned two children, so any fantasies they had ever had, from Linda's childhood doll play through to last week's discussion of girls' names, ended abruptly. No girls. But Mathew was to have a brother, and that's awfully nice. And they could reuse the blue panda-bear quilt and all the "Li'l Slugger" stretchies.

Mathew knew, as well as a two-and-a-half-year-old knows such things, that there was a baby "growing in mommy's belly." Now he learned that the baby was going to be a brother, Zachary. When Mathew outgrows a pair of overalls now, he knows they're put aside for Zachary. And when he says goodnight to Mommy, with just a little prompting, he also says goodnight to Zachary.

John and Linda are Jewish, not observant, but they did have a *bris* for Mathew, and plan one for Zachary. A bris is the ceremonial circumcision held on the eighth day after a boy is born. There is no comparable ceremony for a girl. For the first eight days after birth the child is in some ways more like a fetus, not yet fully recognized as a person, not yet fully welcomed into the community. But Zachary's bris, three months ahead, is planned. They know he's a boy, his birthdate is set—there will be no traditional last-minute flurry of activity preparing for this bris. One friend, invited to the bris of a child not yet born, was caught between horror and laughter: "What now, engraved invitations and booking a hall for a bris?" The eight-day waiting period seems meaningless, planned from three months ahead. All that's left of the tradition is the celebration of the penis, the special welcome for a son.

Zachary, it seems, is as good as here. John, as a matter of fact, won't be around for the birth. As long as Linda and Zachary will be in the hospital for a week recovering from the section, he figures he might as well take care of some out-of-town business. He's not needed for this birth, he says, as he was to "coach" the first labor. And as for actually seeing Zachary—well, he'll be back in a week, in time for the bris. He doesn't say so, but Linda thinks maybe it would be different if it were a girl this time. It's only their second child, but it seems the novelty has worn off.

Somehow the birth of Zachary has become just the transition from the inside to outside, and doesn't seem all that important. Now that they have had the amnio, John and Linda believe even less that anything could be wrong, could go wrong, with this baby. They won't have a sick, imperfect, or damaged baby. This is all too well planned, too well organized; they've been too careful for things like that to happen.

Reality tells us something different. Reality tells us that the caesarean section is more dangerous, certainly to Linda and probably to Zachary, than a vaginal birth would be. And even though Zachary does not have Downs Syndrome, or any of the other conditions for which he was tested, he is no less at risk for other disease, deformity, or accident of birth than any other baby. But to John and Linda, this birth feels somehow cleaner, more controlled, and so safer. They know exactly what to expect. There will be no grunting, sweaty, scary labor. They expect their healthy baby boy to be lifted out by caesarean section, as planned. They have photographs of Zachary's sonogram pasted in the baby album.

John and Linda expect no surprises. If all goes well, Zachary's birth will be routine, almost anticlimactic. The celebration came the night they got the amnio results, and drank a toast to their new son. Birth isn't going to make all that much difference in the creation of Zachary. This chick will have been counted for four months.

"It's a girl!" "It's a boy!"

That used to be the first thing people said when a baby was born. Now that that statement can precede birth by months, it has taken on a new meaning. It no longer means that a child has been born; it means that a fetus has been sexed.

When I was pregnant with my second baby, I went to my son's school, where a kindergarten-age girl asked me if I was going to have a boy or a girl. In a sweet, probably patronizing, talking-to-a-little-kid voice, I explained that I couldn't know that, that the baby was inside, and I couldn't tell. "Oh sure you can," she told me. "My aunt had this test at the doctor's, and she knew." Fetal sex is no longer the mystery it once was. All of the folk tales about carrying high or carrying low, about rings on strings swinging clockwise or counterclockwise—all those ways of figuring out fetal sex are *passé*. Now one can scientifically know. Even a kindergarten kid knows that.

So what? What difference does it make if the sex of the fetus is known months before its birth? Does that change anything? The knowledge makes a difference, the knowledge changes things, because with *sex* comes *gender*. Sex is the biological fact of maleness or femaleness, the chromosomal and anatomical identity. Gender is the social identity, our different expectations for boys and for girls, for sons and for daughters. Gender goes beyond the X and Y chromosomes, beyond genitalia, to our ideas about the kind of person the fetus will become.

Some changes brought about by knowing sex, and so assigning gender, have been fairly obvious to anyone involved in the baby business. Salespeople in infant clothing departments, pregnant women now tell me, have started asking if the woman is expecting a boy or a girl. With knowledge of fetal sex, a baby's room will perhaps be decorated one way for a boy, another for a girl. Since clothing, furnishing, wallpaper, and the like for boys tends to be in brighter colors with stronger lines than it is for girls, perhaps knowing sex ahead of time will eliminate some small amount of extra stimulation from the environment for girls, add some to the environment for boys.

There are other changes I wonder about that may be more

subtle. How does knowing the sex of the fetus change the feelings a pregnant woman has about the baby, even feelings about herself? Before I did this research, I wondered if women would perceive fetuses of known sex differently: would the boys be felt as more active, stronger somehow, and the girls more delicate, softer in their movements? Then, too, it might not only be perception that changes. A pregnant woman can stimulate fetal movement with loud noises, certain positions, activities such as leaning against the washing machine. These can all encourage fetal movement. Or she can soothe fetal movement: lowering the rock music, shifting to her side in bed, and so on. Are women more likely, I wondered, to stimulate fetal sons and soothe fetal daughters? And if "real men don't eat quiche," then do women pregnant with male fetuses eat more "male" foods—more red meat, more protein, maybe just plain more food, while women carrying female fetuses might eat more delicately, worry more about weight gain? In other words, I began to wonder if gender might not become a self-fulfilling prophecy earlier than ever, with boys created bigger, stronger, and more active, even before birth.

Not everyone who has amniocentesis chooses to learn fetal sex. I am troubled to think that the ones who will do the strongest sex-stereotyping are the ones who are most likely to want to know, while it might be those who are the least likely to be influenced by knowing sex, those who think sex does not set boundaries for personality and interests, who do not ask.

So these are the questions I began with in my research on the implications of this new technology that allows us to learn fetal sex. I wanted to know how women decide whether or not to ask about the sex of the fetus, and how, if they did ask, knowing changed their feelings and behavior in the pregnancy.

I also wondered about the effects this technology might have, not on the individual pregnant women, but on the society at large. Many people have voiced concern that the information regarding fetal sex will be used for selective abortion, to enable parents to achieve children of desired sex. A single mother, planning to raise a child alone, for example, might want only a daughter; a traditionally minded family might welcome a son as firstborn; a couple wanting only two children might want one of each sex. A number of social scientists have pointed out that parents' choices of the children's sex could have terrible social consequences, creating strange imbalances and potentially forcing basic social restructuring.

In thinking about and exploring sex selection, I learned some surprising things. I found that learning the sex of the fetus during pregnancy may not be the same thing at all as learning sex when the baby is born, or thinking in the abstract about what sex child one would want. I learned that women who learn fetal sex during pregnancy have feelings and reactions that may surprise even them.

So in the end this chapter will turn back to the experiences and the feelings of the women themselves. Because it is all well and good to talk about the effects of technology on society—but we must always remember that "society" is an abstraction, and these individual pregnant women, the ones who are directly confronted by the technology, are very real.

THE IMPLICATIONS OF ASSIGNING FETAL GENDER

Choosing to Learn Fetal Sex

About 80 or 90 percent of women who have amniocentesis ask the sex of their fetus.[1] Some ask for the thrill, the excitement, that in a traditional pregnancy had to await the birth of the child. They want that excitement "as soon as possible." And when women ask *not* to be told the sex, it is this same quality of fun and surprise that they talk about: ". . . we felt life had to hold *some* surprises," says one; and another explains, "it would be more fun *not* to know, more of a surprise when the baby arrived." Alison, with a definitely unwanted pregnancy, facing an equally unwanted caesarean section, didn't ask sex because "I'd have nothing to look forward to."

The excitement and fun of learning the sex is a reward women can give themselves for having gone through the emotional trauma of the amniocentesis. Katherine, who had gone for week after week of unsuccessful amnio taps, said:

At first I wanted some "naturalness" left. Then after all the problems with the amnio tests, I decided whatever certainties I could get out of all this unpredictableness, I'd take.

There seems to be a point at which people have had as much trouble, anxiety, or uncertainty as they feel able to take, and any place it can be resolved or eliminated is appreciated. Jackie felt that "There were enough surprises having twins," and Theresa, having lost a baby the year before with anencephaly, said, "I didn't feel the need for any surprises—I just wanted a baby to hold and love."

Being able to know the sex somehow trivializes *not* knowing: it becomes seen as a "need for surprises," even a "game." While one woman asked not to know because she thought it was part of the "miracle and mystery of birth to have sex revealed at the time of birth," for most the "mystery" and "miracle" come to be seen as contrived. "It's one thing not to know the unknowable," women say, "and another to sit opposite a doctor who has it written right there on your chart." Some women get told sex "by accident" or mistake, after having asked not to be told. In most labs the information on sex is included in the report to the doctors, even if the woman requests otherwise. Virginia did not want to know the sex, and said she found it easier because the obstetricians were also not told the sex. But given that the knowledge of fetal sex is inevitably learned by someone in the course of chromosomal testing (remember, one cannot check for the presence of extra chromosomes without observing which ones *are* there, including the x and y), the most common and often repeated reason for asking the sex of the fetus is, How can one *not* ask?

It is not simply that the information is now knowable. It is also that it *is known*. It is known to the medical personnel, and once the sex of the fetus becomes part of the medical record, it makes sense to treat it just as one would other information on that record. Nancy said she asked the sex because: "I want all the information available to the physician to be available to me."

From knowable information, to part of the medical record, the sex of the fetus finally becomes part of the "patient's condition."

Spelling it out most clearly, Martha says she asked to know the sex of her fetus because "I believe a patient has the right and moral responsibility to know as much as possible about his or her condition." In this way sex itself is medicalized. The pregnant woman by virtue of her pregnancy is a patient, and the sex of her fetus, by virtue of its place on the medical record, is part of her condition. Sex is a diagnosable chromosomal condition.

Not all women are comfortable with this medicalization of pregnancy and of fetal sex. In a French study of 65 women having amniocentesis, and 25 of their husbands, most of the respondents "tried to pass off their advance knowledge of the child's sex as something simple and ordinary."[2] But the researchers noted that there were lots of jokes about the secretary typing it wrong. No one thought mistakes regarding abnormalities were likely. The researchers felt the joking was a sign of "a deep-seated uncertainty involved in lifting the veil from what would ordinarily remain a secret."

It does of course raise the question of what one takes as "normal." I found some women, with strong objections to the medicalization of pregnancy, and with moral qualms about the amniocentesis and its implications, wanted not to know the sex so that, as one said, "I can just pretend this never happened." If fetal sex is not known, the pregnancy can proceed "normally." Once it is known, the fact of the amnio intrudes into the second half of the pregnancy as it did into the first half. In an interesting juxtaposition of words, Rita said, "We decided not to ask to keep some feeling of spontaneity and control." Spontaneity and control—in learning sex, medical control takes over and spontaneity is lost. In choosing not to know, the woman remains, or can feel she remains, in control of her own pregnancy, which can then proceed "normally" and "spontaneously."

Making It Real: My Fetus, My Son

Knowledge of fetal sex is something to reckon with, something which by its very existence changes the pregnancy experience. Knowledge of sex helps turn a fetus into a baby, makes the baby-to-be more *real*, women say. "Knowing my baby is a girl made her more real to me," said Caroline; and Bonnie echoed her words: "It didn't really matter, but it made the baby more real."

Following as it does upon the tentative pregnancy and the anxiety of the waiting period, learning sex and making the baby "real" can have a powerful emotional impact. Says one woman:

> Finally at five to six months pregnant I got the phone call that all was okay and the baby was a girl. I suddenly realized all the tension that I'd been under for so many weeks. I wanted to rush out and buy baby clothes and look at little-girl outfits. My first child, a son, I had conscientiously dressed in unisex clothing. I could no longer even think about what I would have decided to do had the results been less cheerful. I was as happy as if I'd just given birth—but without the tiredness, discomfort and overwhelming responsibility.

Several childbirth educators shared with me their experiences with women who have had amniocentesis and learned sex. One of them noted:

> These women, these couples, refer to the baby as he or she. It has a much more specific identity. It's direct, not as abstract a connection to the baby. I became very aware of that.

It is not just for themselves that women talk about knowing. Joanne asked sex: "to help myself and the rest of my family to visualize the baby better." Knowing the sex is a way of making the baby seem as "real" to others as it may seem to the woman within whom it moves. A sexed fetus, a "real" baby, can be shared more readily—with husband or children or friends—than the abstract, unknown, imagined baby; and knowing the sex also, some women think, changes and makes "more intimate" their own relationship with the fetus within. Jackie, expecting twins, said she wanted to know their sex because:

> We wanted to talk to them, stroke them, sing to them prior to their birth and use their names.

Other women spoke of feeling "closer" to the baby once they knew its sex. Nancy said:

> I also wanted to know the sex of the child so as to be able to relate to it on a more intimate and knowing basis. We named her very shortly after that and felt she grew in our mutual consciousness as a person.

In a number of cases it was the husbands who wanted to know sex, and wives, more or less reluctantly, went along with their husbands' need to know.

There are other ways in which the fetus becomes a baby when sex is known, and learning sex comes to serve some of the same functions that birth itself has served in the past:

> I was not going to ask at first, but my father was then very ill and we decided he would like to know in case anything happened. (It didn't—he's seen Katra twice with a third time coming up at Thanksgiving.) (Bea)

> Also my father-in-law was dying of cancer and I thought it would be good for him to know. (Phyllis)

These two women used knowledge of fetal sex as a way of "presenting" the baby to its—no, to her or his—grandfather.

It is most assuredly not new for women to think about the sex of their babies before birth. Ann Oakley followed sixty British women through pregnancy and early motherhood and reported:

> Most women spend months imagining what the baby will be like. They may conjure up mental images of the baby's appearance, its personality, its habits, its behavior in later childhood, adolescence, and adulthood. Such pictures cannot be formed without some notion of the baby's sex.[3]

In a traditional (non-amnio) pregnancy different women handle the uncertainty regarding sex in different ways. Some just seem quite sure of what sex the baby is, and while many women do indeed have what they "knew" they were having, certainly many women are wrong. Other women handle the uncertainty by having two different sets of fantasies, alternately imagining themselves mothering a boy child and mothering a girl child. For such women, whatever the sex of the baby, something is gained and something is lost when at birth one set of fantasies is supported and the other denied. In that sense, birthing even the healthiest and most delightful and wanted of babies may involve a bit of grieving for the lost fantasy baby. That same grieving can occur when the baby is assigned its sex earlier in the pregnancy.

What is the difference between *fantasizing* about a baby and *planning* for a baby? Or more specifically, what is the difference between fantasizing about, say, a girl and planning for a girl? One difference has to do with being able to act on the fantasy. Daydreaming a little girl's room is different from buying a pink rug. For many women, knowledge of fetal sex, making the baby "real," allows them to make the transition from fantasy to planning: "I have been buying 'boy things' which I wouldn't have done otherwise," says one woman.

The next question then is what is the difference between *planning* for a girl and actually *having* a girl? What does "having" mean now? To "have" the baby used to mean to have had the birth occur. Once born, one had the baby. Before the birth, one planned for, or simply fantasized about the baby. Painting the child's room before birth is part of planning and getting ready for the baby. Painting a child's room once it is born is part of taking care of and raising the baby. But once women know the sex of the baby they carry, experience that baby as "real," the line between "expecting" and "having" may blur, even disappear. Consider what Valerie has to say about learning she was carrying a female fetus:

> How wonderful to know! Right away she had a name; I got a rose pink carpet for her room; we had a DAUGHTER. I bought her many new clothes, crocheted her a pink blanket, even bought and addressed her announcements. In her journal, I used her name. . . . It was a form of *knowing* our child in advance.

She was no longer expecting a daughter—"We *had* a daughter."

Gender Characteristics in Utero

When I first began researching genetic counseling, I went on a tour of a laboratory where prenatal diagnosis was done. There was a book there, a large ledger. It was full of columns of 46XX, 46XY, 46XX, and on and on, all normal, XX or XY, all 46 chromosomes. All healthy normal male and healthy normal female fetuses. The overwhelmingness of sex/gender got to me then, staring at that book. *All* we know about each fetus is that it is male or it is female. It is not that this particular baby, the one with the folded-down ear or the tiny toes, not this particular baby with your mother's chin and your husband's ears is male, but rather that this totally unknown, undeveloped fetus is male. Maleness then stands alone, with no context. We are left with nothing but the abstract image of maleness or of femaleness. The fetus is invested with the weight of gender, without the balance of particularity, of individuality.[4] Sex tells nothing. And it tells everything.

If one listens to the way women describe stillbirths, miscarriages, or late abortions, there is a pattern that emerges. The story follows the chronology of the experience, and then stops at the announcement of the passage of the fetus. Just as at a birth, the statement of sex is made, though in the past tense: "It was a little girl." That is the moment in the tale when a heaviness descends, as homage is paid to the humanity and the reality of the fetus by both the teller and the listener. In a tale told fresh with grief; it is the point at which tears come.

The assignment of sex does two different things. First, it particularizes, specifies the fetus. If there is another remarkable feature about the fetus, it too may be used in the same way: "It had curly hair" serves the same symbolic function of particularizing and thus rendering real and human. The assignment of sex, however, does something more: it implies gender, with the images of personality that attend to gender. It is not just the chromosomal or anatomical differences we learn when we learn sex. It is also the social role expectations—not only what the fetus is, but what we expect the child to become.

It is just luck, and I do truly believe bad luck at that, that sex is such an obvious chromosomal difference. There are other very obvious anatomical differences between people that are as yet invisible on chromosomes: skin color and height are examples. The difference between two five foot, eight inch, 140-pound white people, one a man and one a woman, is chromosomally dramatic. The obvious body differences between a five-foot, 100-pound black woman and a six-foot, 200-pound white woman are physically striking, but chromosomally invisible.

If, say, height, or better yet, curliness of hair, were readily noticeable on chromosomal testing, that too would come to take on meaning during pregnancy. If women learned that the baby would have curly hair at the same time they learned it did not have Downs Syndrome, I'm sure they would go through pregnancy with images of curly-headed children, would gaze at the curly-headed kids in the schoolyard, would think of their babies just a bit differently. But it is not hair curliness we learn: it is sex.

And so the fetus is not only made to seem more "real," or more of a person, it is also made male or female, a son or a daughter in our minds. Two women who refused amnio and who would also choose not to learn fetal sex even from a blood test, spoke directly to this issue—how knowing the sex of the fetus changes the way one sees, and relates to, the child to come:

> For me, not knowing the sex of the baby to be born is part of that specialness of pregnancy. It's the only time we relate to that spirit in a totally pure and objective way—that is, relative to its sex.

> I feel I'd form all sorts of expectations based on sex. I feel not knowing keeps you off balance a little, and more open to accepting the child for itself.

These two women are right. Knowing the sex does influence our perceptions of babies.

I used to say, along with most social scientists, that gender socialization begins at birth. Even though no one could tell their sex just from looking at diapered babies, knowing the baby's sex made people see the babies differently. They may *look* the same, but they are not *seen* the same. Babies' gender attributes, like their beauty, are in the eye of the beholder.[5] You have probably heard people speak this way: the hands of 7½-pound baby girls are described as "so delicate, such tiny little fingers"; the hands of 7½-pound baby boys are described as "adorable little fists." The "firm grip" of that little fist contrasts with the "tight cling" of those delicate little fingers. That much we know, had come to expect—people think of infant boys differently than infant girls, and in turn treat them differently.

And now—what of our fetal sons and daughters? I asked all the women I interviewed, both those who had and those who refused amnio, to describe the movements of their fetus during the last three months of pregnancy. The words "active" and "very active" were used by almost all of the women; so often did they come up that they were like background noise or static. I will screen out those words (only those words) and show you the other words used by women who had amnio and learned the sex of their fetus.

Mothers of daughters said the movement was:
    very gentle, slow, more rolling it seemed than kicking
    moderate, reassuring but not violent
    strong, stretching kicking
    very few due to breech position
    not terribly active—moved around mostly late at night
    lots of rapid kicking, rather small movement
    very uncomfortably active
    reasonably active
    lively
    vigorous
    severely active
    more nearly a squirm
    quiet in the mornings and afternoons
    seemingly constant jerky large turning moves
    lively but not excessively energetic

Mothers of sons said the movement was:
    many somersaults and very vigorous movements
    pushed a foot in the ribs a lot

a saga of earthquakes
very strong
stretching of skin as if the baby were rolling or turning
calm but strong
rolling around from side to side and little kicks and punches up
   and down
a constant jabbing under my rib cage
vigorous
kicking me in ribs, turning
felt most vigorous movement when I sat down or lay down
very strong
not altogether pleasant
very strong

What do these lists tell us about the perception of fetal gender? The word "lively" was never used to describe a male's movements, only a female's. *Not* violent, *not* excessively energetic, *not* terribly active were used for females, and nothing similar for males. "Strong" was used much more often for male than for female fetuses, including what I think of as the "John Wayne fetus"—"calm but strong." Vigorous was used several times for males, and only once for a female, by a woman who said she did not want to know the sex, but her husband did, and he "is a tease." She said, "I truly do believe that gender is not the most important attribute a person possesses." No other woman used "vigorous" to describe a fetus she knew was female. Notice, too, that while some more masculine-sounding descriptions were given for female fetuses' movements, there were never feminine-sounding descriptions for male fetuses' movements. This is a common enough observation regarding gender—it is more acceptable for women and girls to be in some ways masculine than it ever is for men and boys to be "effeminate."

Among women who refused amnio (and the few women who did not learn sex from amnio), on the other hand, all these words—lively, vigorous, strong, and such—were used, but without any pattern by the sex of the fetus. This is true even though at the time they were describing the movement to me, most of the women had already had the baby and knew the sex. This knowledge does not appear to work retroactively to redefine fetal movement in gender-appropriate terms. The "vigorous" move-ment of a fetus was not, as one might have suspected, redefined as "lively" after the fetus showed herself to be a girl, nor the "lively" movement redefined when a boy was born. Fetal move-ments, when sex is *not* known, are part of the woman's preg-nancy experience, and need not be made appropriate to the sex of the fetus. The woman who does not know the sex of her fetus is able to describe her *pregnancy* without describing her *baby*.

And so the assignment of fetal sex creates a new phenomenon: fetal gender. A new category of person has been called into being: fetal sons and fetal daughters.

Beyond Amnio: New Technology and Fetal Sex

At the moment that I am writing, there are three ways—no, four—of learning fetal sex. One is by amniocentesis. Another, still classified as experimental at this point, is by chorionic villi biopsy (the first-trimester chromosomal test); and a third is by seeing the genitals on the ultrasound screen. The fourth, a tech-nology we may soon be seeing the last of, is by observation at birth. And still another promising technique is being developed that may make waiting for birth the minority experience: the analysis of fetal cells in maternal blood. A simple blood test on pregnant women may someday provide information on fetal sex. Some women who would not be willing to have invasive test-ing—that is, would have no testing that enters the uterus—would have their own blood tested to learn fetal sex. The physicians who are hesitant about routinizing amniocentesis or chorionic villi biopsy for their side effects, and even those few physicians who are concerned about the potential side effects of routine use of ultrasound, will probably be perfectly willing to make use of maternal blood testing. Because it would be so "safe" there are few barriers to the routinization of such testing.

Among the women I interviewed who were "eligible" for, but who refused amniocentesis, about half said they would be in-terested in learning fetal sex from a simple blood test. These are probably the most resistant of populations: they are women who have refused what is generally accepted as "standard" medical treatment. Several of those who said they would have the test to determine sex made a point of saying that they would have it repeated because "I would not trust the first results." This is clearly *not* a population enamored of medical technology. So if half of *these* women would have the test, we can anticipate widespread acceptance.

The reasons these women gave for wanting the test, for wanting to learn fetal sex, were pretty much the same reasons as those women gave who chose to learn fetal sex from amniocentesis. They want the fun and surprise; they don't want others to have information about their fetus that they do not have; and they want to plan. They also see the potential for a different kind of relationship with the fetus if sex could be known:

> I'd like to know the sex of the baby—the baby would be named and part of the family before birth.

> For mental preparation, visual therapy, to create a mind set for the baby's environment.

The women who refused amniocentesis who would also choose *not* to learn fetal sex even from a simple and noninvasive blood test also speak of "surprise." About one-third of them specifically said they like the surprise. Quite a few also spoke of the "mystery," but often in a context that showed a spiritual side to the mystery, more than just the "game" aspect:

> It's all such a wonderful miracle—I'd rather let it unfold before me and if I'm supposed to know, it will come to me in a dream or intuition.

In a related vein, some spoke of learning sex before birth as having a negative effect on the childbirth experience itself:

> Because I feel it would deintensify that moment of discovery and deflate the spiritual quality of giving birth generally.

Lorraine, a licensed practical nurse who works in the Labor and Delivery (L&D) area of a hospital, said she would not want to know the sex of her fetus:

> Half of the excitement of pregnancy is what sex it will be—working L&D, the women who already know seem kind of low—no excitement or anticipation to their labor—just labor!

There is, in sum, some hesitation about using such a technology—practical, spiritual and other reasons for not using it. But given the pressure toward knowing the knowable, it does seem likely that someday soon, most women will learn the sex of their fetus during pregnancy. Will this knowledge, especially if it comes early in the pregnancy, force a kind of sex selection on parents? And what will this mean—for the children, for the parents, and for society?

CONCERNING SEX SELECTION

The libraries are piled high with studies showing that both women and men prefer boys to girls as their first child. In three-child families, they prefer two boys and a girl to two girls and a boy. This finding shows up in surveys when the question is posed abstractly, say, to college students about the "ideal family." It shows up in action when we see that all-girl families are more likely to go on to a next pregnancy than are families with the same number of children but including a son; and when we see shorter birth intervals following the birth of a daughter than following a son.

The existence of son preference is further substantiated in the more detailed studies of women's experiences with pregnancy and early motherhood. Myra Leifer, a psychologist who closely followed nineteen women through their first pregnancies, found that fourteen of them reported a preference for a boy, and two hoped to have a girl. Three women expressed no clear preference.[6] Ann Oakley, interviewing sixty women in-depth and repeatedly throughout their first pregnancies, found less willingness to report boy preference ahead of time. Fifty-four percent said they wanted a boy, 22 percent a girl, and 25 percent said they didn't mind which it was. But she found a very great difference once the baby arrived. The women said they were unwilling to admit a preference beforehand, but once the babies were born, 93 percent of the mothers of sons said they were pleased with the sex of their babies, and only 56 percent of the mothers of daughters said they were pleased.[7]

In all of the reported instances where sex selection techniques are offered—from a Singapore clinic using temperature charts for determining optimum time for conception, to the Chinese experiment with chromosomal testing and selective abortion—it is boys people try to achieve.

Given this widespread, international boy preference, what happens when sex selection techniques become readily available? The first serious American public discourse on this issue came in response to an article in *Science* by Amitai Etzioni, back in the late 1960s.[8] Etzioni had three sons, and he and his wife were contemplating another child. He wondered if he couldn't make use of one of the sex-selection techniques based on timing of intercourse which he had read about to have a girl. While he found no technique to meet his needs (and had a fourth son), he did "learn more about the question of sex choice than I ever cared to know." He found that various sex selection techniques were being developed, even if not yet ready for him, and judging from what he thought to be "surprisingly reliable data,"

> . . . if each set of parents got what they wanted, a considerable "male surplus" would result. The social consequences of such a surplus, I concluded, ranged from the unfavorable to the undesirable. There would be a growing proportion of the population unable to find marriageable partners: homosexuality and prostitution would probably increase. Furthermore, since there would be fewer women, there would be fewer persons interested in culture (books, theater, art) or charged with the moral upbringing of children (which is still a woman's specialization); and there would be more people engaged in competitive, materialistic pursuits (still,

more of the man's world). For the same reason, violent crime would rise.[9]

Every discussion of the social implications of sex selection techniques since has similarly debated the consequences of an over-abundance of men, and its corollary, a shortage of women. Much of this literature, along with probably more than you ever wanted to know about sex selection, too, has been put together in an excellent scholarly book, *Sex Selection of Children*, edited by Neil G. Bennett.[10]

In his introduction to that volume, Nathan Keyfritz of the department of sociology at Harvard assures us that the fear that boy preference would eliminate girls and thus pose a threat to the existence of society is absurd. A girl shortage, he claims, will give rise to a girl preference, and so things will balance out. Eventually. A number of social scientists have made that same prediction: that boy and girl preferences will follow each other in waves for a while, with an eventual return to a balanced sex ratio.[11]

It sounds good, but "it ain't necessarily so." A "shortage" is socially defined. If for example a "shortage" of women were to make male homosexuality and female prostitution more socially acceptable, as Etzioni predicts, then the fact that there would not be enough women to be distributed in heterosexual monogamous matings might very well come to be "a fact of life," and not a shortage or a problem. "Facts of life" are social problems or *issues* when they present challenges to belief systems and values.[12] If the beliefs and values change, lo and behold, the problem disappears. Religious intermarriage, working mothers, and brides who are not virgins are all examples of social problems that have been "solved" in many social circles by a changing value system. They are "facts of life" and not problems.

The question that arises when we think of any kind of shortage is the question of purpose: what purposes are not being met when a shortage exists? If something doesn't serve any particular purpose, then it is hard to imagine a "shortage" of it. It is always a *shortage for what?* that we ask. Sexual partnership, the first purpose of women that Etzioni alluded to in his list, is probably the easiest aspect of a woman shortage to "solve" with a changing value system. Women as biological mothers may be a bit trickier. Those of us who have been casting an uneasy eye in the direction of current reproductive research can have our paranoid fantasies flourish. In a "woman shortage," technological research into artificial wombs should be well funded.

A boy preference won't translate into a woman shortage to the same degree all over the world. Societies in which boy children are most strongly favored are (almost by definition) the most patriarchal, those in which women are most subordinate to men. Keyfritz builds on this to say that boy preference and a girl shortage will "be a major force for sex equality." Wrong again. He says:

> If as a result of sex selection women become fewer, their relative position will change. They will become more desirable in marriage, and the dowry that has to be paid along with a daughter to obtain a suitable husband will drop, perhaps to zero, perhaps being replaced by a bride price.

True enough, but since when is being purchased a measure of equality? The existence of a bride price is not a sign of an egalitarian society. Keyfritz goes on:

> This drastic change in the marriage market will have effects on equality within the family—a woman who is badly treated will leave her husband, knowing she can easily find a new one.

Maybe, but probably not if she has been purchased. Slaves, even in a "shortage," were not free to leave because they were in high demand among masters. Fewer women may work out very differently than Keyfritz and others have predicted: women may indeed be "more desirable in marriage"—and *less* desirable outside of it. In a real woman shortage, would nonsexual and nonreproducing women be tolerated? If men defined women as being valuable, scarce commodities, we might well be protected, and valued in that way, but that is not the same *at all* as equality with men or even as human independence.[13] Protected species status is not the opposite of patriarchy and female subordination, but just another facet of it.

In the United States and in most industrialized Western societies, the son preference is less dramatic, and a severe "woman shortage" is not predicted. Keyfritz says:

> But in most societies the preferences are mild: initially parents may want a boy, but after they have one they want a girl. In short, sex selection would effect more the order within individual families than the ultimate sex ratio obtained.

No small thing that. Birth order appears to be a powerful shaping force in personality development, as well as in the ways family resources are distributed. Tabitha Powledge points out:

> If it [sex selection] is widely used to achieve the storybook two-child family (a boy first, a girl second) then a pernicious pattern already present in these (industrialized) countries— anxious, overachieving men and passive, accommodating women—might be substantially reinforced, because those personality patterns also tend to be characteristics of, respectively, first- and secondborns.[14]

Besides the replication of gender roles within the family of birth (for every girl a big brother, for every boy a little sister) with sex selection for males we would also expect to see gender patterns reproduced in the interaction between sex and class. Medical technology to regulate fertility is more likely to be used by the upper class and middle class rather than by poor families. Thus if there is to be a "woman shortage," it is likely to be class specific. Middle- and upper-class men will, under such circumstances, probably choose for marriage women of lower classes, who will have a strong economic incentive for "marrying up." That pushes the woman shortage down to lower-class men. It also reinforces the patterns of male dominance and female dependence in marriage.

But I agree strongly with Powledge that the worst consequences of sex selection lie not in changing sex ratios or birth
orders, but in the direct perpetuation of gender stereotypes. Parents who went to some time, trouble, and expense to achieve a
son, Powledge notes, are not likely to be happy if he becomes a
ballet dancer.

Here we can see the fine shadings in the two meanings of sex
"determination": first, as ascertaining sex; and second as causing
a particular sex child. When parents have "determined" the sex
of a fetus—using the word in its meaning of learning its sex—
then sex-role expectations for that fetus lock into place: boys
move "vigorously" in utero, and girls "squirm." But when you
start from the premise that one can "determine" fetal sex in the
sense that it can be chosen, then the stereotypes predict the
choice: people who want an active, vigorous, achieving child will
have boys. And when they want a sweeter, quieter, more loving
child, they will have girls.

If everyone really did choose the sex of their children—and I
do not believe such a day will come—we would lose the lessons
to be learned from "wrong sex" children, lessons that probably
cannot be learned as well in any other way. When a man who
truly yearns for a son has instead a daughter, he may just have to
make the best of it. If his images of life with his son include such
classics as a day at the sea, leaving at dawn and teaching the kid
to fish, and life offers him instead a daughter, he has two choices.
He can go fishing alone—and many men do. Or he can take his
little girl, albeit with some misgivings, and give it a try. My fon-
dest memories of my father include those fishing trips.

Parents take a special joy in living over parts of their childhood with and through their children, trying to get it right this
time. That is surely one of the greatest reasons we have for
wanting same-sex children. But women who have sons and men
who have daughters have the opportunity to see how much of
their children's experiences are really the same, how much of our
lives, even in a world dominated by gender, cut across gender:
making friends, shyness, learning to read, finding out where
meat comes from, having a pet die—all of the successes and fail-
ures, accomplishments and losses of life. When you go through
these with a same-sex child—especially, I would think, with a

chosen same-sex child—how can you see their universality? They get tossed in with the few gender-based things, the Little League or dollhouse or whatever, and we think we are seeing girlhood or boyhood, not childhood. If we chose the sex of our children, not only would we lose the felt necessity for "making do" and teaching the girl to fish, the boy to bake, but also the ability to see childhood beyond gender.

Given half a chance, reality will intrude in gender stereotyping much as it does in racial or ethnic stereotyping. One may entertain all sorts of stereotypes about, say, Jews. And if one meets Jews only in the few roles the stereotype permits, then the prejudice is reinforced. But when Jews and Gentiles meet in other situations, as patients in the same hospital, as neighbors fighting for the same street sign, then some of the universality of the human experience breaks through the barriers.

So it goes with gender. If all the men in our lives are in men's roles, and all women in women's roles, then the stereotypes remain unchallenged. If our sons are chosen as sons and our daughters as daughters, we will see them entirely through their gender.

Abortion for Sex Selection

There has been much concern voiced in the media about the use of amniocentesis and abortion for sex selection. It is most assuredly happening. The Chinese pressure to limit family size to only one child has certainly encouraged the use of selective abortion to see to it that that one child is male. And it happens in the United States, too. I observed a genetic counseling session with a 43-year-old Indian woman. She had three girls, the youngest of whom has Downs Syndrome. She said:

> I have three girls, enough. . . . In my culture it's very important to have a boy, to keep the family name.

She also said, "Any kind of retardation, I don't want it." She was clearly and openly intending to use amniocentesis and selective abortion to see to it that she produced a healthy male child. It distressed the genetic counselor terribly—she knew that as a 43-year-old mother of a child with Downs Syndrome, this woman had every right to have the test. And the counselor knew that once the results were available the woman would go ahead and make a decision based on sex as well as on Downs.

So I am not going to say that it does not happen. I am not going to deny the fact of selective abortion for the purpose of achieving chosen sex, and usually male, children. But I will say that I do not see the widespread use of amnio for that purpose. I say this for several reasons.

In societies in which the number of children is very tightly limited, with China's one-child policy as the extreme, then a patriarchal influence shows itself in boy preference and the abortion of females. This is part of the whole "perfect child" syndrome. We want to cut down on the numbers of children we have by eliminating or "weeding out" the "undesirable" children, which includes not only the physically and mentally damaged, but also the "excess" by sex. In most modern countries, the demand is for not one child, but for two, allowing a "one-each" balance.

But it is not that simple.

The many and varied studies of sex selection have oversimplified the situation. These studies have asked people about "family composition" as if it were a completed design, and not an ongoing production. At its extreme, researchers discuss how many extra pregnancies and abortions are necessary to achieve desired sex composition, and then how many more for desired sex sequencing—the boy first, say, then the girl.[15]

All of this assumes a level of rationality that bewilders. It assumes that people have the pregnancies they have in order to achieve the families they want. As simple as that.

Wanting or not wanting to be pregnant, wanting or not wanting a baby—these aspects of this decision are completely ignored. There is an assumption being made about a "finished family" that may not reflect the way real-life decisions are made. Just what is the "goal" of a finished family—when is it complete? Is there some moment for which we are striving, perhaps when the boy is twelve and in Little League and the girl is nine and in ballet? Decisions about pregnancies and babies are made to meet *current* needs and desires, not only to reach some five-year-plan, to construct some ideal family.

Consider: If someone thinks a family of four children is the best, with two of each, and now has one boy and two girls, even if you could give her a written guarantee of another boy, does that mean she's going to get pregnant to achieve that family? Maybe she thinks it's perfect, and a great idea, but she's too busy right now to have another baby. Or what of women who think two kids is a fine family size. And they have their two. And then they face returning to work at low-level, dissatisfying jobs, the kinds of jobs most women face—and go ahead and have a third child as a way of avoiding an unfavorable job market. One of the genetic counselors I interviewed had her own third child because she couldn't face the idea of going back to work as an elementary school teacher. She had a third child and then a career change. Or, more positively, what of "baby hunger"? Some people just love babies, love little children. One woman told me that she and her husband decided to have another child when they realized that there was not going to be a 3-year-old in the house any more.

Not all families feel equally compelled to limit family size. A third child, even a fourth, is a possibility, especially for women in more traditional families. And it is among the more traditional families (by definition) that the strongest push toward producing a male child is experienced. If a family is prepared to have "a few" children, then they can expect to get their boy at some point. It may only be with the third or even the fourth child that a family may face the reality of it being quite entirely possible that they will *never* have a boy, or *never* have a girl. It is less traditional women who are most tightly limiting family size, to one or at most two children, who face that possibility with the first pregnancy.

So who is it that is going to be having abortions for wrong-sex children? I do not see traditional women in patriarchal family settings in Western societies using sex selection with the first pregnancies to achieve male children. I certainly do not see them going halfway through pregnancy and then aborting a firstborn daughter. And, having completed pregnancies, women find abortion an even more difficult prospect. "Trying again" is going to be a more acceptable alternative, with success coming half the time with each try. Among the less traditional women, on the other hand, while family size is more tightly limited, the pressure toward sons is not as great. It will happen sometimes, but all in all, I do not think we are facing a wave of late abortions for sex selection.

But the technology is changing. Early on, in discussions of sex selection, there was an assumption that a technology would be developed that would be used specifically for differential conception. Some kind of "boy pill," or pink and blue diaphragms, or some such, was anticipated. We are a long way from that. Instead of sex selection coming in through the front door, with specially designed technology, I think it is going to sneak in the back, the therapeutic door. That is, in order to screen for disease, genetic testing will be taking place earlier and earlier in pregnancy—the chorionic villi biopsy that is already available on an experimental basis, the blood tests we may soon see. The period of the "tentative" pregnancy will shorten. Appropriate entry into pregnant status will require medical confirmation, as it now does, but that confirmation will come to include genetic testing. Thus with the pregnancy confirmation will come information about the status of the fetus. Including its sex.

A decision to continue or to terminate a pregnancy is always complex. It is based partly on external circumstances, and partly on the woman's feelings about herself and her pregnancy. For many women, early pregnancy is a difficult time. Feelings of exhaustion, nausea, the physical effects of the pregnancy, combine with feelings of ambivalence, fear, unreadiness. It is a time of great vulnerability. Amnio results have come after that time, after women have come to feel physically better and usually emotionally in tune with the pregnancy. The problem with amnio results, the tragedy of amnio, is that results come at a time when it is so very hard to abort. The problem with earlier results may be that they come at a time when it is hard to continue.

I think that almost every pregnancy is met with ambivalence.

Unwanted pregnancies often carry a wisp of desire for a baby, and wanted pregnancies a twinge of regret, of unease at having taken this step. If we toss in knowledge of fetal sex at that ambivalent point, I cannot but believe that it will have an effect on decision-making. Probably it will have the least effect on the truly unwanted pregnancy. But what about the third pregnancy that was an "accident," an unplanned but not necessarily totally unwanted pregnancy. A woman has two boys, learns she is carrying a girl. A woman has two boys, learns she is carrying a third. Such a conception, when it takes place when it was not planned, or when it was not planned "so soon," will inevitably take on added meaning with knowledge of sex. Decisions will be phrased as timing issues, as not wanting a third child, and so on—I do not think that the decision will be consciously made or overtly stated to abort for wrong sex. But there it is: the decision will be influenced by knowledge of sex. As everything is influenced by knowledge of sex.

Jean: Testing Moral Limits

Jean was not planning on having any more children, but became pregnant. She has four sons, and has always dreamed of a daughter. Amniocentesis could tell her if she is carrying a male or female fetus. She is deciding whether to abort right away and have her tubes tied, or have amniocentesis and continue the pregnancy if it is a female fetus.

I have presented this scenario to all sorts of people over the past year. Most are women, most mothers. I can say nothing about the representativeness of this sample. I won't even tell you what percentage of them held what view about what Jean should do. It would be meaningless, and worse, it would be misleading. But I will share the varied ways people have of thinking about this issue. Sometimes they overlap the categories that philosophers and theologians have mapped out—and sometimes they seem to be marching to a different beat.

Some women would go ahead with the plan as outlined. They would have amniocentesis, and abort a male fetus. Some people who responded to this scenario were in a particularly good position to relate to Jean's dilemma:

> Her situation is the only one I feel anywhere near to—but still I can answer only for myself. We have three boys and our fourth child is due (in five months). We want to stop with four children. We plan to do a vasectomy after this baby is born and I think it would be nice to have a girl. But whatever sex this baby is inside of me, I love him/her already.

And another mother of sons said:

> I can understand her wanting a girl (I have three boys) but I would *not* have the test done just to check the sex. She has to decide whether she wants another *baby* and the impact that would have on her life and whether or not that's a compelling reason for terminating the pregnancy.

Not everyone in that situation is so very sure what they would do:

> Perhaps if I already had a house full of boys I'd be more inclined to consider aborting another male. But without a doubt I'd find out first whether it is male or female and healthy. Then decide. Perhaps she'll be pleasantly surprised and won't have to decide anything!!!

Some people follow the "it saves a life" argument one hears from some of the philosophers on this and related issues, which says that the test and *possibility* of abortion are justified because it spares the *certainty* of an abortion. It is one of the arguments put forth in favor of amniocentesis itself: that it spares some fetuses from abortion by allowing some women to continue pregnancies they would otherwise terminate.

> If I were Jean, I would have amniocentesis. I don't believe in it to determine the sex of a child but in Jean's case she has already decided to abort and amniocentesis could save the

child if it is a girl. If it's a boy, things would be no different since she will abort anyway.

Some people who present this argument also present their discomfort with it:

> Since amniocentesis may *prevent* an abortion, I say yes, okay, have it done! But there is something pretty weird about aborting a fetus just because he/she happens to be the "wrong" gender.

And some present it only to end up rejecting the argument:

> Tough question. I generally don't believe in doing amnios to determine sex, but in this case it might prevent an abortion. Still . . . to abort a child because of its sex is pretty hard for me to accept, even if the alternative is abortion regardless of sex. So I would choose not to have the test.

A few people came up with adoption as an alternative solution for Jean. She could continue the pregnancy and give an unwanted son up for adoption, or, if she "wants a daughter guaranteed, she should adopt."

Most people who responded to this scenario did reject the idea of amniocentesis and selective abortion by sex. And yes, even though I am not claiming my sample is generalizable, this finding I do believe would hold among most American and Western women. It may not be the way people will think in another generation or so, but for now, abortion for sex is largely unacceptable. This is true whether one thinks of abortion as killing a baby—"To kill a baby because of its *sex*—I can't even imagine such a thing. God help us all"—and it is *also* true for those who think of abortion as an acceptable solution to an unwanted pregnancy—

> If I were Jean I would not have the amnio. I would not abort the fetus just because it was male. I would abort because I didn't want any more children period.

A lot of people see aborting for sex as selfishness: "pure selfishness," and "the ultimate selfishness and cruelty." That word
was used often. Jean, in choosing to abort a baby because it does
not meet her own needs, is acting in a way that many see as self-
centered. It is not a very different argument than that used by
those who say aborting a potentially disabled fetus because it
would be hard to care for is also selfishness. Jean's case is seen as
a clearer example of "pure" or "unmitigated" selfishness, because there is no inherent problem with the fetus. This then gets
put as a "pro-fetus" argument, with selfish Jean set against her
fetus.

As often seems the case, some people take a righteous pro-
fetus type of argument, while at the same time seeing the baby as
an appropriate punishment for its mother's behavior. For example:

> She has no right to deprive her fetus of life, especially on
> the basis of sex. I think she should have the baby because
> it's her own fault for not having her tubes tied sooner.

Other people have a rather more pleasant view of babies, and
think the baby will carry its own reward; like the woman who
said, "If I were Jean I'd not be ridiculous—and have the baby. A
baby is a baby and is a joy."

But when all the posturing and righteousness and philosophical arguments are said and done, the woman whose voice sounds
the common theme is the one who would

> cry for a while and feel sick and put upon and miser-
> able and bitchy but have no amniocentesis and carry the
> child.

Others would go through the same set of feelings, and abort the
pregnancy. But very few, even under these circumstances, would
use amniocentesis to select sex:

> Grow up. This is too complicated to answer here.

ATTACHMENT AND SEPARATION RECONSIDERED
MY DAUGHTER, MYSELF

The first part of this chapter explored the women's decision to learn the sex of the fetus, and then their perceptions of the fetus when sex was known. It is my understanding, based on the way the decision is made, and the pressures toward learning the knowable, that with new technology that is being developed, in the not so far distant future most women will go through pregnancy knowing the sex of their fetus.

The second part of this chapter examined the research that has been done to date on sex preference, and considered the implications of that research for sex selection. That leaves us with only one last loose end to tie up. In light of all the research on boy preference, one would predict that women learning sex from amniocentesis results, like women learning sex at birth, would be more pleased with boys than with girls.

Not so.

Girls brought pleasure, and boys disappointment.

Fifty of the women I interviewed learned the sex of their fetus from amniocentesis. Ten were disappointed. All ten were carrying males.

At birth, according to the studies that have been done, most women are pleased with the sex of their babies. Among the woman I interviewed who refused amnio, over 90 percent were pleased with the sex of their babies, whether sons or daughters. A few women expressed brief disappointment, usually with a second or third same-sex child. Since the women who have had amnio have just gone through a period of particular stress regarding the health of the fetus, one would all the more expect most of them to experience pleasure. And thirty-two of the fifty women were pleased—but twenty-four of them were having daughters. When daughters were announced, over 90 percent of the women were pleased. When sons were announced, only one-third of the women were pleased.

I asked the women if they were pleased, disappointed, or neither pleased nor disappointed when they learned the sex of their fetus. Given the cultural value of wanting any baby "as long as it's healthy," and the relative unacceptability of admitting disappointment, any indication of neutrality may be a polite expression of disappointment. Of the eight women saying they were neither pleased nor disappointed, or otherwise indicating mixed emotions, six were carrying sons.

Let us look separately at the responses of women told they were carrying females, and those told they were carrying males. Twenty-six of the women learned that they were having daughters, and twenty-four were pleased, often adding "delighted" or "very!" Only two of the twenty-six were less than pleased at the announcement of a girl. Both were to be third daughters: one of them in an all-girl family ("mixed emotions at first, then pleased"); the other with one older brother as well ("we'd have been happy either way"). But birth order does not explain the pleasure with girls, nor the differences in response to sons and daughters. The twenty-four other women told they were having girls were pleased with daughters in *all* birth orders: they were pleased with firstborn daughters (twelve women); with second daughters in all-girl families (six women); with third daughters in all-girl families (one woman); with a third daughter in a four-child family (one woman); as well as first daughters with one or more older brothers (four women).

A very different story is told by the twenty-four women expecting sons. Only eight of them, just one-third, were pleased. Ten were disappointed. The remaining six were "neither pleased nor disappointed" or otherwise ambivalent. Like the mothers of daughters, twelve of these women were expecting their first child. But unlike the firstborn daughters, with whom *all* of the mothers were pleased, only two women, just two out of the twelve, were pleased with firstborn sons. Five women were disappointed, and five claimed neutrality. Women were, in fact, disappointed with sons in almost all birth orders: with firstborn sons (five women); with sons with older brothers (two women); with sons with both older brothers and sisters (three women). The only women pleased to learn they were carrying sons, in addition to the two of the twelve women expecting firstborn sons, were women who already had daughters but not sons (four women); the second son in a five-child family; and the second son in a seven-child family (one woman). Boys were welcome

when they "balanced" a family. Girls were almost always welcome.

Quite the turnaround that is.

How can we explain this? Is it a problem in sampling—could I
somehow have reached the most nontraditional, most feminist
women? Are women having amniocentesis more likely to be
nontraditional and more accepting of daughters than sons? That
is certainly an intriguing possibility. Other studies of sex preference have not effectively controlled for women's willingness to
use technology to achieve reproductive control. While these
women are not using sex control technology, they are demon-
strating their willingness to use modern medical technology to
master the outcome of reproduction. Are such women more
nontraditional or feminist than other women? Let us consider the
women involved to test this hypothesis.

Looking at the overwhelming pleasure with girls tells us nothing. Both groups, those who had amnio and those who refused
amnio, were pleased with their daughters. Besides, the opposite
of pleased with a daughter is not necessarily disappointed with a
son. The woman who runs off crocheting pink blankets when she
learns it is a girl might have done the very same thing, with just
as much joy and blue yarn, had it been a boy. We must direct
our attention specifically to those women who actually were disappointed with sons. The ten women do not conform to stereotypical images of "new women." They are married women, in
traditional lifestyles. Most are full-time mothers, and the few
who are working outside the home are in traditional women's
occupations: one nurse, one social worker working part-time,
and one self-employed potter. These are not women one would
have expected to experience disappointment at the birth of sons.

There is even stronger evidence that women who choose amniocentesis are the same as other women in their preference for
boys. Brenda Seals, a sociologist at the University of Iowa, interviewed women who chose to have amniocentesis *before* they had
the procedure. She found the same strong boy preference (42
percent prefer boys, 25 percent prefer girls, and 33 percent no
preference) that researchers have consistently found among
pregnant women.[16]

The real difference, the important difference, between the

women in my study who had amnio, and were mostly disappointed to learn they were having sons, and those who refused
amnio and were mostly pleased with both sons and daughters, is
when in pregnancy the information comes. All the studies of son preference, all the questions asked by all the researchers, have been
about having sons. None have been about the experience of
being pregnant with a male fetus.

It is one thing to have given birth to a son. It is another thing to
be told that the fetus growing inside your body is male.

When women have been asked about boy preference and girl
preference, the questions have focused on the idea of sons and
daughters, not on the actual pregnancy experience. Even asking
pregnant women whether they prefer to have a boy or a girl does
not tap their experience of themselves as pregnant with a boy or
a girl. To be confronted with the ongoing reality of a pregnancy
with a known male fetus is a different experience than "wanting
a son." Males and females are culturally defined opposites. To
have a male growing in a female body is to contain your own an-
tithesis. It makes of the fetus not a continuation and extension of
self, but an "other."

To explore this issue further, return to the two lists of words
used to describe movement by the women who knew fetal sex
(page 129). The two lists do correspond closely to sex stereotypes: males as stronger, more powerful ("a saga of earthquakes"); females as quieter, more circumscribed (not terribly
active, not excessively energetic, rather small movements). But
there is a hint of something else in those lists as well. The male
movements are also described as more invasive ("constant jabbing under my rib cage") and as more differentiated ("pushed a
foot in the ribs a lot").

Two things may be affecting women's experiences of their
fetal sons and daughters. One, at the simplest level of analysis, is
the perception of the fetus in gender-appropriate terms. Sex-role
stereotypes are used to screen the meaning of fetal movement.
The second is the possibly greater differentiation or separation
from the male fetus. It is possible that while any fetus, however
welcome, is to some extent experienced as an intruder, an
"other" within, and a fetus particularized by the assignment of

sex especially so, perhaps the most foreign "other" of all is the male child growing in the female body.

Thinking about it then, it is not so surprising after all that women were more often disappointed with the announcement of a male fetus. It is not really a contradiction of previous findings. The women may indeed want sons. They may be very happy to have given birth to sons, to be raising sons. That does not mean that they are happy being pregnant with male fetuses. In fact, the more traditional, the more dichotomized a woman's ideas about masculinity and feminity, the less comfortable she may be with the thought of carrying a male fetus. Freud thought women longed for sons, longed to produce a penis from their bodies. He was wrong. The fetus who is male is *other*, an intruder in the female body. The more patriarchal, the more traditional the woman, the more that is true.

The content of the gender stereotype is also relevant. Little girls are filled with sugar and spice and everything nice, they are delicate, small, passive, nonthreatening. Boys are filled with snakes and snails and puppy-dog tails, they are rowdy, rough, demanding. Which would *you* like to have growing inside your body, to be captured within you for months to come? The more traditional the woman's ideas of sex differences, the less appealing a male fetus becomes.

Why do women say they want sons? Some feel that giving birth to a son seems more "clever" somehow, meets greater social approval;[17] or they are responding to a real or perceived preference on the part of their husbands.[18] One of the tasks that women engage in in pregnancy and motherhood is trying to establish bonds between their children and their men. Producing a child that meets the approval of the husband is part of this task. Many of the women choosing to have amniocentesis made it clear that their husband's needs for a child without handicap or defect was a motivation for amnio. Producing a daughter may be a failure similar to, if less severe than, producing a "defective" child. Note that this does not mean that either the women or the men necessarily view girls as "defective," or even as less worthy than boys. If women want very much to involve men in child-rearing, they have incentive for producing the most enticing child. For each of us, for men as well as for women, that may be the same-sex child.

But there is more than the social acceptability of the child, or its meaning to the husband/father to be considered. Leifer, in her study of new motherhood, learned about the meanings that sons and daughters have for the women themselves:

> ... mothers of daughters were more likely to emphasize that they felt "closer" emotionally to a girl than they thought they would to a boy, that there was a greater sense of identification and empathy with her, and that there was less ambivalence about showing affection and love. . . . There was a pervasive belief that to show one's son, even as an infant, too much affection would make him a "sissy" and perpetuate a dependency that would impair his further development. . . . These women more often talked about wanting to foster competence, independence, and autonomy in their infants (sons).[19]

How can these feelings possibly translate to the pregnancy experience? It is difficult to foster independence in an infant son— but in a fetal son? We are brought back again to the demands of separation and individuation.

The process of mother-infant differentiation is two-sided. Not only must the child come to define the mother as "other," so too must the mother come to define the child as other. When male, this child is growing from being part of her body to being something we perceive culturally as being her opposite. Of course men and women, compared to anything else, are much more like each other than unlike. But we see them in contrast to each other, and define them as opposites.

The identification across gender lines would be hard enough to make at any time—but in pregnancy and early motherhood it comes at precisely the moment when a woman is most aware of her own femaleness, the potential, and the power, of her female body. At no point in our lives is either biological sex or social gender any more salient to us than it is in pregnancy and new motherhood. To deny the importance of female biology while pregnant is impossible. If there is ever a moment in her life when a woman is going to be aware of the otherness of males and her identification with females, it has to be during pregnancy. Over and over we hear women say how their feelings toward their own mothers changed during pregnancy, how they came to identify with and understand her better. Pregnancy is a time when women come to feel a connectedness with other women, with mothers, even with nonhuman mothers. I remember sitting in a car by the side of the road once, suckling my weeks-old son, and watching a suckling calf. I stroked my son's head and watched the cow butt gently at her son.

For a woman experiencing pregnancy, and the absolute female-ness of her body, that sense of connectedness with the stream of life that is motherhood, and the connectedness with the fetus within, are reinforced by the femaleness of the fetus, threatened by the maleness of the fetus. Fetuses of unknown sex contain both potentialities—it both is and is not part of self. Fetuses of known sex dichotomize and a sense of identification or a sense of otherness dominates. This is precisely the point Chodorow makes about the mother-daughter identification, but moved back in time to before birth.

When women do not know the sex of the fetus, the identification with the baby as part of themselves can shape the birth experience. One woman I heard years ago expressed the feeling women may have while bringing forth the baby as, "I felt as if I was giving birth to myself." When they have birthed daughters, women sometimes give expression to a continued sense of oneness with the child. Joanna, always called "Jo," looked at her newborn daughter and whispered, "Joanna." One of the women Oakley interviewed said about her daughter:

It's extraordinary. When I first, in the first week, I thought she *was* me; it was really strange, such a strange feeling. I could just see myself and it was as if I was feeding myself.[20]

In contrast, one of the very few women in Oakley's study who said she wanted a girl and was disappointed at the birth of a son said:

He's just a baby at the moment. He's becoming more of a boy, slowly. I *feel* that he looks more like a boy. I'm sure he doesn't—I'm sure he just looks like a baby. But I'm beginning to recognize him as a boy. I just hope it's not going to make too much of a difference.[21]

The feelings of oneness, of giving birth to one's self, of reproducing oneself are challenged by the knowledge that the fetus is male. A baby of unknown sex is "just a baby." But assign sex, even before birth, and we come to "recognize him as a boy." And it does make a difference.

In and of itself, this finding is distressing. But it also points to something else, which may be even more distressing. No one has suggested that male fetuses are in any way inherently "defective" or "less perfect" than are female fetuses. They are simply different—maybe even, to some, better, but surely different, different from their mothers. If part of what disturbs or disappoints women when they learn the fetus is male is the simple difference, the "otherness" of the fetus, then what of the response to the fetus whose otherness is based on its perceived flaws, its "defect"? All that we know about disability, the experience of being disabled and the response to the disabled, highlights the experience of estrangement, of otherness. Our response to disability appears to be not only a response to the specific lack of ability to perform some task or tasks, but to the perceived "otherness" of the disabled.

Prenatal diagnosis does not only discover conditions that are profoundly disabling, conditions that seriously compromise the quality of life of the potential child. Prenatal diagnosis also uncovers conditions that are not generally considered serious. Perhaps we should think of sex as one of those conditions: a diagnosable chromosomal condition, and a condition that may make the fetus perceived by its mother as more of an intruder, more of an "other," more alien to her.

Can we apply the lessons we learn from women's reactions to male fetuses to reactions women may have to other "diagnosable chromosomal conditions?" The next chapter explores women's responses to a variety of diagnoses less "serious" than Downs, but more disconcerting than "wrong sex."

6

AMBIGUOUS
DIAGNOSES

While in some ways amniocentesis to test for chromosomal abnormalities is quite sophisticated, in other ways it is a
terribly crude diagnostic procedure. When all of the elaborate
equipment has been used, when all the complicated processes
completed, the final step of the diagnostic procedure uses scis-
sors and glue. At the final station on the diagnostic line a person
sits at a table with pages of photographs of cells with their scat-
tered chromosomes made visible. She cuts and pastes the chromosomes into karyotypes, pictures of ordered, paired
chromosomes. Most of the finished pictures show twenty-three
matched pairs, in size place from the largest (1) to the smallest
(22) with the sex chromosomes, the Xs and Ys, at the end. When
there is an extra chromosome, three rather than a pair of any
number, that is called a trisomy. An extra twenty-first chromosome, Trisomy 21, is Downs. Some of the other trisomies are

fatal early in fetal or even embryonic development. Some trisomies occur not in every cell, but only in some—the splitting of
the extra chromosome began after the fertilized egg began its development. These mixed conditions are called mosaics. Individuals with a mosaic trisomy are generally less severely affected
than those who have the trisomy in every cell.

The objective nature of the diagnostic process, the very clear
picture of the extra chromosomes, gives a misleading impression,
as if one knew in a scientific and objective way just what would
be the condition of the fetus and potentially of the adult it might
become. Some geneticists and genetic counselors take comfort in
the objectivity. Their diagnoses are not based on a set of self-re-
ported symptoms and clinical impressions, but on the very clear
reading of the karyotype. One genetic counselor contrasted other
medical practice with genetics:

> Lots of medicine is so unscientific—if you put on a mask
> and danced around the patient it couldn't be any less scien-
> tific.

But genetic counseling, says this counselor, is different:

> It has boundaries—emotional, intellectual, psychological.
> It's the art of a science. . . . This is based on hard science.

What gets lost here, in her thinking, are the ambiguities of the
prognosis. The diagnosis may be clear enough, but what does the
karyotype really tell us about the person? "Normal" people have
a 46-chromosome karyotype, and normal people vary enormously in physique, abilities, intelligence. That variation is also
there for the different diagnoses. Two-thirds of the Trisomy 21
conceptions do not survive the pregnancy, even without selective
abortion. Some of those that have survived to the point of amniocentesis would have died later in pregnancy or in infancy.
Some would live to be severely retarded and unhealthy. And
some would be in relatively good physical shape with mild retardation. The diagnosis is clear, as clear and as objective as the
picture of the extra chromosome. The prognosis is something

else entirely. In that sense, *any* chromosomal diagnosis is ambiguous. But as true as that is, it is also true that some diagnoses are yet more ambiguous, and less easily understood, than are others.

Technical Ambiguities

One set of ambiguous results arises from laboratory errors and technical questions in interpreting results. Polly and Rebecca each received disturbing results from amniocentesis; not bad news, but not good news either. As Polly tells it:

> We were called with the results of the amnio: "No Downs, no spina bifida, but—there's a twist and nobody knows for sure what it means." My God!

A "twist" is a translocation: the chromosomes are all there and accounted for, but things may not be in the right order. There is a great deal that is not yet known about the varieties of normal chromosomes. Fetuses are probably the largest population to have their chromosomes tested, so when something unusual shows up, it becomes almost impossible to interpret its meaning for health and growth. What the geneticists did was to ask Polly and her husband to have *their* chromosomes tested. In the informed consent statements clients sign, this potentiality is listed. The results of Polly's and her husband's tests took three more weeks.

As it turned out, Polly also had a "twist," a balanced translocation. Since she seems healthy, it is assumed that so is the fetus. But her doubts linger. She qualified the ultimate good-news report she received when she told me, "My patterns turned out the same—as far as they could tell." She then pointed out her own doubts, as expressed in that statement. Doubts, fears, anxieties have been raised—with unknown effects on Polly and her fetus. Then the doubts and fears have been lain to rest. More or less. Told essentially, "never mind," Polly cannot be expected to simply ignore the incident. As Irving Kenneth Zola has rightly stated: "Don't worry, when expressed by a physician, must be among the most noncomforting messages in the English language."[1]

Rebecca got another kind of troublesome news, with similar not-quite-reassuring reassurance:

> I had amniocentesis specifically for age-related Downs risk. And I was informed of a fetal abnormality—or the possibility of one. I was told that since the condition, one extra chromosome 8, is so extremely rare—occuring once in a million—that it may be more likely to have been a lab error—occuring once in a thousand times. It was all tremendously upsetting.

Rebecca did not know quite what to make of these results. At first, she was going to abort, but then with a better understanding of "the odds" she agreed to a repeat test. She found the whole situation terribly confusing: if the second test did not show any extra eighth chromosomes, no one could tell them that there were none in the fetus. The first test could not be proven wrong. There was no way of getting definitive reassurance from the second amniocentesis. More weeks of pregnancy went by, waiting for the results of the new test. By then, since no one could tell them what it might mean if the fetus *did* indeed have some cells with an extra eighth chromosome, Rebecca and her husband decided to continue the pregnancy even if the second test results confirmed the condition.

The second test did not show the extra eighth chromosome. When I interviewed her, late in her pregnancy, she said:

> It's really hard. I wish I never had amniocentesis in the first place and had gone with the one percent risk factor of Downs. I had real reservations about the long-term effects of ultrasound—but my husband felt raising a handicapped child to be avoided, and that the test was worth it.

I heard from Rebecca again when her baby, Maren, was several months old:

> I had thought that I'd come to some peace about Maren three months before her birth, that whatever the outcome

that would be fine. But I immediately got into another case of postpartum depression. Maren seemed inattentive, a very sleepy baby, wandering eyes—I found myself thinking she was retarded, and wondering why the doctors wouldn't admit it when it was so *obvious*. That's the condition I was in—awful. Actually, Maren seems quite healthy—in spite of a heart defect which is unrelated to Trisomy 8. The genetic department offered to do a blood test when she was born—the result of that was normal. She's been seen regularly by two pediatricians who both think she's fine. I can't say that I haven't worried—for example, she's turning out to be long and thin, as I recall one of the physical symptoms associated with Trisomy 8. . . . Everyone else—her dad, grandparents, our friends, have said to me to forget that trisomy business, which obviously was an error.

So there Rebecca is, and there Polly is, "waiting for the other shoe to drop," waiting for some further sign of abnormality.

These kinds of results are inevitable: laboratory errors do occur, and not all chromosomal patterns look like they have come out of the textbook. The results cause stress, and may raise more anxiety than can be alleviated with further testing.

Technical ambiguities such as these are certainly distressing in and of themselves. But that is just the beginning. The technical ambiguities point to some of the more profound ambiguities that are built right into the diagnostic process, ambiguities that are obscured by the medical language used to report results.

In the language of amniocentesis, a negative result means a normal 46-chromosome finding; a positive result is an abnormality. Many of the women I interviewed had a hard time keeping that straight—they said that they worried about what they would do if they got negative results. Obviously, what they worried about was what their doctors would call positive results. I avoided the confusion by talking not about negative and positive results, but simply good news and bad news. Negative results were good news, and positive results were bad news.

By translating the medical "scientific" or supposedly "neutral" language into more overtly moral language, the language of goodness and badness, I both clarified and perpetuate the problem of interpreting results. A healthy, normal, 46-chromosome baby is what is hoped for. Learning that the baby is other than that is bad news. But good and bad are not absolutes. There is more or less good, and more or less bad news one can get: a diagnosis can be made that is not good, but not, by the parent's standards, that bad. Thinking about these ambiguous bad-news results lays bare the moral system, or the values, underlying definitions of "good" and "bad" news. Positive and negative are presented as opposites. Good and bad, as we use them in our everyday life, are shaded. What is the criterion by which we rank and order good and bad news? How much less-than-good must results be before we consider them bad news?

Evaluating Disabilities

If "normal" is good news, then what makes news bad? One answer lies in how far the condition varies from normal: the less normal functioning to be expected from the individual, the worse the news. That answer oversimplifies the situation, because there are many dimensions on which to measure functioning. Our most common and our broadest distinction is between physical and mental functioning.

When people seek prenatal diagnosis, they are entering into a process of evaluating disabilities, deciding which disabilities make life not worth living for the disabled person, and also which disabilities demand too much or are beyond their competence as parents. Individual women entering the process may or may not fully anticipate how difficult these decisions will be. Most are not informed enough to anticipate the range of possible diagnoses, or the ambiguity inherent in the diagnostic process. Genetic counselors, however, do have the knowledge and the experience to know what prenatal diagnosis can, and cannot, offer, and have had the opportunity to think about the kinds of choices presented.

When I interviewed genetic counselors, and asked them questions about disabilities, I expected them to make important distinctions in what the problems were with raising a child who was mentally retarded, and one who was physically disabled. For the most part, they did not. Discussing the difficulties in raising both the physically disabled and the mentally retarded child, the same issues came up repeatedly: time, money, dependency, and the future. Although only one gave "the expenses" as her sole answer, another said "probably money would be a very big thing," and about a third said "the financial burden" was one of the problems. A number of counselors, approximately one-fourth, specified the time commitment, the amount of time it takes just to do simple tasks, as one of the hardest parts. One discussed the problem of time not with regard to the direct care of the child, but with regard to another, crucial aspect of raising a disabled child:

> advocating for them, getting the things they require and deserve from agencies, which can be a royal hassle.

Time was often related to the issues of dependency involved in raising a child with either a mental or a physical disability: the pressure of "not being able to lead a normal life—financially, physically, emotionally, being so wrapped up in the child's life." As one counselor put it, "You're so involved, it's a symbiotic relationship, almost like a parasite." "Exhaustion," "the burden," and the overwhelming changes in one's life were repeated: "It changes your life," several said, and specifically from one counselor, the awareness that it is a woman's burden:

> Most of the responsibility falls on the woman—the husband is more enmeshed in work.

But the dependency and the perceived burden outlive both parents. Concern for the future was a common theme: "Who's going to take care of this baby when I'm gone?" One counselor said:

> The future of the child is always important, because the parents are not going to be there to take care of the child. For both the physically and the mentally handicapped, the

emotional and physical trauma the family has to endure is terrible. As a parent—the parent always worries about the future of the child.

These concerns—money, time, dependency and concern for the child's future—are essentially the same, regardless of the disability and regardless of the child's own awareness, own suffering. They are, in fact, the general concerns of parenting—simply, or not so simply, less solvable with the disabled child. Every parent worries about money, about time, about the dependency of the child, and what the future will hold. The stakes get higher with a disabled child, but the issues are the same. To rank a given disability or given diagnosis as "good" or "bad" news means placing it on scales of time, money, dependency, and concern for the future. When we try to do that, we can see that these issues lie in a social context, not a medical context. How much money a particular disability will cost parents depends on the amount of state support for services. How dependent a child will be will depend on the environment in which the child lives. This is true for "normal" children, and it is true for disabled children.

While seeing the basic issues as the same, regardless of the disability, the counselors did make distinctions between physical and mental disabilities. For one thing, there seemed to be more emotional identification with the physically disabled: the child's suffering, and watching the child suffer, were mentioned more often with the physically than the mentally disabled. Counselors mentioned the "fear of what the kid would go through with friends," and the "pain and grief over the child's loss and problems." One conjured up this image:

> You'd feel for your pretty daughter sitting in a wheelchair, can't get up and dance, may be looked at as an object of pity and scorn—identifying with the child.

There was also some tendency to paint retardation in the darkest possible terms: those of "not being able to communicate, and the lack of control of bodily functions," or "the physical— changing diapers on a 10-year-old, wiping drool."

In fact, only a very small proportion of the retarded, the very most severely retarded, do not get toilet trained and cannot communicate. The same counselor who talked about diapers and drool with a mentally retarded child fantasized watching the daughter not able to dance as the hardest part of the problems raising the physically disabled. Diapers are at least as likely in the wheelchair bound as in the mentally retarded.

In contrast there were a few cautiously optimistic statements about the physically disabled:

> [Physical disability is] not as hard—depending on the degree, there can be a good prognosis, good chance that the person will be a contributing member to society.

This counselor went on to mention a newspaper article of the day before on the successes of the physically disabled, and to say, "A physical handicap is not as terrible as a mental one, as Downs."

No optimistic word was said by any counselor about any aspect of raising a mentally retarded child. When asked about their own decision-making, and under what circumstances they would or would not have aborted (eliminating the one counselor who said she probably would not have an abortion at all because of religious beliefs), only one was even unsure regarding an abortion for Downs Syndrome; all would abort for severe retardation; and all but three for mild retardation.

The women I interviewed who had amniocentesis saw things somewhat differently. Most of them, like the counselors, were prepared to abort for Downs Syndrome. But there is a notable difference. Some of these women who had amniocentesis apparently did not understand the limits of the diagnoses they would receive. They said they would decide about abortion "depending on the severity." The diagnosis of Downs Syndrome in a fetus cannot predict the degree of severity of later mental retardation or other problems. The problem of ambiguity shows up very clearly in the women's attitudes toward mild retardation. While the genetic counselors saw mild and severe retardation as almost the same, and overwhelmingly said they themselves would abort for either, that was not so for these women who had

amniocentesis. Almost all said they would have aborted for severe retardation, but less than half for mild retardation. Thus for
the genetic counselors, a diagnosis of Downs Syndrome is a clear
enough indicator for abortion, but for the women I interviewed
who had amniocentesis, there is an inherent ambiguity in this
diagnosis.

Regarding physical disabilities, there were also differences between the genetic counselors and those women who had amniocentesis, though the differences were less pronounced. The
questions I asked went beyond what amniocentesis can diagnose,
because I am trying to get some sense of the meaning of disability for those who provide the genetic counseling services and
those who receive them. About two-thirds of the genetic counselors said they would abort for a condition in which the potential child would be "wheelchair-bound." Most of the remaining
third of the counselors were unsure. Among the women who had
amniocentesis, about half said they would have aborted for such
a diagnosis, and over one-third said they would not. The remaining few were unsure. Approximately half of the counselors
said they would abort for a diagnosis of potential blindness,
and almost one-third for potential deafness. Among the women
who had amniocentesis, no such distinction was made between blindness and deafness. Approximately one-third of the
women said they would probably abort for either of these conditions.

The greater willingness to abort for retardation than for physical disability on the part of the counselors, and the distinctions
they make between disabilities, reflects the general cultural
values regarding disabilities and their relative social acceptability. In part it reflects the very active campaigns on the part of
some groups of physically disabled people to achieve greater social acceptability. The women who had amniocentesis reflect
these same cultural values, but with an important difference regarding mild retardation, and overall, less willingness to abort.
These are the women who did agree to have amniocentesis, expecting for the most part to abort for Downs Syndrome, the specific condition for which most of them were told they were at
risk. They began the process expecting clear-cut good or bad

news. They often found themselves facing far more ambiguous
results.

A Diagnosis in Search of a Syndrome

While its severity varies greatly, most of us have some notion of
what Downs Syndrome is. It existed as a socially identified
problem long before the diagnostic tests were developed. Medicine recognized a problem and went looking for a cause. Much of
the popular and even the scientific literature confuses the discovery of the new scientific technique, identifying the karyotype,
with having discovered the cause of Downs Syndrome. But we
still do not really know what the cause is: we do not know what
causes the extra twenty-first chromosome, nor do we know why
an extra twenty-first chromosome causes the eye fold, the retardation, or the physical problems associated with Downs Syndrome.

The pattern of moving from a recognizable condition, or a
"syndrome," to a diagnosis, is repeated on the individual level as
well. When a child is born with observable abnormalities, parents and doctors seek a cause, a diagnosis. Because prenatal
diagnosis is really a *screening* program, it circumvents this usual
process of searching for the cause of abnormalities, by providing
the diagnosis before the symptoms can be observed. For conditions which present startling and dramatic symptoms, such as the
facial stigmata of Downs Syndrome, prenatal diagnosis serves to
move the time of the diagnosis forward by just a few months. For
conditions whose signs are considerably less clear, or come much
later in life, prenatal diagnosis has the effect of diagnosing conditions that may never have presented symptoms. As the diagnostic technology develops, more and more such conditions may
be diagnosed. The best current examples of conditions that may
otherwise never have been diagnosed are some of the mosaic
conditions, and some of the sex chromosome abnormalities.

Trisomies that occur in the sex chromosomes are rarely fatal to
the embryo or fetus, and so are relatively often seen in amniocentesis and among live-born babies. Like Downs, the sex chromosome abnormalities appear to increase with the age of the

parents. Rather than XX (female) or XY (male), a fetus may develop with some variations. The most common are trisomy X (three X chromosomes), Kleinfelter's syndrome (XXY males), or XYY (males with an extra Y chromosome). There may also be not an extra, but a missing second sex chromosome, and the fetus develops as a female with only one X chromosome, a condition called Turner's syndrome. Other, more complicated variations also occur. No one of these sex chromosome abnormalities is quite as common as Downs Syndrome among live-born babies or in amniocentesis, but when considered all together, a fetus is more likely to be diagnosed as having a sex chromosome abnormality than as having Downs Syndrome. And like the other chromosomal abnormalities, mosaics are possible with the sex chromosomes too. The fetus may have some XXY and some XY cells, for example.

Like Downs, these sex chromosome abnormalities are absolutely striking on a karyotype. One could no more miss seeing, for example, an extra X than one could miss seeing an extra twenty-first chromosome. But an extra X has no striking facial or other features associated with it, no remarkable effects on fetal development. Trisomy X, the condition of a female with an extra X chromosome, did not exist as a "syndrome" whose "cause" was discovered. It exists as a "cause" whose syndrome is now being explored.

Deborah had her amniocentesis because "it was the thing to do." She was over 35 and wanted good medical care in her pregnancy. The diagnosis she received was Trisomy X, a female fetus with an extra X chromosome in her cells. Her response to the news was much like the women's responses to Downs Syndrome and other bad news:

> I just went crazy with it. Hysterical. . . . I could not stand for the baby to move, just could not stand it. My emotional rejection of the child came early—embracing her and rejecting her at the same time. Crying for her. Not knowing if I could deal with birthing her knowing what I knew about her. They told me not to tell anyone [the diagnosis]. What could I tell her?

The reason the counselors told Deborah not to tell anyone about the diagnosis was that they felt it might stigmatize the child. Amanda, as Deborah had named her, would have no visible sign of any problem. Indeed, what problems could Deborah expect for Amanda? She learned:

> There is very little on that disorder. We have a technology which could tell us what was wrong, but not what its meaning would be in our lives.

Deborah and her husband spent over two weeks, two precious and agonizing weeks as the pregnancy advanced, researching Trisomy X. They got different answers from different sources. They found that there was no definitive literature on Trisomy X, not even a summary of all the existing literature. They put together what they could from one small study here, one there. Deborah was told to expect that Amanda would be "sterile." It distressed her. It is a particularly difficult time to learn that your daughter will not ever be able to be pregnant, while you are still pregnant with her. If you say that the daughter's fertility is important, then you are saying that she is disabled in an important way. If you say her fertility is not important, then you are denying the importance of the experience you and she are currently sharing.

But more serious was the research that told Deborah to expect a chance of some retardation. And what really frightened Deborah was a report that there was some chance that a Trisomy X woman would become schizophrenic:

> We ended up—I ended up, I could not deal with all of that. The fear that when she got to be an adult, she'd have been schizophrenic.

Deborah was incapacitated by this information; she was made incapable of mothering Amanda. How could she mother the child "knowing what I knew about her"? The information was considered damaging enough so that she was told not to share it. How could it not damage Deborah?

Deborah terminated the pregnancy:

> I never would have thought that I'd have done that. If some-
> one told me I'd have aborted a child that didn't have a se-
> vere thing, I'd have said no, never. . . . I guess I'll deal with it
> the rest of my life. Not guilty, but it will be an issue. I don't
> know whether it was right or wrong, just what I had to do.

Deborah did what she had to do. One reading of what she did,
one way of looking at it, is that she rejected an imperfect baby.
This diagnosis was not, as Deborah herself says, "a severe
thing." But talking to Deborah, listening to her anguish over the
decision, the abortion, her continuing grief and distress, I never
had the sense that she rejected an imperfect baby, that Amanda
wasn't good enough for Deborah. Rather I had a strong feeling
that Deborah felt incapacitated as a mother. That word, incapacitated, keeps coming to me: she felt incapable of proceeding with
this pregnancy and mothering this child.

Deborah became pregnant again, with twins, and again she
had amniocentesis. Only one sac was penetrated. As the doctor
did the amniocentesis, he told her that they would only be able
to give her results on one of the twins. Her reaction?

> I was relieved that the choice was taken away from me. I
> would never abort not knowing what the other baby was.

She said she could relax then—even if they gave her bad news
about the twin they could test, she could continue the pregnancy
for the sake of the other. So what was it that Deborah feared with
Amanda? Apparently not the possibility or potential of problems, the lack of "perfection." It was *knowing* that made continuing intolerable. To have a child be retarded, schizophrenic, that
is indeed tragic. To wait for it to happen is torture.

Other people have had the same kind of reaction, the same
sense of incapacitation. Consider the diagnosis of XYY. Some
years ago, the XYY pattern was "discovered" as a syndrome.
XYY men, it appeared, were unusually tall. They were also over-
represented in jails. The media took up the news that a "gene for

criminality" had been discovered, particularly that the extra Y chromosome made men more aggressive. If Y chromosomes produce men, the reasoning went, and men are more aggressive than women, then an extra Y chromosome should produce extra maleness, extra aggression. Several years and many studies later, it appears that the extra Y chromosome's only demonstrable effects are to raise height and lower intelligence, though not either one to such an extent that one could pick out XYY males from other males without doing a karyotype. Lots of perfectly ordinary, reasonably bright men are living perfectly ordinary lives, never punching anyone, with an extra Y chromosome in their cells.

Similarly, there may not be a lot of truth to the idea that XXX women have a higher chance of schizophrenia. These studies are so hard to do definitively. But true or not, the "information," the *expectations* are planted in the parents' heads, and can be incapacitating, can make them feel that they are incapable of raising the child "knowing what they know." The specter of violent, aggressive behavior in XYY males dies slowly. A genetic counselor described a recent session with a couple who received the XYY diagnosis for their fetus. They chose to terminate the pregnancy. The potential father said:

> It's hard enough to raise a normal kid. If he throws the blocks across the room will I think he's doing it because he's two or because he's XYY?

To the counselor who described the session to me, the decision made a great deal of sense. When I asked if she thought it was helpful for parents to get this kind of information, she said:

> You can't do screening with selective telling of parents, tell XXX, not XYY—having a kid wind up in jail is worse than a kid who can't have a baby.

This counselor prides herself on sharing all information, even translocations, the "twists" that are in themselves appar[e]nt[ly] harmless. She says she herself would abort for *any* chromos[ome] abnormality. Since she had no fertility or miscarriage problems, she said, she could always "start over." But even for those who would choose not to abort, she sees the information as important. Where I see the parent as incapacitated, unable to parent the child knowing what they know, she sees the parent empowered by information. Concerning a diagnosis of Trisomy X without an abortion, she said:

> Parents should really know about this information. If you knew you have a kid with Trisomy X you'll be more aware of what's going on with Trisomy X, more alert.

She cited as an example a piece of research suggesting a possible link of Trisomy X to epilepsy, information parents would have if they knew their child had Trisomy X. It seems not unreasonable. On the other hand, what good does it do? If the parents are alerted, they will be aware of the possibility of seizures. But it is hard to imagine that seizures would otherwise go unnoticed. The usual approach of moving from the symptom to diagnosis would work anyway. It is not parents of Trisomy X children who need to know of the link to seizures: rather, it is those who treat children with seizures who should be aware of a possible link to Trisomy X. Always assuming, that is, that the knowledge made any difference at all in the management of the seizures.

For some people this kind of information is incapacitating. Once they know these potentialities for the fetus, they feel incapable of parenting it. For others, as the genetic counselor so firmly believes, the information makes better parents, parents more aware of their child's possible special needs.

Roberta helped me to explore further the meaning of an ambiguous diagnosis. Like most of the women having amniocentesis for age, Roberta expected to hear that the fetus either did, or did not, have Downs Syndrome. When she heard the doctor's voice on the phone, she knew the news was not going to be good. She remembers his exact words: "The results are puzzling." Some of the cells had missing X chromosomes. It might mean, he said, Turner's Syndrome full-blown, or Turner's Syndrome mosaic.

The doctor who gave her the news did his best. He gave her lots of detail on the phone, spoke to her husband later in the evening on the phone, made himself available for them to come in early the next morning and talk. But for all of his goodwill, he did not have much to offer. They went, as Deborah and her husband had, to the medical literature. They were also able to find a doctor who works with children with Turner's Syndrome. The medical literature, Roberta found, was "way behind." The older literature says that women with Turner's Syndrome will be retarded. The doctor at the clinic for Turner's children told her that is not true, or not usually true. There are concerns about a variety of physical problems, especially kidney problems. Another sonogram determined that May, Roberta's fetus, did not have any apparent problems with her kidneys or any other sign of abnormality.

Roberta says it took her about a week to come to terms with the diagnosis. Based on all she learned about Turner's Syndrome, she decided:

> Even in the worst case, I could handle it. Whatever it is, it's going to be okay. Once I made that decision in my head, I really relaxed, didn't worry about it any more.

When I spoke to her, she described May as a beautiful, healthy baby girl of ten months, with no sign of any abnormality. Girls with Turner's Syndrome are usually very short. So far May's size is normal, but they will know more when she is around 5 years old. Then the next hurdle will be at adolescence. Girls with full Turner's Syndrome do not generally develop secondary sex characteristics without hormone treatment. So they watch and wait.

> I am not sure if it has been helpful or not to have had this unique diagnosis. Certainly it would have been easier to not know and to not have the anxiety, stress, and uncertainty. However, if May does later have some of the problems associated with Turner's, we are more prepared by having known. I guess I really feel that unless the outcome is truly

knowable and clear it is more humane and ethnical to not share this information—but that doesn't feel right either.

Certainly at this point Roberta has made it clear that she does not want any more ambiguous information. Once May was born, Roberta could have had her retested. At any point now, they can do a new karyotype and tell more definitively what percentage of May's cells are missing the second X chromosome. Roberta has chosen not to have the test redone, since no one can tell her what it would mean if 15 percent, or 25 percent, or 35 percent or whatever other percentage of cells were abnormal. If May is having growth problems at 5, or does not enter puberty, then Roberta will be willing to have further testing done.

So what did Roberta gain out of this diagnosis? She will be prepared if certain problems develop. She is looking out for those problems. I asked what would have happened if she had not had the diagnosis, and at 5 May did develop growth problems, or at adolescence did not enter puberty. What if the diagnosis came at that point?

Then there would be something real to deal with, something real with the kid. It'd be a shock then, but something you could do. This way, it's all speculation.

Roberta gained preparation, at the cost of anxiety. If the child does not have any of the problems associated with Turner's Syndrome, if indeed many of us are missing the odd X here and there, all was for nought. If the child does develop the problems, then that might have been a more appropriate moment to do the diagnosis. One cannot help but think about the tension of the household until May passes each of the developmental milestones in question. Lots of children are late going into puberty. I hope May is early. And there is almost no end in sight. The geneticist told Roberta that if May does appear to develop normally, and someday becomes pregnant, then May should have genetic counseling and amniocentesis.

The cost, I believe, is more profound than just anxiety. When the results first came, Roberta recalls:

Initially, I felt this alienation—from the pregnancy, from, from the fetus. I didn't want to put my hands down on my stomach.

Alienation—making something alien, strange. The diagnosis created of this part of Roberta that was her fetus, her pregnancy, something alien, something other. Unlike Deborah, Roberta felt she could handle it, that whatever it came to be, it was okay. Maybe the difference lies in the personalities of the two women, maybe in the diagnoses. Deborah could not go on, but Roberta continued. She will probably do a fine job of raising her child. But I cannot see how this diagnosis made that job any easier.

Roberta does not believe that the missing X chromosome will cause retardation. She worries about some physical problems, especially extreme shortness and lack of sexual development. These are characteristics that are probably fairly resistant to social influence.

But what of the potential parent who learns the child might be "slow," or "aggressive," or "schizophrenic." How does one watch for signs of something like that without doing damage? How can anyone raise a child under those conditions without looking for signs, fearing signs, reading dread meanings into every ordinary developmental variation? The process of expectation becomes part of a self-fulfilling prophecy. The "slow" child is treated so as to make her slow, the "aggressive" child aggressive. The stigmatized child can grow to fit the diagnosis.

Normal, ordinary kids sometimes throw blocks, hit, even bite. Ordinary kids talk to themselves, have imaginary friends, stare into space, and won't respond. Ordinary, bright kids sometimes do not learn to talk for a long time, have trouble with their letters, fail math. What does it do to a parent, what does it cost a parent, to see each of these stages of development as possibly related to a diagnosis, a diagnosis that preceded the child's arrival in their lives? What does it do to a child to arrive in the world as the embodiment of a diagnosis?

We are caught in a bind. It may indeed be more humane and ethical, as Roberta said, not to share such ambiguous information—but no, as she added, that doesn't feel right either. How could someone else decide what a parent should know about a child? How could someone else determine what a woman needs to know to decide whether to continue or to terminate a pregnancy? What right has anyone to withhold such information? But what do we do with information that at best arouses our anxieties for nothing, at worst makes us incapable of parenting?

On Knowledge and Foreknowledge

There is another direction that bad news can take: not the degree of disability, but the very disturbing question of life expectancy. While many of the decisions discussed so far have had to do with the quality of life, others address the quantity of life: how long must a life be to be worth living?

When women abort because the fetus was not going to survive, they say there is no point in continuing a pregnancy that would lead not to birth but to death. Hidden in that statement is the most basic, and the most unanswerable, question of them all: what ever is the point of life? If it doesn't pay to continue a pregnancy when the fetus won't survive the birth, when does it pay to continue a pregnancy? How long must a life be to make it pay, for there to be a point to it?

Not all fatal genetic diseases wreak their havoc in the fetus. Tay Sachs disease allows up to six months or so of normal infancy before the dying process begins. Children with cystic fibrosis most often survive infancy and early childhood. Huntington's disease, the disease Woody Guthrie had, doesn't show its effects usually until halfway through a normal life span. As diagnostic powers expand, cystic fibrosis, Huntington's disease, and more will be diagnosable prenatally. How will any mother begin to decide how long a life must be for her to continue the pregnancy?

The existence, or the potential existence, of this information forces us to confront these unanswerable questions. Once a woman can know whether her child will die in infancy, or die in childhood, or begin its dying early in adulthood, she is forced to make decisions that challenge the very meaning of life. It is the nature of living to feel that it is worth doing, that life is worth living. We know what happens to people who stop thinking that way—they kill themselves, they see no point in going on.

All our children are going to die. We birth all of them into the passage to death. But it really doesn't do to think about it. When a woman is forced to confront the inevitability of her child's death, she must evaluate the meaning of her child's life. One very human response to the inevitable is to see that it may as well already have happened. A child who will not live might as well be dead. In that sense, we might as well all be dead.[2]

But am I saying a child should be brought into life only to die? Truly, no. For myself, I cannot believe in the sanctity of all human life, any human life, however short, painful, horrible. But where, when does the cut-off come, the point at which there is no point in going on with a pregnancy? It is, I do believe, an absolutely unanswerable question.

I spoke to a woman who lost a child in mid-childhood after a fairly long—how long was a winter when you were 10?—inevitably fatal illness. I talked to her about the decisions some women are now going to have to make about how long a life must be. She said she never, ever thought to regret her son had been born. Her regret and grief was only that he had died. But, I pressed on, had she known, if someone could have told her this would be the end of it, could she have brought the child to life? She sagged. No, no, she wouldn't have been able to do that, she said. Where would the strength come from, to bear a child to die? The act of love and hope that is birth would be turned to ashes.

Such knowledge is incapacitating. We have no framework for handling foreknowledge such as this. A life we know is leading to death we say is doomed. What are we to do with this knowledge—how can we not end the life now before it begins?

This knowledge, more than any, incapacitates us as parents, makes us unable to do the job. If you know the child will be dying before the end of the pregnancy, do you still avoid alcohol because it might damage the fetus? What's the point? What's the point of nurturing this life? If you know the child will be dying in just months, how do you respond to colicky weeks? Do you comfort all the more because this is all the life it will have? Do you pull back and harden yourself for what is to come? What you do *not* do is judge your actions toward your child in terms of their effects on the growing child, usual parental concerns such as whether it grows up feeling secure or being "spoiled"—what's the point? If you know the child will be dying in childhood, how do you raise it? What do you teach it about the world, about growing up? I was once horrified to hear someone say of the parents of a young man who had died in a car accident, "what a shame, what a waste—they're still paying off his medical school tuition." I guess, had they known, there would have been no point in sending him to medical school.

People do parent dying children. Few things can be harder. I understand, clearly, trying to avoid that. Seeing the inevitable end of a life at the threshold of that life cuts us at our essence. But knowledge does not always empower.

In Ursula K. LeGuin's science fiction novel *The Left Hand of Darkness*, Genry comes to a world in which some can tell the future. He asks Faxe, one of those who can, why he does not use this gift more often:

> "The unknown," said Faxe's soft voice in the forest, "the unforetold, the unproven, that is what life is based on. Ignorance is the ground of thought. Unproof is the ground of action. Tell me, Genry, what is known? What is sure, predictable, inevitable—the one certain thing you know concerning your future and mine?"
>
> "That we shall die."
>
> "Yes. There's really only one question that can be answered, Genry, and we already know the answer. . . . The only thing that makes life possible is permanent, intolerable uncertainty: not knowing what comes next."[3]

7

GRIEVING THE GENETIC DEFECT

The Tragedy of Choice

I want each person reading this to be able to feel it—I want you to hear the grief, hear the voices of the women who have experienced the new solutions brought by the new technology. Maybe I will sometimes sound morbid, "wallowing" in grief. I sit at my typewriter with tape recorder, interview forms, index cards, stacks of yellow paper, and I cry. There is pain here, and I hear it, and I want you to hear it, too.

Whenever I try to share this pain that wells up at me from these women, it seems to some people as if I am saying they should not have aborted. The women themselves find the very same thing—when they voice their grief and loss, they are reminded of how lucky they are to have had the choice. One ge-

netic counselor told me she always points that out to women
who get a bad diagnosis how lucky they are.

Some women *do* feel lucky. Andrea was carrying a fetus with
Tay Sachs, doomed to slow death in early childhood. She had an
abortion, another pregnancy with a good diagnosis, and now has
a baby:

> As bad as everything was, I have to say thank God there are
> tests like this because I do have a happy little child. It was
> worth going through everything, to have her. I guess I am a
> very positive person, and I knew all along that eventually
> things would turn out all right for me. Every day I say thank
> God that they do have these tests because I don't know what
> people did years ago.

But Andrea grieves—she does not deny her pain. She grieves,
and she feels lucky to have avoided other grief. Some women are
having a harder time feeling "lucky." Maybe it has to do with the
diagnosis: Downs Syndrome presents harder choices than Tay
Sachs. Anna said people were

> basically supportive, though many people said thank good-
> ness you had a way to find out—like it's all one-sided. My
> reaction to that comment was an internal moan—"I wish I
> didn't find out—or do I?"

Beryl too talks about the difficulty of dealing with the "little plat-
itudes":

> "You know you've done the right thing," or "at least you
> have two lovely daughters," or worse yet, "now you have to
> put the past behind you, forget about it, and look at all the
> good things you have," etcetera, etcetera. I knew these
> comments would come, but they still grate on me. The other
> one is, "Aren't you *glad* you found out ahead of time so you
> could have this done?" Thrilled, of course.

When I talk about the pain these women experience, and it
seems to people as if I am saying they should not have aborted,

that angers me. When the women themselves try to talk about their pain, people do not want to hear it. Gratitude is acceptable, grief is not. Is it *our* unease that makes us not want to hear their pain? Beryl says:

> Somehow the world—which really didn't want to think about the implications of our problem even at the time— feels now we should be all "over" our grief and surge ahead happily.

Why must we deny grief for the tragedy that *is*, as we ac- knowledge the tragedy that was avoided? When a woman has to lose her breast to save herself from cancer, isn't she allowed to grieve for the breast? When a teenage boy has to lose his leg to save his life from cancer, isn't he allowed to grieve for his leg? The loss of this body part that was the fetus, that was to have been her baby, is also a loss, also a source of grief. Grief is appro- priate. This is a tragedy.

Does rationalizing, controlling, and in some sense choosing a tragedy make it less a tragedy? In the novel *Sophie's Choice*,[1] the horrors that make up Sophie's life unfold before us: the horrors of concentration camps, the horrors of relocation, the horrors of starvation, exhaustion, illness, abandonment, and evil. But the ultimate horror, the horror that explains her suicide, the horror that overshadows all horror, is the horror of her choice. The choice: she pleads with a concentration camp official as she ar- rives, a Polish Christian, with her son at her side and her daugh- ter in her arms, to spare her children. They are not Jewish, they are good citizens, the children are beautiful Aryan children: spare them. The guard says: very well, we will spare one child. Choose which one. Don't make me do this, she pleads. I can't. Choose, he insists, or we will kill them both. She hands over her daughter. She has chosen.

It is a mockery of the concept of choice. It is a lesser-of-two- evils choice, a devil-and-the-deep-blue-sea choice, a no-choice choice. It is totally cruel, totally evil, what has happened to So- phie. Had someone simply shot one of the children, it would surely have been a kindness. Perhaps it would have been less cruel to have shot them both. It is hard to imagine what would have been more cruel. In choosing, she has become responsible. She has saved her son. She has killed her daughter. Of course she did not kill her daughter: the Nazis did. The one who gave her the "choice" killed. But she chose. And so she killed.

We are not now living under such a regime of cruelty when we make reproductive choices. I am not claiming that the choices I describe here are on the order of Sophie's choice. But there is an underlying element in both, the element of forced choice. In choosing between the tragedy of a disabled, defective, damaged, hurt, "in-valid" child, and the tragedy of aborting a wanted pregnancy, a woman becomes responsible for the tragedy of her choice. Whichever "choice" she makes, it is all the worse for having been chosen. If she chooses to keep the pregnancy and have the baby, she is responsible for its suffering. After all, she chose to have the baby, she could have avoided this tragedy, but chose not to. If she chooses to abort it, if she chooses a fetal loss, then she grieves for the loss of a baby none the less because she has chosen its loss. In adding in the element of choice, her burden grows no lighter. Yes, we can sit here and weigh tragedies and say that the tragedy of a baby's death is less than the tragedy of disability. Or the other way around. And whichever tragedy one chooses as the lesser is the one you get. The chosen tragedy.

I keep hearing a rather strange expression from the women caught up in all of this—the ones choosing whether or not to have their fetuses tested, the ones who are choosing whether or not to continue a pregnancy after a bad diagnosis. The expression is: "my only choice." Whatever a woman chooses, she often experiences it as "her only choice." What precisely is an *only* choice? An only choice is when the other choices are yet more horrible, too horrible to choose. Not everybody agrees on what the "only" choice is: but they are agreeing on the experience of no-choice in a choice situation. That may just be the nature of life and of "free will." Maybe we all make our only choice all the time. But these women are in a position where the elements of choice and of no-choice are both heightened. The whole thing about the new technology that they are offered is that it gives choice. That is what it is all about, after all, the opening up of new reproductive choices. But for most women the choices are all so dreadful that trying to find one she can live with is terribly hard. Taking the least-awful choice is not experienced as "choosing," not really. It is experienced as being trapped, caught. She enters into a rational seeking of information and choices, and finds herself trapped in a nightmare.

Responsibility

How does anyone decide whether to continue or to terminate the pregnancy when given a bad diagnosis? The overwhelming majority of women who get a bad diagnosis do terminate. In part, that is because most of the women who would choose not to terminate sensibly avoid having the tests and facing the decisions.

Even though the decision to have the amniocentesis implies, for most women, the willingness to abort for a bad diagnosis, the actuality of the diagnosis often requires that the decision be made anew. There are several reasons for this. Some women are pressured into the amniocentesis. They sometimes give in because the chances of a bad diagnosis are so remote that it is easier to go along with it than to argue with husband or doctor. Some women postpone the decision purposely, wanting to "get the information, and then decide." Some actively seek out amniocentesis fully expecting to terminate for a bad diagnosis, but find themselves more deeply affected by the pregnancy itself than they had expected. The lateness of the results changes their readiness to abort, and they have to decide again. And some women get unexpected diagnoses, not the bad news for which they were prepared, but other, surprising bad news, requiring new decisions.

It is generally agreed that the most straightforward decision-making occurs when the fetus is diagnosed as having a fatal condition. If the fetus is going to die at birth, then there is often understood to be "no point" in continuing the pregnancy. Six of the thirteen women I discuss in detail in this chapter were in essentially that position. Laura carried an anencephalic fetus, a fetus without sufficient brain development for it to survive more than days after birth. Laura herself, however, remains unsure that the condition was inevitably fatal. The rest of these six women were convinced that their fetus had no chance. Fern's fetus had a diagnosis of a genetic kidney disease and a 99 percent chance of dying even before the end of the pregnancy. Donna's fetus had a blood and bone disease in which the baby bleeds to death. Her third child had the disease and died at five weeks. This was her fourth pregnancy. Shirley never got a clear diagnosis, but it was obvious that her fetus was dying, and making her very sick as well. She aborted to save her own life. Denise carried a fetus with Trisomy 18 and spina bifida. She was told it had a small chance of survival and would lead only a minimal kind of existence at best. Andrea's fetus had Tay Sachs disease, which kills not in utero or in infancy, but does invariably kill within the first years of life. The remaining seven women carried fetuses with the extra twenty-first chromosome that is Downs Syndrome.

Is it any easier for those women whose fetuses would die anyway? I am not sure. That knowledge does not take away the sense of responsibility the women feel. I specifically say *responsibility* and not *guilt*. Some women express feelings of guilt, but all of them express "the inescapable sense of deep responsibility." Listen to Fern, who knew her fetus was dying of kidney disease:

> There are times that I really curse modern technology. No one should have to make these kinds of decisions. There are occasional flukes of nature where things don't work out, or at least they don't seem to, and yet I very firmly believe that there is always something good to be found in every situation, no matter how grim. I also think that most women know in their hearts whether or not their baby is going to be normal, and that emotionally they are prepared for it before the baby's born.

Having articulately expressed the same feelings and beliefs held by so many of the women who *refused* amniocentesis, Fern at this point apologizes for "rambling" and being "not coherent." She goes on to say that it is an individual matter, and each time the decision needs to be made all circumstances need to be evaluated. It is not that Fern feels she should not have done what she did. She is angry at the local hospital that refused her admission for what they called "abortion on demand," making her seek an outpatient facility:

> They were bound and determined for us to have this baby regardless of the pain and suffering he would have to endure prior to and after his birth.

Making the baby suffer would be wrong. The abortion had to be done, yet she wished that "the baby would just hurry up and die so that we wouldn't have to murder it first." She compared the abortion with a spontaneous miscarriage she had, saying it is the same because "it is a life lost and with it all the hopes and dreams of that new being." But the spontaneous miscarriage was different, "because I was not the one that actively murdered my baby." With the abortion, "I had good reason for doing it, but it was still a conscious decision to end that life."

Andrea, who terminated for Tay Sachs disease, also expresses this sense of responsibility: not guilt, but certainly responsibility:

> This is your responsibility. You have to make the choice. No one makes that choice for you.

But even believing that the fetus would die does not protect entirely from guilt. While all the women echo the theme of choice and responsibility, Denise remains the most troubled. Though she thought the amniocentesis was "a very intelligent thing," she says:

> In retrospect, I have wondered if it might have been easier on me just to carry the pregnancy to term and lose the child that way. I think emotionally it might have been—well, that's guessing. Maybe it would just have dragged it out for a longer time and made it just as hard if not harder, for a longer period. Yeah, this was a real person to me, and all the rationalizing in the world is not going to change my feeling. But my husband doesn't consider that the baby was a person.

Denise comes back again and again to the ultimate responsibility in the decision: "An abortion is a choice that you make and despite what other people say to you, it's ultimately your own choice, it's something you do, and—I kind of feel like I committed a murder."

When the fetus will suffer and die, then the abortion can be seen as a painful obligation the mother has toward her fetus, toward her baby. Even Denise wonders only whether it might have been easier on *herself* had she continued the pregnancy "and lost the child that way." Fern, fighting her local hospital for admission for the abortion, is no different than the mothers of infants in neonatal intensive care units who fight to let their suffering babies die in peace. A sacrifice is occuring, suffering is happening, but in many ways it is the socially accepted sacrifice in mothering: the mother suffers to spare her child.

The question of responsibility and obligation, of choice and of sacrifice, becomes more complicated when the diagnosis is Downs Syndrome. As Eleanor describes the dilemma:

> The baby can live to a mature age, and have a rather good life, so there's a tremendous amount of guilt involved—that you're getting rid of it because it is not a perfect human being—and it's your decision—it's not God's decision, or nature's decision, it's yours and yours alone, so it carries with it a heavy weight.

The responsibility when the diagnosis is a fatal condition is the responsibility for determining the timing and the mode of the baby's death. With Downs Syndrome, the responsibility is more directly one of life and death.

No one can predict in detail the condition of the baby just by seeing the extra twenty-first chromosome. Some women are left wondering if the baby might have been only mildly retarded. But one of the sadder ironies in the diagnostic process is that some of the fetuses that are aborted would have miscarried shortly, and some would have died in infancy. The woman has the experience of shouldering responsibility for a decision that "God or nature" might have made for her. Sondra had the comfort of learning that the fetus she carried did have many physical problems:

It made me feel better in a sense, that it wasn't just Downs Syndrome, but heart and lung damage. I never read the autopsy report; [the doctor] told us that, and it made me feel better.

It may have made her feel better, but:

The first few months were really horrible. . . . Guilt feelings, feelings of emptiness—it was terrible. My husband was really great—he had to drag me out of bed, I would just lie in bed. Didn't want to talk to anybody, didn't want to move, really didn't want to do anything.

Sondra did not know about the heart and lung problems before she aborted; she had to come to a decision based on only the information that the fetus had Downs Syndrome. She thought about the kind of life the world would offer her baby:

I have a handicapped sibling and I'm very conscious of how our society deals with the handicapped. I couldn't in right conscience at that time decide to bring a handicapped individual into the world. It's a tremendous decision.

Sondra is painfully aware of the seeming contradiction that exists between her commitment to the rights of the disabled, and the decision she made. "On the one hand you say the handicapped deserve all these rights and then on the other hand say that this child doesn't deserve to live." In addition to her experience with her sister, who had polio as a child, Sondra teaches emotionally disturbed children:

I had trouble dealing with the kids, sort of like, "They're alive, and they're going to go out and kill somebody one day, half of them, and Downs Syndrome people don't. They're not doers, they just need a lot, they don't really take a lot." I was angry.

Even more than Sondra, Beryl understood what the world held in store for her fetus with Downs Syndrome, should she have continued the pregnancy. Beryl has a master's degree in special education, specializing in mental retardation, and worked for thirteen years teaching the moderately, severely, and profoundly retarded:

> How ironic to choose to terminate a pregnancy which, left to nature, I was thoroughly prepared to cope with! . . . I told my geneticist I almost envied the relatively uninformed who could conjure up an image of the fat retardate on the street corner, mouth sagging, etcetera, and make their decision in the recoil. I think being aware of the tremendous steps which have been made with the retarded was less than an asset to me at times and merely introduced more irony into an already complex decision.

So how did Beryl come to the decision to terminate a pregnancy for Downs Syndrome? She does not "recoil" from the retarded; she clearly takes great satisfaction in her work and plans to continue in it. It seems, for Beryl as for Sondra, it is not what she knew about the *fetus* that determined the decision, but what she knows about our world:

> If all of society—including extended family—shared the enthusiasm and confidence in the retarded that we in my work field share, decisions such as ours would be fewer. . . . When I read accusations of being like the Nazis, having no room for anyone but the "perfect," etcetera, I sizzle. . . . Actually, if I were the only one involved, I would have kept the baby and used the best of my training to raise him. But to me the burden placed on the rest of the family, and on society, as I age or die, and the burden which in turn would fall upon the child, is too great to justify satisfying my ego.

Is this really any different than the decision that the other women faced, those whose fetuses were going to die? There is going to be pain and suffering, there is going to be a sacrifice made. Once again, the woman chooses to take on the burden herself, to bear the responsibility for the choice. She lives with the pain of her choice, with her grief and loss, to spare her child.

But it is not only their babies that they spare. While the abortion calls forth pain and grief, so too does the experience of mothering a child with Downs Syndrome. Knowing that the sacrifice of the fetus has not only cost the mother grief, but also spared her other grief, becomes a source of guilt. Since "goodness" for a woman is often measured by her willingness to give of her self,[2] how can she be sure of her own motives in this complex decision? Sacrificing self for child is "good," sacrificing child for self, "wicked."

Guilt looms large for Anna. Months after her abortion, her car swerved as she and her husband drove in the rain. The thought flashed through her mind: "If we get killed, we deserve it." She sees what she avoided by aborting, and thinking about that, says she decided "for very selfish reasons . . . [to] take the choice encouragingly offered to me—to abort the kid." Having made the choice, having terminated the pregnancy, "I felt sad but resigned, and a bitterness about these terrible choices set in that I'm still shrouded in. . . . I feel brittle, with an icy sheath around my heart. I'm on guard."

Elisabeth too speaks of guilt, and openly questions the rightness of her decision. She had the amniocentesis because:

> It seemed unkind to knowingly bring a Downs child into the world, and unkind to not find out if the possibility existed. There was no education for the hell of waiting for the results, or the excruciating continuing sadness and guilt at killing our child.

Elisabeth did what she did out of kindness. But now:

> The question I wonder about now is, is our assumption correct that it is unkind to knowingly bring a Downs child into the world. The Downs child can know and express love and joy and pain. Isn't this enough? By killing a Downs child I bow before the false god of intelligence. Isn't intelligence overvalued in our society at the expense of other values?

She remains isolated in her guilt and grief—she has never been able to talk with anyone who has made a similar decision. When I thank her for giving of herself to me, she says:

> I would talk with anyone, anytime, who has questions. It was the saddest, most guilt-producing anguish of my life.

Unlike those who seek comfort in another baby, Elisabeth and her husband "gave up our dream of a biological addition to our family." Her husband had a vasectomy. She did not want to face these choices again:

> I do not want to terminate the life of another child. I do not want to bring a Downs child into the world. I will not have another pregnancy.

It still seems wrong to Elisabeth to bring into the world a child the world so clearly does not want and will not care for. When both having the child and not having the child would be wrong, guilt is inescapable.

What does it do to a person to make a monumental decision, and not ever be able to be sure of its rightness? Heather says:

> I don't know what it is, but you lose a little bit of your beliefs—it changes you in many ways. Your outlook on life changes, the moral concept—I would say it affects everything. I'm not going to say what I would have been two years ago.

Heather had the abortion because it was the "mature" thing to do. She was visiting relatives when the results came:

> You go through all stages, crying and resentment, it cannot be. . . . Some nights were sleepless, you toss and turn, angry, and then something tells you just be mature and approach it from the mature point of view. And so I just packed up my suitcase and went home. Sunday I flew in and Monday morning I was already in the hospital.

Maturity, morality, religion—all of her basic values were challenged:

> Morally, there is a question—you have to battle with your-
> self. . . . Here we talk about life, what is life, do we have a
> right— . . . [My religious beliefs] changed dramatically. In
> fact, I drew away from the church. Because how can I justify
> myself? . . . You never forget, your life is never the same,
> but it's still a life. Sometimes it seems like a movie, it just
> happened, it's not affecting you. My life is straightened out
> now.

With all of her own anguish, Heather still supports amniocentesis.

> I would only encourage the amniocentesis even though I do
> not think it is the most accurate testing and there is a lot of
> pain involved too—and—the pain you cannot really de-
> scribe. . . . It's a grieving process. . . . And emotional tur-
> moil—there's a lot of whys asked, and questions asked. But
> I guess if you feel secure in your relationship and your en-
> vironment, you can overcome it. You can cope with it, too.
> But you don't believe it's happened to you—it stays with
> you and you feel like you're a victim.

A victim. These women are not the villains some would have us
believe, aborting fetuses it would be inconvenient to raise,
searching for the "perfect" child. They are the victims. They are
the victims of a social system that fails to take collective responsibility for the needs of its members, and leaves individual
women to make impossible choices. We are spared collective responsibility, because we individualize the problem. We make it
the woman's own. She "chooses," and so we owe her nothing.
Whatever the cost, she has chosen, and now it is her problem,
not ours.

Getting Bad News

Waiting for the phone call is bad. For most women, it is the
roughest part of their pregnancies—for some, it is the roughest

part of their lives. For women who get bad news that phone call, that moment of truth, is devastating, shattering, overwhelming.

Rayna Rapp[3] has described her experience with amniocentesis and a diagnosis of Downs Syndrome:

> When [the genetic counselor] Nancy called me twelve days after the tap, I began to scream as soon as I recognized her voice; . . . I knew only positive results (very negative results, from a potential parent's point of view) are reported by phone. The image of myself, alone, screaming into a white plastic telephone is indelible. Although it only took twenty minutes to locate Mike and bring him and a close friend to my side, time is suspended in my memory. I replay the call, and my screams echo for indefinite periods.

The world stops with an announcement like this, an impending death, the death of one's baby. Anna's husband took the phone call. She never saw him so serious, so solemn: at first she thought he was joking when he told her to sit down, he had something to tell her. Then she understood.

> Initially, [I felt] incredible sadness—I immediately identified with the baby inside me and thought poor thing, you'll not make it—then recoiled from that knowledge. But my feelings toward my pregnancy and the baby were immediately altered. I spent the next day crying and grieving over what I hadn't lost yet, and what I had lost at that point—a normal pregnancy and the expectation of a healthy baby.

Anna had no real reason to expect bad news. Like Rayna Rapp, she had her amnio for "advanced" maternal age. The chances of Downs had been less than one-half of one percent. No real preparations had been made for giving her bad news, since none was really expected. Andrea, however, was being tested for Tay Sachs disease. She knew, since she and her husband were both carriers, that there was a one-in-four chance that each pregnancy they had would produce a baby with Tay Sachs disease, a baby who would develop normally for several months and then slowly deteriorate and die within a few years. With the chances one-in-four, Andrea and her husband were brought into the hospital to receive their results:

> The doctor was there in the hospital when I got my results. It was 9:30 in the morning and they said to me, we're going to do a termination. I thought I was going to have to wait two or three days. I couldn't accept the fact. I knew it was going to happen, but I guess I wanted the time to really think about it. He said to me: you have 45 minutes to go back, get your clothes, and come back to the hospital. . . . It was really awful. My husband was going to college and he had registration that morning so we went from the hospital to the college, we went to register. I was sitting there, I couldn't believe it. We came here and then we had to make phone calls because everyone knew I was pregnant, everyone knew I went for my amnio—everyone meaning my brothers and sisters—I was back in the hospital, I was like in a daze. I remember them taking me back and forth. I wasn't crying or anything. I cried when they initially told me. It was awful.

Alone, or in the privacy of your home with your husband, or in the hospital with husband and doctor—the simple fact is there is *no* good way to get bad news. But there are some ways worse than others. Much has been written about the inability of doctors to communicate in a sensitive way. Sondra really likes her doctor—she even went back to him with her next pregnancy. But she is not likely to forgive him for the way he told her the diagnosis. The genetic counselor, unable to reach Sondra, called her obstetrician with the diagnosis of Downs Syndrome. She arrived at his office that afternoon for her regular checkup:

> He was going through the beginnings of a regular prenatal examination. For the first time, it was a really stupid move, he put the monitor to my stomach and I heard the baby's heartbeat as he was telling me. He was having a hard time

telling me. "Did you hear from the results of the amnio?"
That day I expected the amnio results and I knew I'd find
out the sex so I was sort of excited. I said, "No." He said,
"Oh." Meanwhile the baby's heartbeat is pounding, you
hear it over the speakers, and I said, "Why, did you hear
from her?" He said, "Yes, she tried to get you today." Now I
figured, I said, "Is something wrong?" He said, "Yes." All
the time the heart is beating overhead. I said, "What is it?"
He said, "I'll tell you in a minute." I said, "Tell me." He
said, "Well, we call it Downs Syndrome." And the heart is
beating away nice and healthy.

Her world stops, crashes around her ears—and he goes through
the motions, on automatic pilot it seems, checking the health of
the baby she is about to lose.

A State of Shock

Doctors and genetic counselors tend to think it important to
make a decision quickly and get the abortion over with as soon
as possible. Andrea, who was given 45 minutes to get her things
and return to the hospital to begin the abortion process, sum-
marizes the doctors' attitudes. They think:

You don't want to walk around with that baby inside of
you. The faster you do it, the sooner we do it, the better off
you'll be. You'll thank me for it later.

For herself, Andrea says it was just too quick. If she had to go
through it again now, now that she's been through it, that would
be different—this time she would want to get it over with. But
then she felt she needed more time to prepare herself.

There does not seem to be an optimum way of pacing this process out. Surely there is no one best way for all women. Eleanor
had less than twenty-four hours between the diagnosis and the
time the termination began, but her experience supports the
doctors Andrea quoted. Once she knew she was going to terminate, "I felt that every moment being pregnant was just a very

heavy moment." She felt, for herself, it was appropriate to do it right away.

Donna too had just one day; she got the results at two one afternoon and was scheduled to go into the hospital at nine the next morning. But for her that was:

> Not enough time to think and plan and physically be strong enough for it as well as mentally. All this time we had been thinking positively and now we had to realize that we weren't going to have a baby. I tried to get some rest. . . . I had to pack and get household things in order. I spent time crying. My husband called the family.

While some women need time to prepare themselves, to "say goodbye to a baby you never knew" (Sondra), some women need time to come to a decision. Elisabeth said:

> It was cruel of the University of _____ physician to inform me of the diagnosis and tell me I needed to decide and schedule the termination in the same phone conversation. I was alone at the time. It was hell. I was informed that no person in the state had received a "bad" diagnosis and not terminated . . . and it was assumed a bad diagnosis would result in termination. For their scheduling convenience I had to let them know then if I was coming. I asked to talk to any other human being who had been in my position, a bad diagnosis after attachment to the baby. Records were closed. There was no possibility.

Like giving bad news, there are very wrong ways, but can there be a right way of handling this? Sondra lays out the inherent ambivalence of wanting something to be over, but not wanting it to happen:

> Maybe it gives you time to think about it—but at the time, you feel a baby, you become attached to the baby, and every time it moves it reminds you that you're going to put an end to its life and it's very hard to imagine taking more

time. It really is. Maybe theoretically it sounds like you should, but in reality it's very difficult. You imagine your baby. This is your baby. Hard to think of it as a fetus—you say fetus, but you imagine a baby. It moves and you become attached to it. Every time it moved those three days, I said, "Please don't move."

The women often describe themselves as being in a state of shock after the diagnosis. It is disorienting. Suddenly, abruptly, with the diagnosis, one's responsibility to the baby and to the pregnancy ends. As Eleanor explains it:

You're going along and wanting this baby terribly, like any pregnancy, you're taking your vitamins and you're doing everything to safeguard this baby and then, in a matter of seconds, this very wanted pregnancy becomes a very un- wanted pregnancy and it just throws your whole system into shock and change. There's no prior kind of buildup to it.

One of the women spoke of suddenly wanting a drink, after all those months of not having anything, of being careful, watching her diet. It is a strange juxtaposition: months of carefully struc- turing one's entire life to protect the baby—and suddenly turn- ing around to destroy it. "Here I'd been doing everything . . . taking vitamins . . . stopped smoking. And now I was going to have her killed."[4]

The Abortion

There is responsibility in the more abstract sense, of being re- sponsible for a decision. Hard enough, that is. Then there is the responsibility of having to carry through the decision. Without exception, the women who have made the decision to abort a fetus based on prenatal diagnosis feel weighted down by the awesome responsibility. But making the decision is not enough. The woman is herself the body in which the fetus lies. The woman must *herself* go through the process of terminating the pregnancy, of killing the fetus. She can deny, or not think about parts of it, but it is unavoidable that she put herself through it. For some women that is made harder by circumstance, by their own knowledge and awareness, or by institutional management.

There are several different ways to terminate a pregnancy after twenty weeks or so. Most of the women I interviewed, as do most American women having late abortions, went through a labor and delivered a dead fetus. A drug, prostaglandin, can be used to start the labor. A related approach is to inject saline solution or urea into the amniotic fluid, which kills the fetus. Labor then starts after the fetus has died. The third, less common, procedure is a "D&E," in which the cervix is dilated painlessly over a period of several days, the woman made unconscious or heavily sedated, and the fetus removed in pieces. That procedure is held to be more difficult for the medical personnel, because it is they who must dismember and remove the fetus. It is said to be easier for the woman, because she need not labor or go through the harrowing experience of the delivery of the dead fetus. Not all women agree.

Anna is a nurse who knows birth intimately. She has been with many, many laboring women. She has herself birthed two babies. She chose not to have a D&E. She understood quite well what her choices were, and chose to go through a labor and deliver the fetus. With a wry, self-deprecating smile, she says perhaps she needed to feel the pain, to punish herself. We talked about the abortion, a prostaglandin-induced labor. She talked about what she felt, and she talked about what she thinks her baby must have felt. Groping for a way to comfort her, I said she had chosen a kind way for the fetus. Yes, she said. It was not dismembered. It was not bathed in saline. "It was my uterus, clamping down, cutting off her blood supply. It was my uterus that killed her."

We have all heard that late abortions are more difficult, painful, and dangerous than are early abortions. Contrasting the experience of late with early abortions makes sense when we are discussing women who are choosing not to be pregnant. Then we rightly focus on the advantages of getting women the abortion services they need as quickly as possible.

For the women I am talking about, contrasting their abortion experiences with early abortions is meaningless. An earlier abortion was not one of their options. It is as meaningless, and ultimately unkind, a contrast as the abortion clinic that made Elisabeth sit through a session on contraception before they would begin her abortion. These women are not facing late abortions because they were careless contraceptors, or because they did not recognize or acknowledge their pregnancies early enough.

While it is inappropriate to contrast their abortion experiences with early abortions, it is virtually impossible to contrast their abortions with childbirth. Is it easier? Harder? More painful? Less? What does one use for a measure? Those women who had had babies usually placed their description of the abortion in the context of their experiences with birth. Some do it in an offhand way, contrasting this with their "other babies" or "other deliveries." Laura puts it succinctly: "Yes, I had labor pains and I delivered practically the baby. I consider it another delivery."

The descriptions the women gave of their experiences reminded me of childbirth descriptions, but mostly of the medical nightmare childbirth often was through the 1950s and 1960s. The women were out of control, drugged enough to be "woozy," but still felt pain. The major difference I hear is that the husbands are allowed to be there through the labor. But with no support services for the husband, with no one to reassure or comfort him, and with no nursing staff staying with the woman to help, there is a limit to what even the most sensitive and loving of husbands can do. Denise describes her abortion of a Trisomy 18 fetus with spina bifida:

They gave me an injection of prostaglandin. I went through what seemed to be a long, all day, extremely difficult labor. They had me in the maternity ward before, during and after, which I think was horrendous. And they just kind of stuck me in the back room and ignored me. My husband was there and I was under a lot of discomfort and was miserable. I had a lot of contractions after the delivery. A lot more painful contractions than I had had after any of my other children. So I laid around for a few days and took a lot of painkillers. I was told it was normal: contractions of the uterus. I cried a lot.

Andrea was also in the back of the maternity floor, but thought "they were very nice" to give her the furthest room down the hall. Andrea had thirty-six hours of painful labor, with vomiting and a high fever. "It was hell. Those thirty-six hours were very bad. I'm really afraid of putting myself through that again. I don't know if I'd be willing to do that."

Anna, having so much experience with birth, planned on dealing with the labor "like any labor," but found the entire experience, including the nausea caused by the prostaglandin, so much worse than birthing a baby. Rather than being up, walking around and managing the labor actively, she took to bed. She felt her recovery afterward was much like after a birth, just "appallingly long without a baby to take up one's time."

Eleanor felt she was fortunate not to have too bad a time with the abortion:

> I got a saline solution injected in my uterus and then afterwards I got some kind of suppository, like about a day later, because the saline solution didn't work. . . . They gave me drugs because it didn't matter—with my other babies I didn't take drugs, I had natural childbirth. So I was in and out of sleep. . . . I was fortunate again, my physical recovery was pretty good. . . . I didn't have any kind of side effects or complications.

Some women are not so fortunate. Some, like Andrea, have experiences they consider hellish: long, painful labors. Others are themselves in physical danger. Deborah woke up to find herself on a table. She asked what had happened, or was going to happen: "They said something about a hysterectomy. I tried to get off the table. It was a teaching hospital—there were interns and residents, all these people standing around, staring at me." Her bleeding was brought under control, and the hysterectomy was not done. She was weak, however, and then, "The medicine to dry up my milk caused my blood pressure to lower, and I had another medical emergency." Hers was a hard, slow physical recovery. Of all the women that I interviewed, Heather appears to have been in the most danger from the abortion:

> This was a living nightmare because I almost lost my life. If you ask now in retrospect would I do it over again, I doubt it. Something went wrong—the medication didn't agree with my system—and I had an internal hemorrhage and I was in the intensive care unit—I had ten blood transfusions. . . . The labor went on forever and ever, I remember, and then I couldn't take the pain anymore, and they gave me some kind of medication to make me feel less pain. That is when the trauma happened. Physical recovery was very slow, really slow, because of the tremendous shock I went through, and trauma. It took me nearly a year to be myself again.

Some of what makes this experience dreadful is inevitable: the contractions of the uterus to expel a twenty-week fetus are going to be painful, just as the contractions of childbirth are painful. The drugs used have their assorted side effects, and the labor should probably be compared with an induced labor, which women almost invariably report to be more painful and difficult than a natural labor. And most important, unlike childbirth, this is a totally joyless experience, and the emotional anguish compounds the physical.

But as inevitably hard as it may be, it would seem that there must be better ways of helping women through it. One obvious problem is the location: there is *no* appropriate setting for these abortions. Women who are in abortion clinics are distressed by the assumptions and the treatment there. Elisabeth was in a special saline induction unit at a university hospital, where about fifteen women aborted each week. Approximately five each *year* aborted for genetic reasons. Not only was she pained by having to sit through a session on contraception, she felt it cruel even to have to answer the intake person's "Why are you here?" And while many of the women, in whatever setting, were angered by the continual reference to their baby as "the fetus," it is especially a problem in an abortion unit. These are *not* unwanted pregnancies, and the abortion does *not* bring a sense of relief.

On the other hand, putting the woman in the back room of the maternity unit is no solution either. Donna remains angry about the way the whole thing was managed:

> I needed honesty from my doctor and I didn't get that. I had asked him about the procedure, the termination, and he had said, "Don't worry about that now." I had no idea what the procedure was. . . . I was also lied to. I was told I'd be put on a gynecological floor, which I found out later there was no such thing at [that] hospital, it's all done on the maternity floor. They did try to accommodate me by keeping me in a single room at the end of the hall, which was hard on my husband, because he would have to walk down the long hall, and see all the babies, the pregnant women, and he had to pass the nursery.

Wherever the women are placed, it is certain that they should not be left alone, or left alone with only their husbands, unless they specifically request that. Someone—a nurse, a midwife, perhaps a genetic counselor—should be available to them. In interviewing genetic counselors and watching them work, it often occurred to me that many of them were able to discount much of the agony caused by bad diagnoses by not seeing the woman for followup. Perhaps if they worked with the women through the abortion experience itself and after, their counseling in preparation for amniocentesis might also become more sensitive.

Donna's anger also raises the issue of preparation: she did not get honest answers from her doctor about what to expect. Sondra too felt not knowing what to expect made it harder. For her second amniocentesis (which brought good news) she felt better prepared:

> Because you know what to expect of the abortion. And even of your emotions, where your head's at. And the initial shock is less. You're out of control the first time. The second time I made preparations—filled out forms to be sterilized in case of another termination, called the doctor and

told him I might be needing his services. I knew. I knew exactly what was going to happen and I knew him and I knew
the procedures. And I would have more dignity maybe.

She knew, she knew what to expect, and thought that would
make it better. Donna, angry as she was at not knowing, thinks
about it now and says it would be harder to go through it again
because:

You're very aware of what is going to happen, and sometimes not knowing is better. Although you want to be informed, there's nothing like not knowing.

Maybe there are limits to the value of knowing. I think of
Anna, acutely aware of what each contraction was doing. You
cannot take that knowledge away, you cannot shield her from it,
but it is surely no comfort. Sometimes the very presentation of
information takes the form of cruelty. Paternalistic protection is
wrong, but consider how Eleanor's doctor kept her *very* informed:

[the abortion] is almost on a hairline when babies start to
survive, so even the doctor told me, because my uterus felt
big to him, he said that they wanted to do the saline just to
make sure that the baby wouldn't be born alive.

Later she said:

The point of most pain for me was when my doctor injected
the saline and I knew that that was the point when I was
killing the baby. That was, for me, the most difficult point.

There must be better ways of helping women through these
abortions.

Closure

Earlier we heard how getting good news, including the news of
the sex of the fetus, makes the baby more "real," more of a

person. Sadly, often so does getting bad news. The abstraction becomes specified—not, this time, as Zachary, a new brother for Mathew, but still as a particular baby with a particular diagnosis and prognosis.

Sondra didn't quite handle it that way—I think Sondra comes close to using the technology in just the way it was "designed" to be used—to achieve a healthy baby. Speaking many months after her abortion following a diagnosis of Downs Syndrome, she held her new, healthy baby on her lap. Asked if she had named the fetus with Downs Syndrome, she said:

> Well, it's really weird—I always liked the name Jan, so when I got pregnant, we figured boy or girl it was going to be named Jan. I kept the name. This baby's name is Jan. My husband sometimes refers to that pregnancy as the other Jan. . . . When you get pregnant, you create a fantasy, like marriage, and the pregnancy ended but the fantasy didn't. This baby in a sense is the culmination of the fantasy anyway. It's *the baby* so it doesn't really bother me, the name— that baby didn't really have an identity. . . . I didn't think of it as a baby, really, intellectually.

But later on, talking about never having seen the fetus, she mused:

> It's like there's no closure. It doesn't seem like it was all finalized. I sometimes think I would have liked to know the sex—sometimes I'm just about to go to the phone and call the doctor and ask him the sex. Maybe it would have helped. I don't know.

Sondra had a D&E. She said that she only recently learned "that it's taken out in pieces. I do not visualize that. I visualize that he removed the fetus."

Like Sondra, Donna too "tried not to think of it as a baby," and although she had a labor and delivered the fetus, "I never even thought to ask if the child would be whole and if I could see it. Although I wouldn't let myself think of it as a baby, of course I did." Well over a year later, with a new baby in her arms, she says:

> The genetic counselor at the hospital told me the baby would be buried, but I honestly don't know for sure if the baby was buried or not—I'm probably going to call eventually and find out.

These are phantom babies—only sometimes do the women who carried them wonder about them—what was the sex? Has it been buried? The information is there at the other end of the telephone they approach and avoid.

Other women need to take a more active role regarding the body of the fetus. Laura felt she needed to see the baby—she wanted to verify the diagnosis:

> I wanted to see that it was true what they told me and—I mean, I saw it in the sonogram, but sometimes doctors make mistakes. For myself, if I didn't see it, I would say, "Is it true? Maybe it could be a mistake, maybe it was this, maybe something else." This way I saw it.

And Laura had the fetus buried:

> We consulted the rabbi and he advised us to, so, well, it wasn't really a service. The limousine picked us up and that had a little box in the trunk with the fetus and we went to the cemetery and buried it. That was all. No one else was involved other than my husband and I.

But even having seen and buried the fetus, its reality is uncertain:

> I said we should have given him a name because when I say "the baby" [my husband] thinks I am talking about Davey [the 3-year-old] so I decided to name him. But I don't think he remembers—I may tell him something about Samuel and he'll say "who's Samuel?" It was something that didn't really exist, he wasn't born.

Seeing and burying the body does not mean the same thing to all women—that of course is true in any death. Some of us feel a strong need to see the body of a loved one. And some of us feel that way only some of the time. When my grandmother died suddenly while far away on vacation, I knew I needed to see her body, to make it real for me. With other deaths, and for other people, it may feel better to remember the person "as they were." The fetus is different because it has never been seen—it has been held and felt, but never seen. Some women are comfortable leaving it just that way. Heather did not see her fetus, nor did she bury it:

> I knew the child would be dead, but I said just give it a blessing, and the nurse told me she did so.

But Beryl said she needed just to see the fetus because "this was the only way I could put closure on this sad experience."

Not wanting to see or to bury the fetus does not mean an absence of feeling about the body. Andrea didn't want to see or bury the fetus, said she was too sick and too depressed at the time to really think about it. But she also said:

> I was really upset because I know they took a biopsy. I felt I just wanted to leave this baby alone.

Fern was the only other woman I interviewed who, like Sondra, had a D&E rather than a labor and delivery. For Fern, it was the most difficult aspect of the abortion:

> Our baby could not be delivered whole and we could not hold him and say goodbye to him properly—more important for me than for my husband. I'm sure I would have been able to get through the grieving process faster if I were able to see him. Because of the [abortion] process he did not come out of it whole—and that has been the worst part of this whole ordeal.

This is not a sentiment unique to Fern. A woman interviewed in a film for genetic counselors also discussed her distress about the piecemeal removal of the fetus:

On top of knowing I had terminated, I had to know I had
mutilated her body.

It all happens so fast—it takes forever, but it all happens so
fast. Decisions are made quickly, and then lived with. Several
women are now sorry that they did not see or bury the fetus.
How can we possibly improve on this? It seems unnecessarily
cruel to make every woman having amniocentesis think through
which type of abortion procedure she would choose, whether or
not she wishes to see the fetus, what kind of disposal of the body
she prefers. For 99 out of 100 women, it will not come to that.
Should they all make the decisions, for the sake of "informed
consent?" The alternative is to make all of these decisions in
haste, at a time of great grief and confusion. Deborah said:

> I regret not having seen her. I was encouraged to do so by
> the social worker at the hospital, but I felt so conflicted
> emotionally that I chose not to [re: burial]. No, I wish I had,
> I believe it is helpful. It seemed so strange to be—to grieve a
> baby I had killed, yet I loved her and wanted her so much.

Eleanor too speaks of the inner conflict that prevented her
from seeing the fetus:

> I feel, yes, I should have seen it. That I regret. At the time—I
> knew I could, but I felt very guilty, and I felt almost that I
> had given up a right to see that fetus—I felt like I had mur-
> dered my baby, so—and now I'm going to look at it and see
> what it was and know it? I just couldn't. I just didn't feel I
> had the right to look at it.

Sometimes it is the feeling of guilt that surfaces, but even
without the guilt, the feelings of blurred reality, the phantom, invisible loss comes through. Shirley's fetus was killing her. The
prenatal diagnosis confirmed that she had to end the pregnancy
to save her life. A priest came into her hospital room later and
told her that what she had done was acceptable in the eyes of the
Church. Hers was as guilt-free an abortion as there could be—

the baby was dying anyway. The abortion simply saved Shirley's own life. But still she deals with the grief, and the unreality of it all:

> I should have told more people, for more support. But it was hard explaining the fact that the child I was carrying was going to die, was not healthy, and was slowly killing me.

At the delivery:

> I didn't want to [see], they wouldn't let me. The nurse held my head so I wouldn't see. But I did see. She was all blue and bloated.

Seen but not seen, glimpsed but not held, real but not real:

> It hurts that I never got to hold her in my arms. That if she had lived for one minute we could have gotten a tax exemption. I know that is a bizarre statement, but it hurts for some reason. . . . No one seemed to want to talk about the experience, or say "I'm sorry." . . . I sorta wish I had [a memorial service] but she seemed most real to me and not "real" to my husband and family.

Not husband, not family, not the society at large recognize this baby and its loss, so very real to Shirley.

Like so many others, Anna told of her anger at the social worker who kept talking about the "fetus," while Anna mourned the baby—"I wanted to throw a chair at her." She saw the baby. She needed to have the diagnosis checked, to make sure. She had the baby cremated, and as we spoke, just two months after the abortion, she said:

> We'll bury or spread her ashes in spring, maybe plant a tree. It's too early to be entirely rid of her.

Elisabeth too grieves greatly, continues to question the rightness of what she did, but was able to take comfort in the burial:

We asked to have our baby's body. They thought we were morbid, but relented if my husband would go to the courthouse and get a birth certificate. John made a small wooden box for Paul Thomas. We buried him in our orchard. We are Quakers. Our pastor, also a personal friend, and a close couple and our two children were with us as we dug the grave and put Paul Thomas to rest. I felt comforted by their presence, by our acknowledging and honoring his life potential and asking his and God's forgiveness. Praying that his spirit-soul be released to come again to earth in a whole not deformed being.

Husbands

All of the women that I interviewed who terminated pregnancies after prenatal diagnosis were married; they had husbands to share this grief with them. Or maybe not.

As long as babies grow in women's bodies, men and women cannot really share this grief. They may both be grieving, but the tragedy is unfolding deep inside her, and it is her body which bears the child, and bears its loss. However much one may be committed to shared parenting, to raising children together, to the abolition of separate "mommy" and "daddy" roles, there really is no shared parenting at twenty weeks of pregnancy. Ultimately, couples do not get pregnant: women do.[5] Rayna Rapp, describing her abortion for Downs Syndrome, recognizes while trying to deny this reality:

For two weeks, Mike and I breathed as one person. His distress, loss and concern were never one whit less than my own. But we were sometimes upset and angered by the unconscious cultural attitudes which precluded acknowledgement of his loss. He was expected to "cope" while I was nurtured through my "need." . . . And yet, having spent fifteen years arguing against biological determinism in my intellectual and political life, I'm compelled to recognize the material reality of this experience. Because it happened in my body, a woman's body, I recovered much more slowly than Mike did. By whatever mysterious process, he was able to damp back the pain, and throw himself back into work after several weeks. For me, it took months. As long as I had the fourteen pounds of pregnancy weight to lose, as long as my aching breasts, filled with milk, wouldn't squeeze into bras, as long as my tummy muscles protruded, I was confronted with the physical reality of being post-pregnant, without a child. Mike's support seemed inadequate; I was still in deep mourning while he seemed distant and cured.[6]

Some husbands, like Mike, are deeply shocked, grieved, hurt. Fern's fetus had a kidney disease; the diagnosis was that it was unlikely to survive to the end of the pregnancy, very unlikely to live beyond its infancy. Her husband, she said, was more shocked than she was: she had the premonition that things were not going well. This was not her first pregnancy: she recognized her body's messages warning her that this was not right. He was less prepared. And he confronted the problem men face so often in our society: isolation from intimacy with anyone but their wives:[7]

I was able to cry on my friends' shoulders, but he really had no one to turn to other than myself. The two people—other males—he did reach out to were so baffled by the situation and that he needed help with it, that they really could offer no help.

Other husbands also report anger at the demands placed on them, the lack of sympathy, the lack of attention to their needs. One said all attention focused on his wife. The hospital staff had "Not so much as an 'I'm sorry' " for him.[8]

While we have a cultural belief that grief and adversity bring people together, the sad fact of the matter is that it more often drives people apart. The very roles that society seems to demand of husbands and wives create some of the tension. Shirley, since divorced, reports that during the time of her diagnosis and the termination of the pregnancy, her husband "played 'macho strong man' for much of the time—supportive, but too shielding. The doctors talked to him, not to me."

Andrea said that the experience of terminating their first pregnancy for Tay Sachs disease brought her and her husband "closer together," but her discussion of her second pregnancy denies that:

> The second time when I was pregnant I think we were both very closed about our emotions. I think we were both really afraid to discuss them. It was funny, we really didn't discuss what would happen if I ended up with another abortion, how we would have reacted. Emotionally I think we were very far apart because I think we were afraid to discuss it.

The very demands made upon them by society, the demands they place upon themselves and upon each other, all may pull the couple apart, make it harder for them to lean on each other. And even when they can "breathe as one person," at some point the ultimate physical reality of which body held the pregnancy surfaces. Beryl said her husband was "completely shocked just like I was," and their responses to the diagnosis and abortion were "similar"—but she reports that after getting the diagnosis on a Thursday, with the abortion scheduled not until Monday, "my husband went away on business over the weekend and I had to go about my usual business with my 18-month-old and my 3-year-old." Eleanor said that after the abortion,

> I kind of felt he was disappointed that we weren't going to have a baby, but I think relieved that it was over with, and I don't think he was at all, as the days passed, that preoccupied or consumed with it like I was.

Somehow, the husbands go back to work, pull their lives together, able by "whatever mysterious process" to damp back the pain, while the wife goes on grieving, holding her full breasts and empty belly.

Denise declares it is impossible for husbands and wives to respond the same way. She begins by saying that she and her husband were "equally very upset," but goes on:

Of course, he didn't feel the baby moving. I don't think anyone can share with the woman. He felt badly. I think it's much clearer with a man. It's hard, but I don't think it's anything like the decision I had to make.

Even without the decisions brought by prenatal diagnosis, we all know that husbands and wives do not always enter pregnancies in the same frame of mind. Obviously not all pregnancies are equally wanted. Earlier I talked about Alison, who did not want to continue the pregnancy, and looked to the amniocentesis as an opportunity to escape the pregnancy on terms acceptable to her husband. Life being what it is, her baby was healthy. Other times it is the husband who does not want the pregnancy to begin with. Andrea said that added another element to her husband's grief and guilt, because he felt "that it was his fault since he didn't want the pregnancy," and he was all the more supportive because of it. Not all husbands react that way. A woman whose prenatal diagnosis revealed the fetus had died, said:

My husband was indifferent because the pregnancy was not planned and he was not supportive to the idea and not interested in having another child at the time.

Some women got into a kind of bargaining situation with their husbands: she will keep the pregnancy as she wants to, but agrees to terminate if anything serious is wrong. The termination for defect is seen as her part of the bargain, the acceptance of a healthy child as the husband's part. As Denise says:

I had promised my husband initially that if the amniocentesis showed anything serious then I would not argue about having an abortion. He wasn't happy about my being pregnant, the pregnancy was an accident and a shock. What I had said to my husband was that I would terminate if there was anything really seriously wrong. I had not made a decision on mongolism.

Denise's fetus was diagnosed as having an extra eighteenth chromosome, a more serious condition than the extra twenty-first, which is Downs, or "mongolism." She agreed to the abortion "when I was convinced that the child absolutely would not survive anyway, and it would just, if anything, have a very minimal, painful existence and it was pointless." It was, nonetheless, "the most difficult thing I've ever done in my life."

Even where the pregnancy has been accepted by both, there is obviously no guarantee that both will feel the same about terminating for any specific diagnosis. Might not Denise's husband have considered Downs to be something "really seriously wrong"? These decisions are so very difficult, so very hard for all of us who even think about them—it would be too much to expect that just because two people are married they would march in perfect time, come to the same conclusions in the same way. Among the women I interviewed it was mostly the husbands who were more sure about terminating the pregnancy, perhaps because the costs of the termination—psychic, emotional, physical—were less real to them than were the costs of raising a profoundly damaged child.

In its strongest form, wives feel that, as wives, they do not have a choice. They do what their husbands insist or need for them to do. Laura says:

> I didn't want to do it of course, but my husband decided not to have a child in this condition. . . . I did want to try, but of course my husband made me see that it really would have brought more pain and more difficulties for us. Yes, I did want to continue. . . . He didn't need this, but I would have tried. . . . So at this point I saw that the best thing would be termination and avoid more pain and problems for my husband.

Most women did not feel compelled by their husbands: most husbands specifically stated that they would support the woman's decision, or such was the implicit understanding. But it still often seemed that it was the husband who was sure, who knew the pregnancy had to be terminated, while the wife wrestled with the choice. Anna said her husband would have supported her decision either way, but:

He felt clearly that he did not want to bring a Downs child into the world. I was in a quandary—it felt wrong to end this baby's existence because it had Downs, yet I didn't feel capable of taking on such a project.

Women sometimes fantasize about taking the baby away and raising it, saving it.

But perhaps it is not as simple as I am presenting it. Mostly, I just spoke to the women. I can tell you not what the husbands said, but how the wives saw the husbands. Perhaps the women feel the need to experience a compulsion to do the deed—that it is just too awful a decision to make for themselves. Maybe they project onto the husbands the determination to abort, so that they can go through it unwillingly, reluctantly, but necessarily. It has been suggested that in cultures that practice infanticide, "some kind of supernatural reason is produced by way of showing that the actions were not wanted but were prescribed, so that the parent responsible could carry them out in grief and deep reluctance, while feeling that she had fulfilled an onerous and agonizing responsibility in the only possible way. The element of stress was reduced by the acceptance of a higher, inscrutable will."[9]

Women facing prenatal diagnosis are not given this support; they are told that they are being given choices, that they are free to do whatever they choose to do. In this situation of "free choice" the genetic counselors and doctors, as well they should, pointedly remove themselves from the decision: it is *your* decision, *your* responsibility, they tell the woman. It is something she truly does not want to do—she grieves, mourns, despairs. Yet she also feels she "must." The only person we as a society invest with the "right" to have any input into the decision is her husband. So it becomes easier on her, if harder on her marriage, if the woman can project onto her husband the certainty that the abortion must take place.

And yet the husband is not a blank slate on which the wife projects. I believe that he is *in fact* urging the abortion—just as the husbands urged the amniocentesis to start with. Researchers[10] who interviewed both husbands and wives following pregnancy termination after prenatal diagnosis found "The interviews with the husbands reveal that their self-images were as the 'realists' in the families. Their decisions seemed to require less soul-searching as compared to the wives."

It goes beyond their own psychological processes. In their interaction the couple recreate the social roles of man and woman, they recreate the structure of the family. He must be the voice of rationality, his grief and emotion denied. She cannot really choose, not really be a free moral agent, but must be guided and supported. The husband aligns himself with the doctor, with science, with the larger society, while the woman aligns herself with the darker forces, with the baby within. The drama plays out, she sacrifices for him, for the family. The family as a social structure, as an ideal, remains intact. The family as a particular constellation of individuals suffers.

Grief

There is good reason to be angry at some of the husbands of the women I interviewed—as at some of their doctors. As a group, they managed to display a remarkable lack of sensitivity to the women's needs: leaving on business the day after the diagnosis, saying they didn't want the pregnancy anyway, asking "who's Samuel?" and the like. But do remember that these wives agreed to the amniocentesis, knowing full well that this could be the outcome. They too, like the husbands, were expecting, most of them, to deal with this "rationally" and "sensibly." Some were pressured in, but most walked in, eyes open, knowing what could happen. Or *could* they know? Especially for those having their first babies, could they know what was coming?

One genetic counselor said:

For abnormal results, they're always in maternity clothes. I'm always taken aback. I'm talking to a woman who's well into a pregnancy. It jolts me every time. For the pre-amnio (counseling), it's jeans, loose clothes. Then she presents in maternity clothes, swollen ankles, sensible shoes—a different person. That upsets me.

In the few months since the pregnancy began, even in the few weeks since the amnio was performed, the woman has been transformed. She is a "different person." The woman who agreed to terminate a pregnancy for a bad diagnosis is not the same person, not faced with the same decision. But the husband *is* the same person—while some men deeply identify with the pregnancy, for many men little has begun to change at this point in the pregnancy. Probably most men do grieve at the loss of the expected baby. But the pregnancy is more for the woman than something she "expects"—it is part of who she *is*. She loses the baby, and she also loses that part of herself: "I was planning my life around it," says Sondra. "It's like, you're not having a baby, you're not pregnant, your identity is all screwed up. You're not a pregnant lady anymore. All of a sudden, in one day, there is no baby."

What Sondra is describing is no different than any other sudden loss of a baby—a spontaneous miscarriage, a stillbirth. Tabitha Powledge, a genetic counselor, says that "Patients and genetic counselors alike report that mourning a pregnancy ended because of an abnormality is almost identical to mourning the death of a newborn infant."[11] We have seen that much of the societal response is the same: the woman is told she should be grateful for the healthy children she does have, that she will have another baby and forget this, and so on. Much of the medical response is also the same as to a stillbirth: notably putting the woman on the back of the maternity floor and, for the most part, avoiding her.

Putting aside all the questions of guilt, of choice, or responsibility, we are still left with grief. And we do not, in modern Western society, deal very well with grief.

A friend recently told me that after the death of her grown son, her only child, someone told her, "You'll never be the same again." At the time, she thought it was an ugly, terrible thing to say. Now, years later, she sees its wisdom. Grief and loss are permanent, they become part of us and they do not go away.

There is a set of myths about grieving and how it should be done. It is partly perpetuated in the way Elisabeth Kubler-Ross's work has been popularized.[12] The idea is that we go through stages, in an orderly progression, winding up at "acceptance," and then it is over. Kubler-Ross worked with the dying. When all the denial, anger and bargaining are over, dying people do often come to acceptance. We believe now they *should* achieve acceptance, and that makes their dying easier—certainly easier on us, at any rate, the living. They die peacefully. But one way or the other, they do die, and their grief is over. But what of the bereaved, the grieving who go on living? All this language of resolved grief, of acceptance, has made many people think it somehow gets "resolved," finished, completed and put away.

Many of the genetic counselors, many of the women themselves, talked about the "stages" of grief, and their progression through them. There is just beginning to appear (and it is about time, too) some discussion in the medical literature of support for the bereaved family. But with it come the inevitable timetables—how long it takes families to "complete" the grieving process. Six months, one year, two years—different researchers come up with different figures, but the underlying assumption is that there is an end to it. That is part and parcel of the medicalization, and in some sense, the trivialization of grief. It is beginning to seem wrong to medical workers simply to abandon grieving families, send the woman home from the hospital, mail along an autopsy report on the fetus or baby, and end it there. So medical and related workers have started to think in terms of support services, an excellent idea. But once they start talking about support services, then they need a determination of what kind of services are needed, and over what period of time. And so along comes the development of timetables, of expectations for "normal," and, hand-in-hand, definitions of "abnormal" or "pathological," grieving processes. Grief thus becomes trivialized when we talk about someone being in "stage 2"—and medicalized when we say someone "should be" in stage 3.

Then, too, now that we feel we have mapped the route, perhaps we expect the journey to be easier. One of the women who had amnio (and ultimately got good news) was a psychologist who said she decided not to distance herself from the fetus in preparation for the results, but to go ahead and allow herself to develop her feelings for it. Then, if she had to terminate, she would do her "grieving work." Grieving work! Certainly—and if I cut myself, I can do my bleeding work. We are a culture that values doing, not being, that respects work, but not grief. Grief cannot be accepted for what it is, but must somehow be "dignified" as work, a job well done.

Real grief is not ever done, not ever "over." It becomes incorporated into one's very being. Anna said she came home from the abortion, went up to her room, sat on her bed, and said to herself, "Okay, now cry and get it over with." Months later we sit in the kitchen and she still cries—and is sick of it, sick of grieving and mourning. She asks me how many months it took the other women I interviewed to "get over it." I think of them, some of them years after the abortion, and none of them ever really done with it, and I say, well it takes time. Give it time.

She is also sick of the irregularity of it, the bursting out in all the wrong places. Her husband, her children, her friends—where she should find comfort, she finds herself irritable, snapping. These women who have amniocentesis for "advanced maternal age," they are called "older," but they are really quite young. For many, this is their first serious encounter with grief, with loss. They are inexperienced. They are learning that people do not sit down and cry for more and then for less time each day about the thing they are mourning. They don't cry because the baby died. They cry because the dish dropped, because they're tired, because a kid broke something or was fresh, because, because, because. It gets kicked off sometimes by some baby reminder—Donna said she "couldn't watch a show that dealt with babies without crying for a really long time. Seeing a child with the same name, the same age, was rough." But the grief also gets kicked off by the feeling of grief, of anger, of sadness, which calls forth this unending well of grief. It is the nature of bereavement. You feel sad about some real, this-minute thing, and you grieve from the depths of your well-stocked larder of grief. You have tears in reserve.

Anna says she will have another baby, and then it will be over. But that won't really work either. Previous children don't make up for it—people say to me of Anna and women like her, "Well, she has two healthy children." And new babies don't make up for it. Eleanor feels she went into her next pregnancy too fast, it was "very much a replacement pregnancy." She advises others to wait, give themselves time. Time, of course, is exactly what the women who have had amniocentesis because of their age do not have. But another baby *is*, for those who have the courage to try again, a very great comfort. Sondra, like several of the others I interviewed, decided to give it just one more try, and made arrangements to be sterilized if there was another termination. She says now, holding her new baby:

> You look at this baby, and you say this baby wouldn't be here if it wasn't for that.

She did have her tubes tied after the birth:

> This is it. Close the book. I succeeded. I had a baby. No more babies.

A new baby is a success, a reaffirmation of one's body and motherhood. A new baby is, in itself, a source of comfort, a source of joy and of pleasure. But a new baby does not replace the lost baby. Talk to an older woman about babies lost decades ago. Those were real babies. They are real, they die, and they are mourned. They are not replaced. The loss of a baby is what it is, a loss, a tragedy. It is not a detour on the route to a healthy baby. It is a tragedy of its own, and its grief must be respected.

8

RECONSIDERING THE ISSUES

New Technology, Same Problems

"Nobody really likes this," said a genetic counselor to me about the entire amniocentesis process—the withdrawal of fluid, the long wait, the agonizing choices and the late abortions. "It's a choice between bad and worse. They'll continue to look for blood tests for early abortion."

At first I would have agreed with her premise: an early blood test, an early abortion, that will take care of it, that will be a good solution. Now I am less sure. Now that I understand the solution, I am beginning to see that the real question lies with the problem. I find myself asking: what exactly is the problem for which prenatal diagnosis and selective abortion is the solution?

Earlier testing will shift the problem around, but it will not make it go away. At twenty weeks, we ask how we can justify the abortion. At ten weeks, a very different question may be asked: how can one justify the pregnancy?

One way to understand this shift in issues that comes with improvements in reproductive technology is to see it in the context of the history of technological improvements. What usually accompanies such change is a rise in the standards of production: that is what has happened in every field that modern technology has entered. With the arrival of mechanized factories, the rates of production went up. With the invention of the washing machine, our standards of cleanliness went up. With new reproductive technology, will our standards for our children rise?

These are some of the social issues that we must consider when we examine improvements in prenatal diagnosis. But at the same time as we see it in its larger social context, we can also think about the technology at the level of the individual woman working her way through the prenatal diagnostic process. What will an early test bring her?

One version of early prenatal diagnosis is already available: chorionic villi biopsy, as described in an earlier chapter. When newspaper articles about chorionic villi biopsy began to appear, a number of people who knew I was studying amniocentesis said, essentially, "Well, that's that." With the newer test, they thought, we are through with amniocentesis. Unfortunately, it is not that simple. Chorionic villi biopsy cannot entirely replace amniocentesis, and it brings problems of its own.

The fetus is not the sole product of conception. The union of egg and sperm produce the placenta, the cord, and the amniotic sac as well. The chorionic villi are part of the early development of the placenta. As early as the seventh week of pregnancy a piece of the villi can be cut off—biopsied—using a catheter inserted through the cervix. Since all of these products of conception develop from the same chromosomal union, the chromosomal structure of the placenta and the villi are expected to be the same as that of the fetus. Downs Syndrome and the other chromosomal disorders can be diagnosed by examining tissue removed from the chorionic villi. Instead of a twenty-week diagnosis, the news can come as early as seven weeks—not that much later than a standard pregnancy test. The long tentative pregnancy can be collapsed into the few, always tentative, early weeks.

But there are limitations to the technology. One of the most important is the risk of miscarriage associated with the technique. Strange as it may seem, there are no clear data telling us the rates of very early miscarriages, and so no real way of knowing whether the chorionic villi biopsy significantly increases the rate. Chorionic villi biopsy is associated with miscarriage rates, depending on who is reporting, of 2 to 10 percent.[1] That may be high. Or it may not.

Not every woman who is three weeks "late," and so seven weeks pregnant as medically defined, *knows* that she is pregnant. Even those who do know that they are pregnant may not have ascertained the pregnancy to their physician's satisfaction. Sometimes a woman is late, feels that she is pregnant, and has an early pregnancy test. The test comes back negative, and then she gets her period. Is that just a late period? Or is it an early miscarriage? The pregnancy test indicated that the woman was not carrying a normal pregnancy, but it does not prove that she was not, at that point, in the process of losing a pregnancy. Many, many women of course wait a few extra weeks before having a pregnancy test, and so can never ascertain whether it was a late period or an early miscarriage.

The National Institute of Health is soon to begin a nationwide study of the incidence of miscarriage in early pregnancy. That should give us a basis for comparison with chorionic villi biopsy. And other studies are now under way that should provide better information about the miscarriage rate associated with chorionic villi biopsy.

Even if the rate of miscarriage is considerably higher than that caused by amniocentesis, that may still be an acceptable risk to many women. Facing even a 5 percent risk of miscarriage at seven weeks may be less frightening than the three-in-1000 risk of miscarriage with amniocentesis at sixteen weeks. And especially, learning that there is no chromosomal problem at seven to ten weeks rather than twenty weeks may be worth a great deal. For many women, the decision will have to do with how easily she feels she can get pregnant again.

But spontaneous miscarriage following the procedure is not

the only problem. Accuracy of diagnosis is another. New research is beginning to indicate that it is possible to discover chromosomal abnormalities in placental material which are not to be found in the fetus: that is, the cells of the placenta may develop with missing or with extra chromosomes while the fetus itself has normal chromosomes. Thus some women will abort a normal fetus because of an abnormal placenta. But that too may be an acceptable risk for many women: it may be easier to live with the knowledge that one aborted a presumably normal embryo with an abnormal placenta at nine weeks of gestation than to go through an abortion of even a severely disabled fetus at twenty weeks.

Earlier abortions are undoubtedly easier, in every sense of the word: physically, emotionally, intellectually. But just as late abortions following amniocentesis are not comparable to other late abortions, so early abortions following chorionic villi biopsy may be considerably more emotionally distressing than are the more usual early abortions to avoid an unwanted pregnancy.

But an even more relevant question than how these abortions compare to other early abortions is how do early abortions for fetal defect compare with early spontaneous miscarriages? Because for many women, that will be the trade-off. As I pointed out when discussing the abortion experience following amniocentesis, some of the fetuses that are aborted at twenty weeks would have shortly died by themselves, sparing the woman the anguish of the decision and the weight of responsibility. While the pain and anguish are less early on in the pregnancy, the numbers are greater: most fetal abnormalities do spontaneously miscarry. An earlier test—a test at, say, eight weeks—will find approximately six times as many chromosomal abnormalities as will amniocentesis at sixteen weeks. Thus with chorionic villi biopsy replacing amniocentesis, six times as many women will face the decision to terminate a pregnancy based on knowledge about the fetus.

In spite of this, women might be willing to face both the possibility of aborting a normal fetus, and the responsibility for aborting a fetus that would have miscarried on its own, all to avoid the prolonged tentative pregnancy and the nightmare of late abortion. But still there are problems.

Not everything that can be diagnosed by amniocentesis can be diagnosed by chorionic villi biopsy. Neural tube defects, the failure of the neural tube to close that results in spina bifida or in anencephaly, cannot be diagnosed that early in the pregnancy. Neither can serious, but late-developing fetal anomalies be measured early. Examples include some forms of hydrocephalus, some kidney disorders, and some congenital heart problems. At this point there is absolutely no way that brain damage can be diagnosed at *any* point in pregnancy.

If the goal of prenatal diagnosis is ultimately to diagnose all which is diagnosable, chorionic villi biopsy will not suffice. It will, perhaps, be useful as a first screen. Pregnancies without chromosomal disorders will be left to continue, and to be further tested as they progress. Maternal blood tests are now available that screen for the probability of spina bifida or anencephaly. This is the AFP, alphafetoprotein, test. If the blood test is positive, it is repeated. If it is positive again, amniocentesis is the next step.

One possible scenario for a prenatal diagnostic screening would be a flow chart, proceeding from a chorionic villi biopsy to an AFP screening at the sixteenth week, repeating the AFP test if it gives bad news, and going on, if the news is still bad, to amniocentesis. Bad news can thus come at two points: after the chorionic villi biopsy, at which time the pregnancy can be terminated, or with AFP screening. Bad news results with AFP screening are very common: on the first screening approximately 5 percent of the women tested will have elevated results, or "bad news," but only 1 to 2 percent of those actually have a fetus with a neural tube defect. The second screening, and the amniocentesis, along with ultrasound testing, are used to find the affected pregnancies. But not all women follow through on the medically recommended process. There is anecdotal data suggesting that some terminate after the first suggestion of bad news from the AFP screening.[2] From the medical profession's viewpoint, that is a foolish overreaction. From the point of the woman who is facing imminent quickening, it makes sense: it might be easier to terminate the pregnancy at once, before the fetus has begun to move, than to wait, living with the anxiety and facing the risk of an even later termination.

There is another possible scenario. Some research is beginning to suggest that while elevated AFP levels indicate a risk of neural tube defects, low AFP levels may be indicative of a risk of Downs Syndrome. With this information, an entirely different flow chart presents itself. Expensive, invasive, and very early chorionic bi-opsy might be used only for pregnancies at very high risk: the one-in-four risk facing a carrier-couple of a genetic disease. For the vast majority of pregnancies the risks of miscarriage, of false positive results, the costs—financial, emotional, and otherwise— of chorionic biopsy could be bypassed. Rather than chorionic villi biopsy for advanced maternal age, AFP screening could be done universally. We are already rapidly moving in that di-rection, looking for neural tube defects. In this scenario, women with normal AFP levels would get their medical all-clear at about sixteen weeks. Those with high or low levels would go on to fur-ther testing, including amniocentesis. The sixteen-week tentative pregnancy would be made all but universal—every woman who presented herself for prenatal care would be prescreened this way.

New Technology, New Problems

While neither chorionic villi biopsy nor, for that matter, any other early pregnancy diagnostic test, will ever be able to resolve all of the problems raised by amniocentesis and the relatively-late-in-pregnancy tests, we must not dismiss the special advan-tages of early testing. With such testing some women would be spared very great suffering—consider what Anna, or Beryl, or Andrea went through. How very much easier it would have been for them to have had the diagnosis come in the early weeks of pregnancy. Anna told me it seemed so ironic to her that she got through the whole beginnings of the pregnancy, that time when she, like so many women, was sleepy, a bit nauseous, and most of all still having mixed feelings, still wondering why she was getting herself into this. It was only after those feelings had passed, only after she had "geared up" for the pregnancy, only after the baby had begun to move, after she had started wearing maternity clothes and really feeling like she was having a baby—it was only then that the bad news came. An earlier diagnosis would clearly have spared her much anguish.

To spare Anna and the others such pain is worth a great deal. What we will have to decide, as individuals choosing to use this technology, and as a society choosing to institute mass screening, is whether it is worth the costs of the earlier testing. To repeat, some of the costs are ultimately avoidable: when safer early testing can be done, then the problems of the higher rate of miscarriage precipitated by the testing procedure itself can be avoided. But some of the costs are not avoidable: to spare each Anna, six other women will have to share some of the pain. They will receive diagnoses of chromosomal or other abnormalities, will evaluate the meaning of the potential disability for their fetus, and will, almost certainly, schedule an abortion. The only reference to this I have seen in the medical literature addresses the additional laboratory costs and financial costs related to so many more unfavorable diagnoses. I am more concerned with the emotional costs to each woman.

Will these women be made aware that the embryo or fetus would probably have miscarried anyway? I tend to doubt it. Many medical procedures are based on statistical evaluations of risk. Not every strep throat requires antibiotics; most would clear up by themselves. Not every inflamed appendix requires surgery; most would be all right. Not every prolonged labor requires a caesarean section; most would end well. The reason for doing the procedure or giving the drug, the reason for actively interfering, is that there is usually no way of knowing with certainty *which* cases would not end well, which would end in disability or death. But when one talks to either the practitioners providing the treatments, or to the people receiving the treatments, that is not what one hears. The message that comes across from those engaged in therapeutic encounters is that the therapy is absolutely essential, that the worst-case scenario would surely have evolved without intervention. Each individual feels that she *needed* the procedure, that she, or her baby in the case of caesarean section, was saved by prompt treatment. Knowing this, it is hard for me to imagine that abortions based on unfavorable diagnoses would be presented or experienced as probably unnecessary. Rather than thinking that the pregnancy would probably have miscarried spontaneously, each woman will be encouraged to think that the medical procedures spared her, and her potential child, a lifetime of pain.

There is another, more subtle, and perhaps more frightening problem with earlier diagnosis, a problem inherent in its advantages. The advantage is that it makes the termination easier, so much easier that even if it is more common it may be worth it. But what will it mean to make the termination decision an easier one?

When discussing sex selection, I pointed out that the difficulty of aborting a pregnancy so late worked against the institutionalization of amniocentesis for sex selection. One has to have very strong feelings about wanting only one or the other sex child to be willing to terminate a pregnancy at twenty weeks. But at ten weeks? A very early announcement of fetal sex makes sex selection a much more enticing option. Add in the knowledge of a "wrong sex" fetus, say a third son or a third daughter, at approximately the same time as pregnancy confirmation, and the very normal early pregnancy ambivalence can take on new meaning.

Does this awareness of the effect of early diagnosis on sex selection tell us anything about the very nature of early diagnosis? The answer lies in how like disability is gender.

Both gender and disability are social constructs, ideas about what people are, based on physical characteristics: the "defect" or anomaly that results in disability, and the biological sex that results in the social construction of gender. In either case, we are talking about a biological difference that matters only some of the time, but which influences our perceptions of people virtually all of the time.

Gender, like disability—or disability, like gender—is a way that we classify ourselves and others in the world. There certainly is an element of truth in saying that we are all disabled in some ways, and certainly we are all *potentially* disabled in all ways, all the time. The vast majority of us will in fact eventually develop at least one disability: in that sense, disability is a normal part of life. But it is also true that each society and social grouping establishes definitions of normal, of acceptable variations from normal, and of deviant or stigmatized variations from normal.[3] While all of us have had the experience of being the stigmatized in the company of normals, some of us routinely have that experience in almost every setting: people who are blind, mentally retarded, in wheelchairs, disfigured. While gender is one of the most powerful ways we have of classifying people as like or unlike us, "normal" and "abnormal" is another. One of the classic scenes in the literature of disability is the confrontation: a confrontation not with others, but with self. There is a moment when the newly disabled person looks in the mirror and for the first time sees *self* as one of *them*. For the child who is born disabled, the moment may occur for the parent, perhaps when first bringing the child into the special classroom, and seeing one's own child as one of "those" children. The wrenching pain of that moment is based on the self/other categorization of the world—a categorization so like gender.

Some societies clearly mark males as normal, females as "other"; in some, the parallel is taken to its logical extreme, and femaleness, like disability, is grounds for infanticide. Those who are worried about the potential uses of sex selection sometimes speak of gynecide, the killing off of females. The President's Commission for the Study of Ethical Problems in Medicine and Biomedical and Behavioral Research, in its report on screening and counseling for genetic conditions, spoke strongly against the use of amniocentesis for sex selection, saying that sometimes it is an expression of "sex prejudice," and that "Such attitudes are an affront to the notion of human equality and are especially inappropriate in a society struggling to rid itself of a heritage of such prejudice."[4] Further, the Commission felt that "parental concern with the sex of the fetus (to the point of aborting one of the undesired sex) seems incompatible with the attitude of virtually unconditional acceptance that developmental psychologists have found to be essential to successful parenting. For the good of all children, society's effort should go into promoting the acceptance of each individual—with his or her particular strengths and weaknesses—rather than reinforcing the negative attitudes that lead to rejection."[5]

When Debby Kaplan, a disabled woman active in the disability rights movement, read this statement in the Commission's report, she thought that that was just exactly the kind of statement she wanted to see about disability: that we are ridding ourselves of prejudice and that, for the good of *all* of our children, we must accept *each* unconditionally.[6]

So gender *is* like disability—and I have shown that women experience the gender of their fetuses in ways similar to the way they experience their potential disability. It is not that women experience their own femaleness as disability—no, quite something else. For the woman, femaleness is self, and the female fetus is a normal extension of self. It is the male fetus who is other. And it is the potentially disabled fetus, the diagnosed fetus, who is other.

At twenty weeks of pregnancy, the discovery of the otherness of the fetus is distressing, alienating, as Roberta said of her fetus' diagnosis of Turner's Syndrome. But at twenty weeks, the fetus is also experienced as one's own baby, and however distressing, however alienating, it is no easy thing to reject one's own baby. But at ten weeks? Just as with sex selection, abortion for potential disability, disfigurement, strangeness, otherness, is an easier option. It may even be an easier option than continuing the pregnancy, allowing the other to grow within, to remain in this most intimate of relations.

In the first chapter of this book I introduced a woman who had learned that a bout of beer drinking she had had early in her pregnancy might have had adverse effects on her fetus. Probably not, of course—while we are becoming more aware of the dangers of alcohol abuse during pregnancy, there is still a difference between a few beers and chronic alcoholism. But the counselor did discuss with her the real possibility that some damage might have occurred. The woman said she'd abort. She was early on in the pregnancy. Her response was, "It will only set us back three months." Why should she continue a pregnancy with a fetus that might have been harmed? She felt, as yet, no commitment to this fetus, no sense of motherhood toward it. She was early in a first pregnancy, and the fetus was still an abstraction for her. She aborted, and I assume she started over, as was her intention.

While I found myself profoundly disturbed by her decision, there is a certain level of rational appeal in what she said. What if she had a more definitive diagnosis—not that there was a possibility of some harm done, but rather, that a diagnostic test, such as chorionic villi biopsy, showed that there was indeed something "wrong" with the fetus. Think about Roberta—would she have kept her fetus with the diagnosis of Turner's Syndrome, a diagnosis she found disturbing, frightening, alienating? What happens to all of the ambiguous diagnoses, the mild diseases, the unclear readings, the less than totally disabling impairments? Will we indeed see a rise in the standards of production for children, seeking, as geneticists and population control lobbies have urged, a more perfect product?

In addition to the psychological factors, there are structural reasons for such a "rise in standards" to occur. Insurance companies might very well begin to refuse payment for conditions that were diagnosed early on, but which parents chose to accept.[7] Even with the late abortions required with our current technology, the pressure "not to bring into the world" a child with a disability grows. One woman I observed in a pre-amnio counseling session spoke of a friend of hers who had refused genetic testing. The baby had what she called "brickly bones": its bones broke with even routine handling. Looking at her friend and the baby, she thinks, "She didn't have to have that baby. I'm not blaming her, but . . ."

Blame begins to insinuate itself. The birth of a severely disabled child, when the disability could have been prenatally diagnosed and the pregnancy terminated, begins to be seen as an act of irresponsibility. The standards of production rise, and we are to be held accountable by those standards.

But is it really a rising standard that we are talking about? Even more than *raising* standards, technological advance *establishes* standards: standardization is a part of industrialization. Deviations of all kinds tend to disappear: will that too happen with children? Will we establish a set of norms of acceptability, and then narrow, and narrow, and narrow yet again those norms?

Where *are* we headed?

On Slippery Slopes

One of the arguments that people use against prenatal diagnosis and selective abortion is the issue I just raised: where are we headed? Jeremy Rifkin, one of the most outspoken opponents of the unlimited development of biotechnology, expresses this concern. Rifkin goes past diagnosis to treatment: one of the hopes for treatment of genetic conditions is to alter the genetic material. Rifkin worries about where this may lead:

> Once we decide to begin the process of human genetic engineering, there is really no logical place to stop. If diabetes, sickle-cell anemia, and cancer are to be cured by altering the genetic makeup of an individual, why not proceed to other "disorders": myopia, color blindness, left-handedness? Indeed, what is to preclude a society from deciding that a certain skin color is a disorder?[8]

Philosophers refer to this kind of argument as a "slippery slope" argument: that once started down, there is no way or place to stop. Sometimes it is called the "camel's nose" argument: if you allow the camel to put his nose in the tent, you will never keep out the rest of the camel.

The argument is appealing in its simplicity. Most people agree that abortions for some conditions—minor impairments like nearsightedness, for example, would be just plain wrong. So what if we just draw a clear line, and say, no, we cannot manufacture children to order, and so we must take them as they come.

Beware of simple arguments.

Some fetuses, with some diagnoses, are doomed to suffer and to die. For some the solution to their problems does not lie in responsive design, greater accessibility, improved services or better attitudes toward disability. Consider the problem faced by this mother, who wrote anonymously to *Ms.* magazine:

> When my husband and I were faced with making the choice of whether or not to bear a defective child, in our hearts

there really was no choice. We already had a beautiful little daughter at home whose frail body and mind were wasting away as the result of Niemann-Pick disease. Few things can be more frustrating or heartbreaking for parents than watching a dearly loved child succumb to an illness for which there is no treatment or cure. We knew that we loved any unborn child I might carry far too much to allow her or him to suffer the pain and total body deterioration that Niemann-Pick would bring. Even so, when that dreadful situation presented itself to us, the grief and anguish were overwhelming . . . but we could never willfully subject any other child to the effects of such a devastating disease.[9]

Think too about Andrea, whose fetus was diagnosed as having Tay Sachs disease, an absolute sentence of early childhood death. Would we in any sense keep ourselves pure, avoid slippery slopes and camels in our tents, if we forced these women to bear their babies to suffer and to die?

Simple answers will not work. In what follows, I am going to speak of Tay Sachs disease, but what I have to say applies to Niemann-Pick, cystic fibrosis, sickle-cell anemia, hemophelia, Lesch-Nyhan—all of the dread diseases and conditions that can cause our children suffering, pain, perhaps death; all conditions for which parents can be "carriers," facing risks as high as one-in-two or one-in-four with each pregnancy.

I spoke to my mother about this. She once worked at what was then called "Jewish Chronic Disease Hospital." Before that it was the "Home for the Incurables," and it is now "Kingsbrook Medical Center." There is a whole history of social attitudes toward disease and disability right there in those names, but that is perhaps another story. My mother was there the night of the big East Coast blackout. She was a dental hygienist, and spent that night in the Tay Sachs ward, hand-suctioning babies. Why, I asked. Why did you do it? Why didn't you let them die? What she said was, "That's a hard question. Let me think. That's what the nurses were doing. That's what needed to be done, that's what they were doing. The babies came from all over the world. They didn't seem to be dying, not right then and there. They were sick babies, all schnuffly and stuffed up, but they couldn't cough. And I was suctioning. I did a lot of that in dentistry, I knew how. So I went from one to the other, as they needed it, all night long, with a bulb syringe. I couldn't just stand there and watch a baby choke to death in front of me. Maybe if it were mine, if the quality of its life, if it were suffering, if it were mine and I had watched it suffer for months or years with no chance—maybe when something like that, the blackout, comes along you take advantage of it to let the baby go. But they were sick babies, and we just did it."

My mother, like every other user of modern technology, got caught up in the technology. We do what we know how to do. How can we not? Yet thinking about it, the only possible thing that could make Tay Sachs more dreadful than it inevitably is, is dragging it out for longer. And that was precisely the only thing medicine had to offer. With modern treatment Tay Sachs babies no longer died in the first two to three years, but lived as long as four or five.

There were twenty babies in the room, my mother thinks. Maybe more, maybe even fifty. It was over twenty years ago. There is nowhere in the world anymore where there would be that many Tay Sachs babies in one room. The tragedies are now private. The abortions are private. The suffering is private. No one will walk into a room full of Tay Sachs babies anymore.

Does that mean that we have solved the problem of Tay Sachs or the other diseases like it? Some think so. For instance, when I interviewed genetic counselors and asked about the seriousness of various conditions, some said the question made no sense, because while a given condition may be dreadful to have, it is nonetheless "not too serious because it can be prenatally diagnosed and aborted." Public policy decisions seem to make this assumption as well; in the 1960s there were two to three times as many people working on research in the field of Tay Sachs, funded by the National Institute of Health and by the Tay Sachs Foundation.[10] Curing Tay Sachs disease is no longer the priority it was. The emphasis nowadays has switched to screening programs.[11] Linda Hoffman, a biochemist who has done research identifying the missing enzyme that causes Tay Sachs, says the problem lies with the technology itself: "We just don't know that much about brain chemistry. I don't think people don't want to look, they just don't know how." That, she says, is true about curing Tay Sachs, and it is also true about locating the biochemical basis for the mental retardation in Downs Syndrome. As we talked, she kept using the phrase, "The technology is just not there yet." I am sure that that is quite true. But is technology something that grows "like Topsy," or does technological change come from social pressure? And where does the social pressure go when the room full of Tay Sachs babies is replaced by fifty individual grieving women like Andrea?

The use of prenatal diagnosis and selective abortion privatizes the tragedy. A baby is real to anyone who sees it. The tragedy of a dying baby is real to anyone who stands there and looks, who holds the baby. The horror of a room filled with dying babies is real to anyone who enters. But a fetus is real only to the woman who claims it as her baby. To others the abstraction may be important—to the "right to life," to the "protectors of the unborn"—but the particular fetus a woman was ready to mother is real only to that woman, and maybe, just maybe, to a few people who are close to her. But early on, when its kicking is hers alone, when its movements and responses, when its dance inside is private for her, then her fetus, her baby, is real only for her. In a world in which women's reality is secondary, is seen as emotional and nonrational, that reality is not credited. Remember the abandonment experienced by the women who terminated pregnancies—they were expected to be grateful, not to grieve. As Sondra said when talking about how people kept their distance: "I wanted company. I wanted sympathy and attention, and everything people have when they lose someone."

When we privatize the tragedy, that is not what happens. The loss the women experience is not a socially recognized or shared loss, and may be treated as no loss at all. Aren't you pleased, we ask.

When I began researching prenatal diagnosis, I think somewhere in the back of my mind I held on to the idea that abortion was just an interim solution, until cures are found. Now I am forced to consider that the technology may preclude going be-

yond itself. If the loss is unrecognized, turned around into a solution, then the pressure is off. The absence of a room full of
dying babies certainly takes away much of the motivation for
Tay Sachs research. The fundraising, the appeals, the pressure
on individual physicians and on researchers—all of that is pretty
much gone.

But we do know that most of the major breakthroughs in medical research have come not from looking for specific cures, but
from basic research. What are our possibilities in that direction?
Let us say that the enzyme lacking in Tay Sachs disease is not
only artificially produced, but the next important step is taken,
and a way of getting that enzyme directly to the brain is developed. That would be the cure. Some version of that story would
be the cure for any number of the diseases for which prenatal
diagnosis and selective abortion is the only current solution. But
on whom are we going to try this cure? The few babies whose
parents are unalterably opposed to abortion? The occasional
baby that slips through the screening net? Even if the cure works
with those babies, how many years will it be before other people
will take the chance? With prenatal testing and abortion, especially early testing and abortion readily available, who would
have the courage to take the chance on an unproven cure? And
so how will cures come to be proven? The symptoms of Tay
Sachs do not show up for the first six to nine months of life. How
long will a "cured" Tay Sachs child have to live without symptoms before others would be willing to risk bearing such a child?
It would in some ways be *worse* if a cure only delayed symptoms
for some years.

It is not just Tay Sachs disease, of course. It is not even only
the recessive conditions for which parents know they are carriers. What of Downs Syndrome itself? What if we routinize prenatal testing for Downs Syndrome so that virtually every fetus is
tested. If selective abortion were to be widely accepted, then
there would be very few Downs Syndrome babies born. Those
that were would be primarily children of women who had no
prenatal care, women who are the poorest of the poor, the least
educated, least powerful people in the society. Where will the
pressure be to find cures for the problems brought by Downs
Syndrome?

If widely used, the technology of prenatal diagnosis and selective abortion is not an interim measure, but locks out the possibility of developing cures. The more conditions we can diagnose prenatally, and especially the earlier the diagnosis can be done, the more we are going to be locked in, with fancier and earlier detection, more and more controlled pregnancies, more and more private tragedies, more and more responsibilities for producing the best possible "product" out of each pregnancy, rejecting all the "defectives."

And here comes the camel again, poking his way into our tent. Can we reject the technology, make the babies suffer? It certainly seems very wrong to do so just in order to have babies around to experiment on to find cures. Are there no solutions to this problem?

Genetic Ties: Rethinking Parenthood

When there seems to be no way out of a problem it may be time to stop looking for solutions, and go back and look again at the problem. Is Tay Sachs disease—or any of these painful, fatal, miserable, devastating conditions—the real problem? Obviously it is, from the point of view of the baby so afflicted, or the parents of that baby. But if we move back a few steps, there is another problem we face, one that might be easier to solve. That problem is: how can Tay Sachs carriers—or carriers of some other such condition—have healthy children?

The solutions that we can come up with are always structured by the way we pose our questions. If we ask, "How can we prevent this *couple*, with their one-in-four chance, from producing a child who will have the disease?" then prenatal diagnosis and selective abortion is the answer. But if we say instead, "How can this *woman* have a pregnancy that will not result in a Tay Sachs baby?" then there is a very different answer: she need not mate with a carrier. Looking at it this way, we see that it limits us to say the disease is the problem. The problem is maintaining genetic paternity. If that were not so, then artificial insemination with noncarrier donor sperm would be readily accepted.

Andrea thought about this. After she had her abortion, the doctor told her that she had three choices: adoption, artificial insemination, or trying again. She and her husband decided that they should try once more and see what happened. She waited ten months and then became pregnant. In her first pregnancy, the one that had resulted in the abortion for Tay Sachs, she had put on weight and started wearing maternity clothes by the third month. She knew that she and her husband were carriers, but "still you don't really want to believe it could happen." Her second pregnancy: "I dieted, I did not go into maternity clothes. They could not do the amniocentesis on time because I did not have enough fluid and weight and all, whereas the first time I had my amniocentesis early. The second time I did not go into maternity clothes except at the very end. I did not tell anyone I was pregnant. It was totally two different experiences."

Why did she put herself through this?

> We were kind of thinking about artificial insemination, but I really can't—I don't know if I could really do it to tell you the truth . . . your husband has to be very—here we have a child from the two of us, and I don't know how he would react to a child that wasn't his, knowing in the back of his mind that child wasn't his.

Did Andrea go through the trauma of a second pregnancy with a one-in-four chance of Tay Sachs and another abortion to avoid Tay Sachs disease, or to maintain her husband's paternity?

While many men, especially men who are infertile, have been accepting of artificial insemination with donor sperm (AID), some men have been unwilling to forgo genetic fatherhood, unwilling to be social fathers to children who are not "theirs." There are women who have gone through repeated pregnancies leading to abortions for conditions like Tay Sachs rather than use artificial insemination. While it is tempting to see that as one of the worst examples of patriarchal dominance, a clear case of women suffering to maintain men's right of paternity, there is perhaps a kinder perspective. By having so discouraged men's active involvement with their babies and young children, we have as a society made of fatherhood a tenuous connection. The emphasis on men's genetic tie to their children serves as a counterbalance not only to the powerful biological relationship of pregnancy, but to the equally or more powerful social relationship of motherhood.

New reproductive technology may bring us new options. Amniocentesis, chorionic villi biopsy, and other techniques for prenatal diagnosis are just a part of the new reproductive technology. Artificial insemination is an older technique, and we now have in vitro fertilization, egg donations, and embryo transplants. As these reproductive technologies proliferate they challenge our definitions of motherhood and of fatherhood, and make us think very differently about the products of conception.[12]

We have grown accustomed to distinguishing social and biological parenthood—our system of anonymous adoption taught us that. But the new technology adds new distinctions: we can now think in terms of "genetic" parents, those who provide half of the genetic material for a child; "physiologic" parents, those who nurture and grow an embryo/fetus in their bodies; and "social" parents, those who rear a child.

Women never before were able to think about genetic motherhood without pregnancy, or pregnancy without genetic motherhood: if we were biological mothers, carrying babies, then we were genetic mothers. But making the inseparable separate is what the technology of reproduction is all about. Now women can carry in their bodies babies that are not "theirs"—not theirs genetically, that is. And women now have the potential for genetic parenthood without physiologic motherhood: in essence, women can now *father* children.

Of all the strange concepts and relationships brought by the new reproductive technology, the idea of women "fathering" children is perhaps the strangest, the idea we have the hardest time grasping. To be a father is to have a child of your "seed" growing in another person's body. A biological father contributes half the genetic basis for the child-to-be, but does not contain, grow, or nurture the fetus. That is the essence of biological fatherhood: the father is a genitor. With the new technology of reproduction, women too can now have their "seed" growing in another woman's body.

Up until recently, women's genetic material was inaccessible without motherhood. Women could not "donate" an egg, without "donating" a child, a baby that they had grown to term in their own bodies. But with in vitro fertilization, in which eggs are taken from a woman and fertilized outside of her body, that is no longer the case. Not that we are yet ready to have babies without mothers—the fertilized egg needs a woman to carry it, to grow a baby out of the egg, to mother it. Closely related to in vitro fertilization is the technology of embryo transplants. In embryo transplants, embryos are removed from the woman in whom they were conceived and transplanted to another woman in whom they are carried and by whom they are born. With this "transplanting" of women's genetic material, new questions arise: who is the biological mother, the "donor" or the "host"? Strangely enough, when we try to figure out who is the "real" mother, we are forced to confront the meaning not so much of *motherhood* as of *fatherhood*—because one of those women fathered the child, and the other carried it.

Like these women who "donate" eggs that doctors plant in other women's bodies, men have "donated" (or sold) their seed to be placed in a woman's body by a doctor. This is "artificial" insemination: a syringe, rather than a penis, placing the semen in the vagina. The continued secrecy surrounding artificial insemination is telling. Adoption is discussed openly, and the first sets of parents of babies fertilized in vitro held press conferences, but very few people who have used artificial insemination seem ready to come out of the closet. Maybe that is because biological fatherhood still means genetic parenthood, and social fatherhood is so ambiguous. It is not really being a child-rearer—so many fathers do so little child-rearing. What makes a man really the father of a child in this society, if not genetics? And a child without a father in a patriarchal society is called illegitimate.

What lessons can be drawn from men's experiences with biological fatherhood to help us understand the meaning of splitting off genetic parenthood from pregnancy for women? And what can the new reproductive technology for women tell us about fatherhood?

If we believe that the *real* mother is the egg donor, and the surrogate is the "host," the "rented womb," then the importance of genetic parenthood—the importance of *fatherhood*—is underlined. If that genetic tie is important for a woman, more important than the pregnancy experience, if it is the ovum that makes the child "hers"—as Andrea spoke of a child of her husband's sperm as being "his"—then the importance of fatherhood is reaffirmed. In contrast, if we say that the "real" mother is the one who bears the child—and I think this is much truer to most women's feelings—then we are minimizing the importance of being the "genitor," and therefore minimizing biological fatherhood.

For women who, like Andrea, carry diseases like Tay Sachs, a new option opens up with this technology. They can sacrifice their own "fatherhood," their genetic ties to their children, and maintain their husband's fatherhood. The women can enter biological motherhood at the point after conception, carrying and birthing what will be their social children. Such a woman might not be a genetic parent, but social motherhood would begin with a biological tie, with pregnancy. Does it make sense to say that a pregnant woman is not a biological mother? Can we look at a woman heavy with child and say the child is not hers?

Thus even though embryo transplants and in vitro fertilization with donor ovum are more expensive, more painful, and more invasive treatments, with much lower success rates than artificial insemination, as these technologies become available they will be used. They will substitute for women's genetic ties to their children, and leave paternity intact. Woman as genitor will be discounted, man as genitor will be reaffirmed. Father as creator of the seed and mother as his vessel will be reified. For individual, committed, heterosexual couples who are identified carriers of serious genetic diseases, a new option will be available.

There is of course no single right answer, no definitive solution for the problems presented by a serious genetic disease, one which causes babies pain, suffering, and death. Some would reject all of these technological solutions. I spoke to a woman in her 80s about this work I have been doing, especially the interviews with women who, in great anguish, terminated pregnancies to spare their babies pain. This woman, who had led a long, full life, a life not without its own tragedies, saw it all differently:

> This amnio, it's just trading one grief for another, it's just a trade, just one for the other. So it would be better not to do it, wouldn't it? You can't take anyone else's pain, not even your children's—don't they know they can't? When I had diphtheria, my mother could comfort me, she stayed in my bed with me, she held me—but she couldn't have it for me.

But what, I asked, of the children who die so young, in pain, what then?

> One life to a customer, one to a customer. You're alone. Ultimately we're all alone, we're each alone.

For some people, this is the answer: we accept our children, we comfort them, we do what we can, but we cannot take their pain and their lives for them. For others, that is not enough. For some, it is better not to have a child, then to have a child who will suffer. For some, the best gift we can give our children is to forego genetic ties. Perhaps, for some, prenatal diagnosis and selective abortion is the best answer. But that answer, the one that our society is rapidly institutionalizing as the accepted solution, is costly. That solution demands the most of women. It asks women to establish all of the ties of parenthood: genetic, biological, and early social ties as we begin to feel like mothers to our babies within, and then be ready to break those ties. If that is the solution we choose, it behooves us to consider the way we have defined the problem.

Motherhood and Morality

And so we come full circle: what exactly is the problem for which prenatal diagnosis and selective abortion is the solution? Is it to allow carriers of genetic diseases to have children of their "own"? Then there may be other and better ways of achieving that end. Is it to prevent disability and create more perfect "products"? Then how will we ever set the standards for children?

Is it to spare women the demands of raising disabled children? Some of the proponents of genetic counseling and prenatal diagnosis would agree with that last statement, would agree that prenatal diagnosis exists to help women who want to be mothers. As one genetic counselor told me, she never sees a child with a recognizable genetic syndrome but that she thinks of some mother she helped spare that heartbreak. And some opponents of prenatal diagnosis also think that its purpose is to spare women: they say it is an attempt by selfish women to avoid difficult-to-raise children.

Selfishness may be the most hurtful accusation we can hurl at mothers. For women in general, but for mothers especially, goodness is in giving, in caring for others.[13] Over and over again, women learn that the time of women, the very lives of women, are unimportant in themselves. We are valued predominantly in terms of how much we give to others. Men and women both learn that women's needs are less important, that women's needs, and especially mothers' needs, come second, if at all. Women's definition of "goodness" as being willingness to respond to the needs of others rather than their own needs reflects this shared cultural value of the expendability of women. The feminist perspective, in contrast, allows us to bring women back in as people whose lives *do* count. That is why feminists have almost universally supported women's right to abort unwanted pregnancies: it is an affirmation that the lives of women are important.

Consider, in contrast, this story, which makes the rounds of the right-to-life movement:

> How would you advise a mother who was pregnant with her fifth child based on the following set of facts: her husband had syphilis, she had tuberculosis. Their first child was born blind. The second child died. The third was born deaf. The fourth had tuberculosis. If you said to abort, you would have just killed the great composer, Ludwig van Beeth_____

In a similar vein, I have heard a number of people wh____ abled arguing against prenatal diagnosis and selectiv___ by saying that had such technology been available, ____ not have been here. It is a compelling argument. But the disabled do not have the corner on that market: lots and lots of us would not be here if our mothers had had better access to abortion. Some of us are the sixth children of women who were tired, sick, had given all they had to give long before we came—women who yearned for peace and time for themselves. Some of us arrived in our mothers' lives far too early, interrupting all that they had planned for themselves. Maybe, for our mothers' own sake; some of us *should* have been aborted. What, after all, became of Mrs. Beethoven? Maybe with one deaf, one blind, and one tubercular child, with her own illness and her husband's, maybe she should have had that abortion.

Trying to justify or to fail to justify any abortion based on the kind of person the fetus might turn out to be is a dangerous thing. How much of a sacrifice can we demand of a woman? And should we determine the extent of her sacrifice based on the potential contribution of the child: are composers worth more of a sacrifice than bakers or street-cleaners—or more mothers? We embark on a dangerous path when we justify abortions on any standard other than the life of the woman contemplating the abortion. Only she can know the sacrifice in her own life of continuing, or of ending, a pregnancy.

How much any given child demands of a mother is based not only on the condition of the child, but even more on the conditions of the mother's life. Any analysis of a woman's right to choose an abortion has to recognize the context in which the decision to abort is made, the circumstances in which the woman is placed. As Rosalyn Petchesky has stated:

The "right to choose" means very little when women are powerless . . . women make their own reproductive choices, but they do not make them just as they please; they do not make them under conditions which they themselves create but under social conditions and constraints which they, as mere individuals, are powerless to change.[14]

We live in a system in which women and children are both devalued, an anti-child, anti-woman society. It is women and children who are poor, whose needs are not being met. In this system, women and children are pitted against each other, competing for scarce resources. The mother finds herself becoming a resource: her own life and, specifically, her own time are to be divided between herself and her children. Whatever the children get, it may very well be coming off the life of the mother—in time, in attention, in emotional support, sometimes in food and basic necessities. It is in this context that she is judged in terms of her willingness to sacrifice. The more she gives of herself to her children, the better a mother the society says she is. The more she holds back of herself, for herself, the more she runs the risk of being the "wicked stepmother," evil in her selfishness.

Especially because women and children are both devalued, to speak for the rights or needs of either to be met contributes to the devaluation of the other. That is why feminists have been accused of being "anti-family," "anti-child." If the mother is the child's main resource, and one suggests that the mother has her own needs, then the implied loss is the child's. If the mother will not sacrifice for the child, what will become of it? On the other hand, those who concern themselves with the needs of the children have been seen as "anti-feminist," against the "liberation" of women. If one deplores the condition of institutionalized day care and says a baby deserves more, if one talks about "maternal deprivation" or the needs of children for love and attention, such talk is seen as reactionary.

The problem with the arguments that babies needs must be met lies with the underlying premises regarding how and by whom the needs are to be met. The needs of the children are set against the needs of the mothers. We speak of *maternal* deprivation, not *parental* deprivation, or more clearly, deprivation of attention and affection. It is not fathers, and certainly not all of us as a society, that are being asked to respond to the very real, quite recognizable, and reasonable needs of infants and children for attention, comfort, love, money, and time. What should be a relatively harmless statement of the needs of babies for devoted care becomes dangerous in a context in which the needs of children are pitted against the needs of mothers.

When one adds to the situation the virtually total devaluation of the needs of the disabled, the "defective," "in-valid" people, the place of selective abortion in our society is highlighted.

Women know that children with "special needs" make special demands. The society as a whole has shown itself unwilling to meet those demands—we are as a society unwilling to meet the ordinary needs of ordinary children. With wonderful and notable exceptions, fathers and other family members have not risen to the occasion. The burden of child-rearing, of all child-rearing, has fallen overwhelmingly on individual mothers. While those in the disability rights movement rightly resent the use of the word "burden" to describe their lives, it is not a description unique to the disabled. Children, all children, can be described as burdensome when their needs fall almost exclusively on one person. Yes, they are also delightful, joyous, pleasures and treasures, whether able-bodied or disabled. But side by side with the joys of child-rearing are the burdens; along with the pleasures come the sacrifices. The individual woman, or at very best, the individual couple or family, can demand more and more from the society for the child—and in fact making such demands becomes one of the chief responsibilities of the parents of a disabled child. But it is clear to us all that the society will not respond with openness and generosity, and most assuredly cannot be depended on to continue responding to her child's needs when the mother is no longer there. Even if the woman were to be willing to sacrifice herself entirely to meet the needs of the child, it may still not be enough.

Carol Gilligan, in her study of women's moral development, said:

When birth control and abortion provide women with effective means for controlling their fertility, the dilemma of choice enters a central arena of women's lives. Then the relations that have traditionally defined women's identities and framed their moral judgment no longer flow inevitably from their reproductive capacity, but become matters over which they have control.[15]

With selective abortion, the potential for deciding not only whether or not to bear a child, but what kind of a child to bear, the element of choice enters directly into the maternal role. Selective abortion means also selective acceptance, a fundamental challenge to the social institution of motherhood. Selective abortion, selective acceptance, selective motherhood—a denial of the myth of the all-giving, all-accepting mother. With birth control and abortion, women were able to choose not to bear children, not to be mothers. But with selective abortion, we ask mothers to decide just what kind of child they choose to mother.

So choice enters a new arena of women's lives. In a world that supports and values neither mothers nor children, we ask individual mothers to look at their individual fetuses, and decide whether this child will be asking too much of her.

Gilligan says that in our moral development, women most especially want not to hurt anyone:

> When no option exists that can be construed as being in the best interests of everybody, when responsibilities conflict and decision entails the sacrifice of somebody's needs, then the woman confronts the seemingly impossible task of choosing the victim.[16]

Such is the nature of choice for women who would now be mothers.

APPENDIX:
GUIDELINES FOR
PERSONAL
DECISION-MAKING

People ask me now, knowing that I have done this research, "Well, what would you do—would you have amnio?" And I answer that I don't know what I would do, that I am just very grateful that I had my children already, that I am through now. I was 33 when my second child was born in 1981, clearly, by the standards of the day, "too young" to have amniocentesis. Thirty-three is no longer considered quite so young. If I was 33 and pregnant now I would have to make a decision about amnio; I could not ignore it as I was able to in 1981.

That answer, that I'm just glad I had my children already, is not at all unique to me. Almost every older woman who hears about amniocentesis and the decisions that women face today has the same response. Those of you who read this while pregnant or planning pregnancies, those who are trying to decide if and how to use the new technology for prenatal diagnosis, are in a difficult position.

It may be that in the greater scheme of things this is just an awkward moment in medical history. Medical expansion into the care of the fetus follows the pattern of earlier medical expansions: diagnosis precedes treatment. The first step in the development of new medical expertise is usually the "discovery" of a disease. The newly discovered diseases or syndromes are named, often after the physician who first categorizes the condition. In later stages of medical expansion, diagnostic techniques are refined. It is usually only then that treatments are developed.

This is the point that medicine has reached in fetology: the ability to diagnose far exceeds the ability to treat. There are now literally hundreds of diseases, impairments, defects, and conditions that are prenatally diagnosable. There are a handful that are prenatally treatable, and those few only on an experimental basis. Thus as things now stand, when serious defects are diagnosed, the only real choices a woman faces are continuing the pregnancy with the knowledge of the diseases or conditions her baby will face, or terminating the pregnancy. It is hard to imagine more difficult choices for a woman to face.

Perhaps someday fetal treatments will be discovered, or perhaps some other solutions as yet unthought will come to be. Or it may be that in fetology diagnosis will always exceed treatment, and these dilemmas will be with women who wish to be mothers forever more. In either case, for the currently pregnant woman, questions about whether and how to use the new technology for diagnosis arise with all of the immediacy and urgency that pregnancy entails.

What follows are my suggestions for issues to consider in making the decision about whether or not to have amniocentesis, and for those who choose to have the testing done, some suggestions for ways of coping with the decision-making and the process. Like the genetic counselors I interviewed, I too want to be "nondirective" about the big issues: no one can decide for a woman whether or not she should have amniocentesis. But I do know some of the issues one should consider in making the decision.

For your convenience, I will review here the basic diagnostic techniques that are available and the conditions which can be diagnosed (Part I) before discussing the factors that should enter into the decision (Part II). I will close with some suggestions for those who have chosen amniocentesis (Part III).

PART I

The Diagnostic Techniques

There are three basic approaches to diagnosing fetal conditions. One is to "see," or to visualize, the fetus in some way. X rays were used for this purpose for many years, although they enable us to visualize only the fetal skeleton and, as we now know, pose serious risks to the fetus. Sonography, the use of sound waves, is the current alternative to radiation. Sonography, unlike X rays, shows the soft tissue, the organ development of the fetus, as well as the skeleton. The long-term risks of sonography are now being hotly debated.

A second diagnostic approach is to measure various substances produced, or failed to be produced, by the fetus. In a regular patient, blood and urine are readily accessible, and so often used in diagnosis. Not so for the fetus. Some fetal substances can be measured in the mother's blood, but most cannot.

The third diagnostic approach is to examine fetal cells to see the chromosomes of the fetus, the basic genetic building material. Again, in a regular patient such cells are easily accessible, but not so for the fetus lying protected within the womb.

The relatively new technique that has enabled the rapid expansion of prenatal diagnosis is amniocentesis: the withdrawal of some of the amniotic fluid, containing fetal products and fetal cells. A needle inserted in the mother's abdomen, below the navel, can be used to penetrate the amniotic sac and withdraw fluid for testing. With the use of sonography, the chances of the needle hitting the placenta or the fetus itself can be minimized, though not entirely removed. By examining this fluid hundreds of genetic conditions can be diagnosed, including the "inborn errors of metabolism," in which the fetus fails to produce or overproduces some necessary substance, and the chromosomal defects, in which the genetic material itself is observably abnormal.

Amniocentesis cannot be done early in pregnancy, because it must await the availability of sufficient fluid for testing, usually at around the sixteenth week. Results take approximately four weeks; the diagnosis is thus not usually available until the twentieth week of pregnancy, or halfway through. From this stem the most serious concerns most women have about amniocentesis. A newer technique is chorionic villi biopsy, which can be done much earlier in pregnancy, but is still experimental. Chorionic villi biopsy appears to be associated with a high rate of miscarriage.

As with ultrasound and with chorionic villi biopsy, the risks of amniocentesis are under debate. Some risks stem from the damage that can be done by the needle that withdraws the fluid, including the risk of infection and miscarriage. Performed by expert workers, the risk of miscarriage is approximately three-in-1000. Without amniocentesis, thirty-two in one thousand pregnancies will spontaneously abort after the sixteenth week; with amniocentesis, the number rises to thirty-five in one thousand. It can be difficult or impossible to tell if any particular miscarriage was caused by the amniocentesis or would have occurred anyway. Other risks come from the loss of fluid, which in some women may not be replaced adequately, and some studies have linked this to orthopedic problems. Unknown risks of amniocentesis include the long-term safety of the ultrasound exposure necessary to place the needle correctly.

The Conditions to be Diagnosed

There are some genetic conditions for which parents can be "carriers," such as sickle-cell anemia and Tay Sachs disease. These and other conditions can only be diagnosed if the laboratory knows what to look for. Separate tests must be done on the fluid in order to diagnose these conditions. Therefore genetic counseling and history-taking by a trained genetic counselor is important if amniocentesis is to be as useful as possible.

For parents who have watched one child suffer and slowly, in-evitably die with a condition like Tay Sachs disease, the avail-ability of prenatal diagnosis can fundamentally change their reproductive options. When both parents are carriers of such a disease, each pregnancy they have has a one-in-four chance of producing a fetus with the condition. But prenatal diagnosis is not the *only* or necessarily the *best* option for people in this situa-tion. See Chapter 8 on the use of other reproductive technologies in this situation.

Very few parents are faced with such high risks of reproduc-tive tragedy. The much more common uses of prenatal diagnosis are for the neural tube defects, including spina bifida, and for chromosomal disorders, especially Downs Syndrome.

The chances of bearing a fetus with Downs Syndrome, which causes mental retardation and is associated with some physical problems as well, rises with the age of both the mother and the father. There is no particular age at which the risks jump dramat-ically, but rather a steady increase. For a woman at age 30, the chances are roughly one-in-1000; at age 35, one-in-350; and at age 40, one-in-100. It may well be that other age-related fac-tors—perhaps diet, general health, exposure to environmental toxins and radiation—are the real causes of Downs Syndrome, and not age per se. But so far age alone has been the only factor demonstrably linked to Downs Syndrome in the general popula-tion.

PART II

Decision-Making

Deciding whether or not to have amniocentesis is a balancing and weighing of risks, costs, and benefits. There is no right or wrong answer, and certainly no medical or technical answer as to whether amniocentesis should be done.

It is often claimed that amniocentesis is appropriate at the point where the risks of the procedure causing a miscarriage are no greater than the risks of the condition for which the fetus is being tested. According to that logic, when both parents are carriers for a condition, amniocentesis makes sense, because its risks are so much lower. For Downs Syndrome, the "balancing-out" point, the point at which the risks of the condition equal the risks of a miscarriage from the procedure, is at age 35: at 35 both numbers are roughly one-in-350. That is one of the reasons that age 35 has been made a "magic" number: women just below 35 have been encouraged to think of themselves as "low risk"; women just over 35 as "high risk," even though the increase in risks is slight and gradual.

But weighing these two risks against each other is overly simplistic. The *meanings* and not just the *probabilities* of both risks must be considered by each woman, for herself and her family. The meaning of disability is not the same to all people, nor are all disabilities the same. Most of us know too little about disabilities to fully understand their meaning in our children's lives.

As with disability, miscarriage means different things to different women. Some women get pregnant fairly easily, and feel that they would not be emotionally devastated by a miscarriage. Other women may have spent years trying to get pregnant, and feel that this may be their last chance at having a baby. And, regardless of the ease with which the pregnancy was achieved, some women feel a strong commitment to *this* pregnancy, to what they feel is their baby, early on, and feel its loss would be a death in the family.

The meaning of pregnancy loss is the basic question in considering amniocentesis. The risk of miscarriage from the procedure is one concern. But more fundamentally, the potential for pregnancy loss, through abortion, is built right into amniocentesis. Terminating a wanted pregnancy at twenty weeks is a profoundly wrenching, painful experience. The potential for such a termination casts its shadow back over the entire first half of the pregnancy, creating the "tentative pregnancy." A woman's commitment to her pregnancy under the conditions imposed by amniocentesis can only be tentative. She cannot ignore it, but neither can she wholeheartedly embrace it. The pregnancy may not be leading to a baby, but to an abortion.

Women usually manage to keep the anxiety under control— we are strong—but there is a cost to that: the cost is in the developing relationship with the fetus, and the woman's developing sense of herself as the baby's mother. The problems and difficulties created by the tentative pregnancy are discussed in Chapter 4. In its focus on the statistics of risk, the medical model blinds us to these other costs of prenatal diagnosis.

Be Prepared?

Some women separate the decision to have amniocentesis from the decision to abort. If a woman is quite sure that she would not abort, she sometimes considers amniocentesis in order to be prepared for the birth of a baby with problems, particularly for the "older" mother, for Downs Syndrome.

On the whole, there is not much one need do immediately to prepare for a baby with Downs Syndrome. Though the chances are greater with a baby with Downs Syndrome, the baby may or may not have physical problems requiring immediate attention—just as is true of a baby without Downs Syndrome. For any birth, medical and neonatal services should be available or on call. The same decision-making issues arise with Downs Syndrome as with any problem: parents have to decide what sorts of medical procedures are appropriate for their baby. These decisions always have to be made—and made again and again—as circumstances develop. Knowing ahead of time that the baby has Downs Syndrome does not tell you what services will be needed in the hours and days after birth. For other, later decisions, there is time after the baby is born.

The psychological benefits of being prepared must also be weighed against the very real costs of preparation. For the minority of women who are completely opposed to all abortions under all circumstances, the knowledge of serious fetal anomalies, conditions that are going to cause the baby great pain, disability, or death, makes continuing the pregnancy and birthing the child enormously stressful.

There are other costs, too. Knowing the baby will be born with a particular disability encourages us to focus on that disability rather than on the individuality of the child. Dealing with an abstract diagnosis is very different than dealing with particular problems in one's own baby or child. This is especially important for the less severe conditions diagnosable by amniocentesis. See Chapter 6 for a discussion of these ambiguous diagnoses.

The Reassurance of Amniocentesis

The final issue I suggest you consider in making your decision is the question of reassurance. Since the risks of finding a disabling condition are usually quite low, some women feel that they may as well have the test and be reassured.

The question of anxiety and reassurance in amniocentesis is complex—so much so that one genetic counselor I interviewed said that she likes best about her job "relieving some of the anxiety a pregnancy brings," and another likes least "causing anxiety." While we must acknowledge the relief and reassurance amniocentesis provides, it is important to place that in the context of the anxiety it generates.

You are at *very* much higher risk of developing, say, breast cancer, than you are of having a fetus with Downs Syndrome. What if a test were developed which women could take at age 25 that would tell us whether or not we were going to have breast cancer? Perhaps we would spend our twenty-fourth year in great anxiety, thinking often about the risks of breast cancer. The test would offer incredible reassurance. We might wonder how women ever managed to go for years and years never knowing whether or not they would have breast cancer. For the 99 or so out of 100 40-year-old women of earlier generations who bore children without Downs Syndrome, that fear did not constantly haunt the pregnancy. But it might now.

Thus amniocentesis is able to allay only those fears it first raises. On the other hand, some women take more reassurance from amniocentesis than it objectively has to give. That is, once told the fetus does not have the abnormalities for which it was tested, some women feel "home free." Such is not the case. Even with perfect accuracy (and particularly with neural tube defects, diagnoses can be missed), only a small percentage of all birth defects, let alone later causes of illness and disability, have been eliminated. The possibility of spending the rest of one's life caring for a sick or disabled child can *never* be eliminated by prenatal testing. I worry about women who say they only dare have children because prenatal diagnosis is available. Motherhood is, among other things, one more chance for a speeding truck to ruin your life.

In Sum

As a medical/technical procedure, prenatal diagnosis can be routinized, the conditions under which it is done standardized. But prenatal diagnosis is very much more than a medical procedure, and can never be routinized or standardized for those experiencing it. The decisions cannot be made on the basis of the statistics of risk, and no cost-benefit analysis will ever be able to quantify the emotional costs—or for that matter the very real emotional benefits which are possible.

As you struggle with this decision, reach out to others. Read Chapter 3 to see how other women have made the choice, but it is terribly important to find people in whom you can confide. No one should be isolated in the decision-making process, and no marriage should be expected to bear all of it. Isolation is no way to enter motherhood.

PART III

Suggestions for Those Who Have Decided to Use Amniocentesis for Prenatal Diagnosis

What follows are my suggestions for ways of coping with the amniocentesis experience. Rather than hedging this with "you might want to consider" and other such artifice, I will write in simple declarative statements—straightforward "do this" and "don't do that." I feel free to write this way because I know that you, as reader, are absolutely free to close the book and ignore me.

My first piece of advice is unusual, coming from an author: *do not read this entire book now.* If you are quite sure that you want to have amniocentesis, or if you have had the test and are awaiting your results, you have no need of Chapter 7, on grieving the genetic defect. The chances of your finding yourself in the position of having a bad diagnosis are so small, so remote, that there is no reason for you to deal with those issues at this point. I certainly wouldn't want to have read it while I was pregnant. In the very unlikely event of your getting bad news from your prenatal diagnosis, you should then read Chapter 7.

Announce the pregnancy. Do not keep the pregnancy a secret while you wait for your results. Announce it just as you would if you were not having amniocentesis. Remember, we do not wait six months to see if a newborn baby will die of crib death before sending out the birth announcements. For one thing, we expect the baby to live: most do. For another, if the baby were to die, we would need all the help we could get.

These same reasons apply in prenatal diagnosis. You should expect good news. Even with the very high-risk situations in which both parents are known carriers of a genetic disease, three out of four prenatal diagnoses will produce good news. For the more usual tests for chromosomal disorders, there will be scores if not hundreds of good-news diagnoses for every bad-news diagnosis. I interviewed genetic counselors who have worked for a solid year without ever finding a case of Downs Syndrome. Yes, you could be the one to get the bad news. You could also fall down the stairs and break your neck, and your house could be hit by lightning. But you have good reason to expect good news.

On the other hand, if you were to get bad news, or even if you were to have a miscarriage and lose the pregnancy spontaneously, you will need support. Denying the pregnancy publicly, or trying to deny it privately to yourself while you wait for results, does not work. If things go well, it is the test that will hardly have mattered, and the first half of your pregnancy, the first bulges in your body, the first flutters of movement, which will matter. Do not deny yourself the pleasures of these experiences. When things do not go well, when the pregnancy ends in an abortion, those women who tried to deny the pregnancy do not seem to escape the grief. Instead, they are all the more alone in their sorrow, and the strains on themselves and their marriages are enormous.

Some people have balanced their needs for privacy regarding the abortion decision with their needs for public sympathy and support in their grief by telling only part of the story. That is the solution a number of women came to, especially for their older children. They told children, distant family, and casual friends that the baby died. More intimate friends and family were told more.

Don't ask what you don't want to know. Most women having amniocentesis for prenatal diagnosis are aware of Downs Syndrome as the reason for the test. Downs Syndrome is one of many, many diagnoses possible. Some of these, like an extra eighteenth chromosome, are more severe than Downs Syndrome. More common, and less severe, are the sex chromosome anomalies: a girl with only one X chromosome (Turner's Syndrome), a boy with an extra X or an extra Y chromosome, a girl with an extra X chromosome. Some of the chromosomal abnormalities that are found in amniocentesis might never show up as a problem, and would otherwise have gone undiagnosed. Others would eventually have shown themselves, but not in a profoundly disabling way. In my interviews with women who have had amniocentesis, I have been struck by the enormous grief women experience with any "bad-news" diagnosis, including diagnoses they might have been better able to cope with had they shown up developmentally.

While we have, with very good reason, focused on our "right to know" in medical care, there is also a right *not* to know. We have not only the right of informed consent, but of *informed refusal*, including the informed refusal of information. That may sound like a contradiction, but it is not. If a woman would choose not to abort for a particular condition, she has a right to ask *not* to be informed if her fetus has that condition. A truly informed consent for prenatal diagnosis would mean knowing about the ambiguous diagnoses that are possible, and deciding ahead of time which information was wanted—and which not.

The question of what to do with "unexpected diagnoses" has long troubled those who do genetic testing. It seems ethically wrong to withhold information that arises in testing, and yet the information, far from being helpful, may be harmful, leading to "labeling" of the child. Such diagnoses, however, are not truly "unexpected." Those doing the tests know that they are possible.

Once the test has been done and the results available, it is too late to ask the woman whether or not she wants this information. But if the informed consent procedure for the test were truly informational, the woman would know such diagnoses are possible, and could decide ahead of time what she wanted done with the information.

The counseling that would be required for truly informed refusal of information goes beyond anything that is currently offered. Such counseling would mean a full educational program. Some would say it is impractical—and maybe it is. But it is neither practical, nor ethical, to provide women with information on the condition of the fetus that they neither want nor need. Just as a woman can ask not to learn the sex of her fetus, so too should she be able to ask not to learn such conditions as Turner's Syndrome.

Two women who read drafts of Chapter 6, on ambiguous diagnoses, before having amniocentesis tried to implement their rights of informed refusal. Since geneticists and genetic counselors pride themselves on providing information, *all* the information available, the counseling sessions were difficult. The women insisted that there were things they did *not* want to know; the counselors insisted the women needed *all* information. When I interviewed genetic counselors, some were and some were not willing to withhold information at the woman's request. If you wish to exercise your right of informed refusal, be prepared to argue the point, and perhaps to shop around for a supportive genetic counseling service or physician.

Do not ask to learn the sex of the fetus. Children are sex-typed early enough. Knowledge of fetal sex limits the way that parents perceive the child-to-be and sets expectations in place before we can know the individuality of the child.

The most common reasons people gave for wanting to know the sex of the fetus were, first, in order to deal with disappointment before the child came; and second, for what were called "practical" reasons. Let us consider each.

If one truly wants, say, a boy, it might sound reasonable to find out ahead of time if the child will be a girl, and come to terms with it. But what I have seen is that the depth of disappointment when sex is learned before birth surpasses the level of disappointment at the time of birth. Birth usually brings its own euphoria, and its own acceptance and excitement about the baby. "Wrong" sex babies are so wonderful, so unique—and so time-consuming—that the "wrongness" of the sex often fades. But presented with that information halfway through a pregnancy, all one can do is brood about it.

The idea of learning for "practical" reasons is intriguing: what practical difference does it make if an infant is a boy or a girl? Practical reasons usually translate into earlier sex-typing of clothing and environment: the pinks and the blues. Just a few generations ago, children were dressed in gender-neutral ways up until as late as three years. Baby dresses and curls were left on boys through babyhood. In the last several generations we have come to expect sex-typed clothing on infants. I am now distressed to see "it's a girl!" or "it's a boy!" maternity T-shirts. Must gender socialization begin in utero?

For these reasons, and others discussed in detail in Chapter 5, I urge you to give your babies a few more months of gender-free acceptance.

Finally, for those few who will receive bad news from prenatal diagnosis, *let no one refuse you your right to grieve.* Whether you choose to terminate the pregnancy or not, something precious has been lost to you. You have every right to grieve that loss.

For those who choose to terminate, there are yet more decisions to be made: the type of abortion procedure, whether or not to see and to bury the fetus, and, ultimately, whether or not to have another pregnancy. Reading Chapter 7 on grieving, and having those closest to you read it as well, can be helpful. Some decisions have to be made quickly. Learning how these other women have made their decisions, and how they feel about those decisions later, may help you in reaching your own. But it is no substitute for talking to others who have been in the same position. Your genetic counselor, midwife, childbirth educator, or physician may be able to put you in touch with women or families who have made the same choices you make. This is a new kind of grief, and we will have to help each other through it.

REFERENCES

Chapter 1

1. I wish to thank Rosalyn Weinman Schram for her insight and wording on this issue.
2. President's Commission for the Study of Ethical Problems in Medicine and Biomedical and Behavioral Research, *Screening and Counseling for Genetic Conditions: A Report on the Ethical, Social and Legal Implications of Genetic Screening, Counseling and Educational Programs.* Washington, D.C.: U.S. Government Printing Office, 1983.
3. According to *New York Times*–CBS polls, the proportion of the population that agreed that abortion should be legal if there is a "strong chance there is a serious defect in the baby" was 79 percent in 1972 and 80 percent in 1984. *New York Times*, October 14, 1984, p. E3.

4. William Isaac Thomas, "Defining the Situation." In Coser and Rosenberg (eds.), *Sociological Theory*, 3rd edition. New York: Macmillan, 1969.

5. Meredith B. Burke and Aliza Kolker, "Amniocentesis and the Social Construction of Pregnancy." Paper presented to the annual meeting of the District of Columbia Sociological Society, Baltimore, MD, 1982.

6. Robert Massie, *Nicholas and Alexandria*. New York: Atheneum, 1967.

7. C. Wright Mills, *The Sociological Imagination*. New York: Oxford University Press, 1959.

8. Richard Titmuss, *The Gift Relationship: From Human Blood to Social Policy*. New York: Vintage Books, 1972.

9. Titmuss, p. 239.

10. Nadine Taub, "An Introduction: A Symposium on Reproductive Rights; The Emerging Issues." *Women's Rights Law Reporter*, vol. 7, no. 3, 1982, p. 169.

11. Ruth Hubbard, "Some Legal and Policy Implications of Recent Advances in Prenatal Diagnosis and Fetal Therapy," *Women's Rights Law Reporter*, vol. 7, no. 3, 1982, p. 210.

12. Irving Kenneth Zola, *Socio-Medical Inquiries: Recollections, Reflections and Reconsiderations*. Philadelphia: Temple University Press, 1983, p. 296.

13. I wish to thank Betty Leyerle for her wisdom and her wording.

Chapter 2

1. Kristen Luker, *Abortion and the Policies of Motherhood*. Berkeley, CA: University of California Press, 1984.

2. Genoveffa Corea, *The Mother Machine: Reproductive Technologies from Artificial Insemination to Artificial Wombs*. New York: Harper and Row, 1985. I am grateful to Genoveffa Corea for making this book available to me in manuscript.

3. Irving Kenneth Zola, op. cit. Zola states that he coined the term "medicalization" in a graduate course (p. 243). The term refers to the sociopolitical process of "making medicine and the labels 'healthy' and 'ill' *relevant* to an ever-increasing part of human existence" (p. 247).

4. Barbara Katz Rothman, *In Labor: Women and Power in the Birthplace*. New York: W.W. Norton and Co., 1982, pp. 45–47.

5. For a discussion of the changing legal status of the fetus and the pregnant woman, see Janet Gallagher, "The Fetus and the

Law—Whose Life Is It Anyway?" *Ms.*, September 1984, pp. 62–135.

6. For a fuller discussion, see Ruth Hubbard, op. cit., pp. 201–28.

7. Watson A. Bowes, Jr., and Brad Selgestad, "Fetal Versus Maternal Rights: Medical and Legal Perspectives." *Obstetrics and Gynecology*, 58: 209–14, August 1981.

8. Genetics and the Law: Third National Symposium co-sponsored by the American Society of Law and Medicine and Boston University Schools of Medicine, Law and Public Health, Boston, MA, April 2–4, 1984.

9. Rothman, op. cit.

10. For a discussion of the abortion of female fetuses, see Rita Arditti, Renate Duelli-Klein, and Shelley Minden (eds.), *Test Tube Women: What Future for Motherhood?* Boston: Pandora Press, 1984. In that volume, see Hoskins and Holmes, "Technology and Prenatal Femicide"; Sangari, "If You Would Be the Mother of a Son"; and Roggencamp, "Abortion of a Special Kind: Male Sex Selection in India."

11. Erich Fromm, *The Forgotten Language: An Introduction to the Understanding of Dreams, Fairy Tales and Myths.* New York: Grove Press, 1956.

12. Sources for history of the eugenics movement include: Kenneth Ludmerer and Marc Lappe, "Eugenics," *Encyclopedia of Bioethics*, vol. 1, 1978; and Daniel J. Kevles, "Annals of Eugenics," a four-part series in *The New Yorker*, October 1984.

13. Sheldon C. Reed, "A Short History of Genetic Counseling," *Social Biology*, vol. 21, no. 4, 1971, pp. 332–39.

14. Ibid., p. 335.

15. Richard M. Frankel and Howard B. Beckman, "Between Physician and Patient: The Medical Record and the Construction of Clinical Reality." Paper presented to the Society for the Study of Social Problems, Detroit, August 1983.

16. Cited in Seymour Kessler, *Genetic Counseling: The Psychological Dimension.* New York: Academic Press, 1979.

17. James R. Sorenson, "Counselors: A Self Portrait." *Genetic Counseling*, vol. 1, no. 5, October 1973.

Chapter 3

1. Meredith B. Burke and Aliza Kolker, op. cit.

2. Irving Kenneth Zola, op. cit.

Chapter 4

1. Patricia Leff, "Routine Lessons." *Mothering*, Winter 1985, pp. 76–77.

2. Barbara Dixson et al., "Midtrimester Amniocentesis: Subjective Maternal Responses." *Journal of Reproductive Medicine*, vol. 26, no. 1, 1981, pp. 10–16; R. S. Ashery, "Communication Openness with Friends, Relatives and Children of Couples Having Amniocentesis." *Prenatal Diagnosis*, vol. 1, no. 2, 1981, pp. 153–56.

3. See for example the work of Natalie Shainess, referred to in Diane Schulder and Florynce Kennedy, *Abortion Rap.* New York: McGraw-Hill Co., 1971, p. 122.

4. Magda Denes, *In Necessity and Sorrow: Life and Death in an Abortion Hospital.* New York: Basic Books, 1976, pp. 158–59.

5. Sheila Kitzinger, *The Complete Book of Pregnancy and Childbirth.* New York: Alfred A. Knopf, 1980, p. 326.

6. Meredith B. Burke and Aliza Kolker, op. cit.

7. Nancy Chodorow, *The Reproduction of Mothering.* Berkeley, CA: University of California Press, 1978.

8. David B. Lynne, "Divergent Feedback and Sex-Role Identification in Boys and Men," *Merrill Quarterly*, vol. X, no. 1, 1964, pp. 17–23; and "Sex Differences in Identification Development." *Sociometry*, vol. XXIV, no. 4, 1961, pp. 372–83.

9. Carol Gilligan, *In a Different Voice: Psychological Theory and Women's Development.* Cambridge, MA: Harvard University Press, 1982.

10. Chodorow, op. cit., p. 167.

11. Lynne, op. cit., 1964 and 1961.

12. Lillian Rubin, *Intimate Strangers.* New York: Harper and Row, 1983.

13. Marshall H. Klaus and John H. Kennell, *Maternal Infant Bonding.* St. Louis: C. V. Mosby Company, 1976.

Chapter 5

1. Tabitha Powledge, "Windows on the Womb." *Psychology Today*, May 1983, pp. 37–40.

2. Danielle Silvestre and Nadine Fiesco, "Reactions to Amniocentesis: An Analysis of 87 Interviews." *American Journal of Orthopsychiatry*, 50:4, 1980, pp. 610–17.

3. Ann Oakley, *Becoming a Mother.* New York: Schocken Books, 1980, p. 118.

4. I wish to thank Judith Lorber for her elegant phrasing of this concern.

5. Jeffrey Rubin, Frank Provenzano and Zella Luria, "The Eye of the Beholder: Parents' Views on Sex of Newborns," *American Journal of Orthopsychiatry*, 44:47–55, 1974.

6. Myra Leifer, *Psychological Effects of Motherhood: A Study of First Pregnancy.* New York: Praeger, 1980, p. 84.

7. Oakley, *Becoming a Mother*, p. 118.

8. Amitai Etzioni, *Genetic Fix.* New York: Harper and Row, 1973.

9. Ibid., p. 16.

10. Neil G. Bennett (ed.), *Sex Selection of Children.* New York: Academic Press, 1983.

11. C. F. Westoff and R. R. Rindfuss, "Sex Preselection in the United States: Some Implications." *Science*, 184:633–36, 1974.

12. C. Wright Mills, *The Sociological Imagination.* New York: Oxford University Press, 1959.

13. See John Postgate, "Bat's Chance in Hell." *New Scientist*, 58:12–15, 1973, for an argument in some ways similar to mine.

14. Tabitha Powledge, "Toward a Moral Policy for Sex Choice," 1983, in Bennett, op. cit.

15. Frances E. Kobrin and Robert G. Potter, Jr., "Sex Selection Through Amniocentesis and Selective Abortion," 1983, in Bennett, op. cit.

16. Brenda Seals, personal communication, November 1984.

17. Oakley, *Becoming a Mother*, p. 118.

18. Myra Leifer, op. cit.

19. Ibid., p. 94.

20. Oakley, *Woman Confined: Towards a Sociology of Childbirth.* New York: Schocken Books, 1980, p. 165.

21. Oakley, *Becoming a Mother*, p. 120.

Chapter 6

1. Irving Kenneth Zola, op. cit., p. 147.

2. I wish to thank Betty Leyerle for her insight and clarification of this issue.

3. Ursula LeGuin, *The Left Hand of Darkness.* New York: Ace Books, 1969.

Chapter 7

1. William Styron, *Sophie's Choice.* New York: Random House, 1976.

2. For a discussion of women's moral reasoning, see Carol Gilligan, op. cit.

3. Rayna Rapp, "XYLO: A True Story," 1984. In Arditti, Duelli-Klein, and Minden (eds.), op. cit. p. 318.

4. This is from a film on selective abortion following amniocentesis, for use by health professionals: *Support for Prenatal Diagnosis*, Division of Genetics, Loma Linda University Medical Center, California, 1983.

5. I wish to thank Barbara Moburg for her clear and emphatic statement of this obvious, but often overlooked truth, at the National Women's Studies Association annual meeting, New Jersey, 1984. It is a truth that is often lost in the "pregnant couples" school of childbirth education.

6. Rapp, op. cit., p. 323.

7. Lillian Rubin, op. cit.

8. Film, *Support for Prenatal Diagnosis*, op. cit.

9. Germaine Greer, *Sex and Destiny: The Politics of Human Fertility.* New York: Harper and Row, 1984.

10. Bernard Adler and Theodore Kushnick, "Genetic Counseling in Prenatally Diagnosed Trisomy 18 and 21: Psychological Aspects." *Pediatrics*, vol. 64:1, January 1982, pp. 94–99.

11. Tabitha Powledge, op. cit., pp. 37–40.

12. Elisabeth Kubler-Ross, *On Death and Dying*. New York: Macmillan, 1969.

Chapter 8

1. Studies are now being done to determine the exact rates of miscarriage associated with chorion villi biopsy. Different sources vary in their estimates.

2. Brenda Seals, personal communication.

3. Irving Goffman, *Stigma: Notes on the Management of Spoiled Identity.* Englewood Cliffs, NJ: Prentice-Hall, 1963.

4. President's Commission for the Study of Ethical Problems in Medicine and Biomedical and Behavioral Research, op. cit., p. 57.

5. Ibid.

6. Deborah Kaplan, panelist, "Genetic Screening and Engineering." Presented at the 14th National Conference on Women and the Law, Washington D.C., April 10, 1983.

7. Irving Kenneth Zola, op. cit., p. 294.

8. Jeremy Rifkin, *Algeny*. New York: Viking Press, 1983, p. 332.

9. Anonymous letter to the editor, *Ms.*, August 1984.

10. Linda Hoffman, personal communication.

11. Madeleine J. Goodman and Lenn E. Goodman, "The Overselling of Genetic Anxiety." *The Hastings Center Report*, October, 1982, pp. 20–27.

12. For a more complete discussion of the effects of new reproductive technology on our ideas about parenthood, see Rothman, "How Science Is Redefining Parenthood." *Ms.*, August 1982.

13. For a discussion of the meaning of morality to women, see Carol Gilligan, op. cit.

14. R. P. Petchesky, "Reproductive Freedom: Beyond a Woman's Right to Choose," *Signs: Journal of Women in Culture and Society*, 5:661–685, 1980.

15. Gilligan, op. cit., p. 70.

16. Gilligan, op. cit., p. 80.

SELECTED
BIBLIOGRAPHY

The following is a highly selective list of books that influenced my thinking. Some were cited as references; some served as background. This is *not* intended as a bibliography for the researcher or scholar. For ease of accessibility, only books are listed, and none of the hundreds of related journal articles or scores of other relevant books.

Arditti, Rita, Renate Duelli-Klein, and Shelley Minden (eds.), *Test Tube Women: What Future for Motherhood?* Boston and London: Pandora Press, 1984.

Bennett, Neil G. (ed.), *Sex Selection of Children.* New York: Academic Press, 1983.

Borg, Susan, and Judith Lasker, *When Pregnancy Fails.* Boston: Beacon Press, 1981.

Chodorow, Nancy, *The Reproduction of Mothering.* Berkeley, CA: University of California Press, 1978.

Corea, Genoveffa, *The Mother Machine: Reproductive Technologies from*

Artificial Insemination to Artificial Wombs. New York: Harper and Row, 1985.

Denes, Magda, *In Necessity and Sorrow: Life and Death in an Abortion Hospital.* New York: Basic Books, 1976.

Etzioni, Amitai, *Genetic Fix.* New York: Harper and Row, 1973.

Evans, Daryl Paul, *The Lives of Mentally Retarded People.* Boulder, CO: Westview Press, 1983.

Gilligan, Carol, *In a Different Voice: Psychological Theory and Women's Development.* Cambridge, MA: Harvard University Press, 1982.

Glaser, Barney, and Anselm Strauss, *The Discovery of Grounded Theory.* Chicago: Aldine, 1967.

Greer, Germaine, *Sex and Destiny: The Politics of Human Fertility.* New York: Harper and Row, 1984.

Holmes, Helen B., Betty Hoskins, and Michael Gross, *The Custom Made Child?,* Clifton, NJ: Humana Press, 1981.

Hubbard, Ruth, Mary Sue Henefin, and Barbara Fried (eds.), *Biological Woman: The Convenient Myth.* Cambridge, MA: Schenkman, 1982.

Luker, Kristen, *Abortion and the Politics of Motherhood.* Berkeley, CA: University of California Press, 1984.

Massie, Robert, and Suzanne Massie, *Journey.* New York: Ballantine Books, 1984.

Mills, C. Wright, *The Sociological Imagination.* New York: Oxford University Press, 1959.

Oakley, Ann, *Becoming a Mother.* New York: Schocken Books, 1980.
———, *Woman Confined: Towards a Sociology of Childbirth.* New York: Schocken Books, 1980.

President's Commission for the Study of Ethical Problems in Medicine and Biomedical and Behavioral Research, *Screening and Counseling for Genetic Conditions: The Ethical, Social and Legal Implications of Genetic Screening, Counseling and Educational Programs.* Washington D.C.: U.S. Government Printing Office, 1983.

Rifkin, Jeremy, *Algeny.* New York: Viking Press, 1983.

Rothman, Barbara Katz, *In Labor: Women and Power in the Birthplace.* New York: W.W. Norton and Co., 1982.

Rubin, Lillian, *Intimate Strangers.* New York: Harper and Row, 1983.

Stinson, Robert, and Peggy Stinson, *The Long Dying of Baby Andrew.* Boston: Little, Brown and Company, 1983.

Titmuss, Richard, *The Gift Relationship: From Human Blood to Social Policy.* New York: Pantheon Books, 1971.

Zola, Irving Kenneth, *Missing Pieces: A Chronicle of Living with a Disability.* Philadelphia: Temple University Press, 1983.

———, *Socio-Medical Inquiries: Recollections, Reflections and Reconsiderations.* Philadelphia: Temple University Press, 1983.

INDEX